The M & E Business Studies

The purpose of this series is to meet the needs of students following business studies courses whether for the Business and Technician Education Council (BTEC) or for the examinations of the major professional institutes. The books have been written to conform with syllabus specifications and are constructed around a series of objectives stated at the beginning of each chapter, with assignments and self-assessment questions where appropriate.

General Editor

Dr. Edwin Kerr
*Chief Officer, Council for National
Academic Awards*

Advisory Editors

K. W. Aitken
*Vice-Principal, South-East
London College*

P. W. Holmes
*Director, Regional Management
Studies Centre, Bristol Polytechnic*

The M&E Business Studies Series

An Introduction to Industrial Relations

T. L. JOHNSTON
M.A., Ph.D.

Former Professor of Economics,
Heriot-Watt University

SECOND EDITION

Macdonald and Evans

Macdonald & Evans Ltd.
Estover, Plymouth PL6 7PZ

First published 1981
Reprinted with amendments 1983
Second Edition 1985

© Macdonald & Evans Ltd. 1985

British Library Cataloguing in Publication Data:

Johnston, T. L.
    An introduction to industrial relations.—
    2nd ed.—(The M & E business studies series,
    ISSN 0266–4917)
    1. Industrial relations—Great Britain
    I. Title
    331'.0941   HD8391

ISBN 0–7121–0450–X

This book is copyright
and may not be reproduced in whole
or in part (except for purposes of review)
without the express permission
of the publishers in writing

Printed in Great Britain by
J. W. Arrowsmith Ltd., Bristol

Phototypeset in Linotron 202 Times by
Western Printing Services Ltd., Bristol

Preface to the Second Edition

It is entirely appropriate that the Business and Technician Education Council should have recognised the need to have a text on Industrial Relations available for students of business studies. Whether students are interested in careers in business, finance, distribution and commerce, or public sector administration, they will have to deal with people. As employees and, in the fullness of time, managers, they will be concerned in a professional way with social relations in the production process, whether that process is carried on in a plant, an office, or a building site.

This text marks out the ground of an introduction to industrial relations as a serious academic discipline, and in addition as a very important branch of applied social and economic knowledge. While it is pitched at a level which is comfortable for the BTEC student, it also straddles the range of interest of the student working for "A" levels, or their equivalent, in government, politics, and social sciences, and of the undergraduate seeking a foundation text in industrial relations. It is hoped that this last group will find the references to the literature and to further reading a helpful signpost to more advanced study of the subject.

As the BTEC option module specification stipulates, the approach in this study seeks to catch the perspectives of a variety of disciplines: history, law, politics, psychology, sociology and economics. As an economist, the author makes no apology for the fact that certain of the core themes of industrial relations have a very powerful economic content. Others, such as those pertaining to the role of government, which is considered in Chapter Three, carry a stronger infusion of law and government.

This edition brings the material up to date by incorporating the most recent statistical information, for example about trade union membership, and taking account of changes in labour legislation, the priorities of public policy, and the major findings of recent research and surveys.

In the space available it has not been possible to embark upon a systematic comparative text which seeks to juxtapose and compare a variety of national industrial relations systems in their entirety. We have concentrated on a basically British core of industrial relations arrangements and analysis. At the same time, there are frequent excursions across frontiers to other systems. It is hoped that the reader will be invigorated by a fresh insight and perspective which is gained from studying the approaches of other countries to particular parts of the industrial relations mosaic.

Current affairs have a strong infusion nowadays of industrial relations matters. Human relationships in industry and commerce also attract the attention of the media. In addition, therefore, to the broad educational and vocational relevance of the subject, a knowledge of industrial relations makes us all more informed members of the community.

It follows that the student should seek to reinforce his or her study of the subject via this text by a critical reading and appraisal of the reports on and analysis of industrial relations situations and problems which are brought to our notice as part of everyday life. There is no excuse for regarding industrial relations as a dry-as-dust academic discipline. It is about us. For that reason, however, the student is under a particular obligation to endeavour to apply his or her critical faculty in an objective way to the subject matter. This study is aimed at developing and sharpening that faculty.

1985   T.L.J.

Acknowledgments

Over the years teachers and students of industrial relations in a number of countries have forced the author to broaden and deepen his understanding of the subject of this text. The learning process has usually been extremely congenial and constructive, and has involved the consumption of numerous cups of coffee. Practitioners—trade unionists, employers, government officials, and that mysterious breed, "neutral third parties"—have also provided an appropriate corrective of practical experience and wisdom which bring an author closer to the real world. The smoke-filled room does exist, and it too can be a stimulating, if rigorous, learning environment. This necessarily anonymous tribute to all of the above is gratefully recorded.

More specific acknowledgment is provided in the footnote and further reading references to the individual sources which have been consulted and cited. The author thanks other authors of books, journal editors, and officials responsible for official publications, through HMSO, the ILO etc., for the access to this rich vein of material.

Contents

CHAPTER ONE

The Nature of Industrial Relations

```
┌─────────────────────────────────────────────────┐
│                 CHAPTER OBJECTIVES                │
│                                                   │
│   After studying this chapter you should be able to: │
│ * ask yourself what is covered by the definition "social │
│   relations in production";                       │
│ * assess the contribution which different subjects, e.g. │
│   psychology, can make to understanding industrial │
│   relations;                                      │
│ * evaluate the problems involved in constructing a │
│   model of an industrial relations system;        │
│ * summarise the characteristics of the industrial │
│   relations system in a country with which you are │
│   familiar.                                       │
└─────────────────────────────────────────────────┘
```

"The understandings of the greater part of men are necessarily formed by their ordinary employments."   *Adam Smith*

THE WORLD OF WORK

Industrial relations is a fascinating subject, for it is about people and about people in the world of work. This world covers a vast range of types of production activity, carried out in all kinds of surroundings in every country. The "terms and conditions" governing people at work, and the way these are arrived at, are the core of industrial relations, and they are obviously of crucial concern to the people actually involved. It is they who are close to the action, indeed immersed in it.

However, it is not only workers and managers "at the coal face" who have interests in something called industrial relations. The Government of the country has an important stake, in part because it is an employer in its own right but also because it is the custodian of the public interest in labour relations policies and practices. This third party at the bargaining table has become an important figure.

Beyond these groups with an immediate concern for industrial relations there is in addition a host of academic students and scholars—from economists, sociologists, psychologists, political scientists, to engineers and historians—who study human behaviour in the world of work in a professional way. Again, it is easy to understand why the subject has such a fascination for this wide range of interested parties. It is topical, practical, and involves studying the working behaviour of a very large proportion of the people in any country, namely the labour force.

We associate industrial relations with the spread of Industrialism, a process which began in Britain in the eighteenth century, with the first Industrial Revolution. It is a truism that Britain was the first workshop of the world, an observation, incidentally, which often leads to the caustic conclusion that we have paid the price accordingly, and are the prisoners of our past. The pioneer is frequently overtaken by the late starter. One of the objects of this book is to place such truisms in a wider setting of analysis and understanding.

Nor are the arrangements in any one country rigid and unchanging. A country's industrial relations system may sometimes experience rapid change, some impetus may alter its course of development. We shall see numerous examples of this kind of push, or change of direction, in industrial relations arrangements as we progress. Moreover, we can often gain a clearer insight into our own industrial relations situation if we look over the fence, and see that other countries have their distinctive arrangements for ordering relationships between management and employees.

Some definitions
If, then, industrial relations has many manifestations, by subject or discipline, historically, and by country, does not this make it extremely difficult to find a focus for studying its structure and content? How are we to set about analysing the subject matter? One typical British response to this key question has been to see industrial relations as the study of all aspects of *job regulation*— making and administering the rules, formal and informal, systematic, or otherwise, which regulate the employment relationship. Job regulation is regarded as the core. Perhaps this is a narrow, static and rather defensive view. If we focus instead on the concepts of work and employment we are likely from the start to become aware that many facets of industrial relations are about changing jobs and moving on to new tasks and work, usually as a result of some agreed adjustment. That can of course be the subject of keen bargaining.

A rather wider definition declares that industrial relations is concerned with *social relations in production*.[1] Notice that "production" can cover a vast range of economic activity, ranging far beyond manufacturing in the narrow sense. Indeed, much production nowadays provides *services*, and the manufacturing base in many industrialised countries is shrinking, both absolutely and in relation to other ways in which people earn a living.

The word "social" is also crucial in the definition. We may well be interested to know how a particular individual feels about his job, for that may in turn affect his behaviour when he is involved with others. But it is primarily on this interaction with other people, workers and employers, that we concentrate when we study industrial relations. In recent years, for example, there has been a great extension in Britain of protective legislation in support of the individual worker; but even a claim for unfair dismissal is fundamentally about inter-personal relationships. There is a social context, a community of work, in factory and office and in other places of employment.

ACADEMIC APPROACHES

This community of work and industrial relations can, we have suggested, be analysed from a number of vantage points. What are some of the academic disciplines or subjects which help to shed light on the subject matter of industrial relations? Take *Economics*. Some of the earliest as well as the most vigorous contributions to industrial relations understanding have come from that quarter. Price theory and the study of forces of demand and supply, and of the use of bargaining power brought to bear in markets, have developed important insights into wage-fixing, pay differentials, and "trade-offs" in bargaining between management and employees. These economic factors are the red meat of much industrial relations.

It is no accident that some of the simplest, but also most simplistic, theories of industrial relations are contained in the wage theories of early nineteenth-century economists. The *subsistence theory* of wages suggested that the pressure of potential population increase would keep wages down to a basic minimum. This theory, closely linked with the population theory associated with T. R. Malthus, simply left no scope for trade unions, whom we would expect to be interested in seeking to influence and control the terms on which employees supply their labour effort to production. Wage theory has subsequently become more realistic, but also more complicated in consequence. In particular, it has had to grapple with the activities of trade unions in the real world, and with important influences in wage determination which are less susceptible to analysis on a narrow economic base, such as notions of fairness and equity, group solidarity, and security of employment.

Other disciplines have thus had plenty of scope to show their paces and to demonstrate that they too have a decided contribution to make. *Sociology* has distilled powerful insights into the nature of work, group behaviour, organisational theory and practice, and highlighted the importance of concepts such as authority, affluence, alienation, authority and conflict, to our understanding of industrial relations phenomena. It is not money alone that motivates people at work. *Psychology* has also enhanced our grasp of motivation, incentives, and such topics as the physiology of shift work.

Political theory or science is interested in principles of government, power and power-sharing, for example within the trade unions, in labour–management arrangements for negotiating, and in examining the role of the state. The idea of "industrial government" was used by the Wisconsin school of industrial relations fifty years ago to focus the subject. This approach also stressed the importance of *Law* as a rule-maker, a codifier, and source of sanctions in the governance of industrial relations. Other schools have undertaken intensive studies of the institutions, such as trade unions, which are parties of interest in labour relations.

From the standpoint of technology, the *engineer* has an evident interest in work processes and in job design. More recently, the recognition that technology has to be matched to people, that job enrichment is important, has produced an awareness that technical and social systems at the place of work have somehow to be married. This was stressed in the pioneering work at the Tavistock Institute of Human Relations, and it has been the centre of much interesting practical and academic work on job reform, not least in Scandinavia.

The insights of the *historian* are clearly very pertinent to industrial relations "on the move". Societies do not stand still, but evolve and adapt. Last, but by no means least, we should be willing to reflect, under the guidance of the *philosopher and moralist, and the theologian*, about the nature of the society whose industrial relations we are examining. "Freedom of the individual", the "work ethic", the "rule of law", and "solidarity" often become clichés, unless we put them under the microscope of some hard intellectual scrutiny.

MODELS OF INDUSTRIAL RELATIONS SYSTEMS

Industrial relations is then multi-faceted, inter-disciplinary, as well as being the stuff of our activities at work. Unfortunately, the more we accept the wisdom of taking a broad and inter-disciplinary approach to industrial relations, the less confident we become about single explanations as to what makes industrial relations tick. We must recognise at the outset that the theory of industrial relations, in the sense of concepts or models which can be applied to problems, in the expectation, or even the hope, of explaining and predicting, is not at all advanced.

We all know that it is difficult to conduct experiments in human relationships. The controlled experiment is unusual, and frequently of limited relevance. Hypotheses are difficult to test, and they often appear stilted and artificial if they are applied to part of an industrial relations system. A lot of work has been done on the theory of trade union growth, for example: but unions do not grow in isolation, and satisfactory explanations require us to recognise that the attitudes of employers, government and the law may be crucial. The system is an interlocking one; everything depends on everything else.

If in addition we distinguish, as the Donovan Royal Commission did in Britain in the mid-1960s[2] between the "formal" and the "informal" systems of industrial relations, our doubts about how to approach an industrial relations system are increased. Donovan argued that Britain had two systems of industrial relations. One was the formal system embodied in the official institutions. The other was the informal system created by the actual behaviour of trade unions and employers' associations, of managers, shop stewards and workers.

Analysis of the informal system is particularly difficult. Are we simply to undertake case studies of actual behaviour and seek to discern inferences or suggested tendencies? As a matter of fact, there is an encouraging growth in survey work which is seeking to map the changing contours of British industrial relations. In the 1970s, when major changes occurred in industrial relations legislation, the centre of gravity shifted substantially to the local level. In due course, an accumulation of surveys will provide more systematic information about trends, and provide a better stock of data against which to test theories. As yet, however, theory in industrial relations is not a well-developed subject.[3]

Karl Marx

Even the most famous of all theories of social development, that produced by Karl Marx, is of little use to us in modelling industrial relations systems. On the basis of his historical analysis of the development of societies, which was essentially materialist or economic in its fundamentals, Marx produced a simple two-class model of mid-nineteenth-century society, as typified by Britain. The bourgeois capital-owning class employed and exploited the industrial working class. This led to the increasing distress of the working class, who ultimately rebelled, overthrew the capitalist society, and installed the dictatorship of the proletariat. The process was an inevitable one, rooted in the laws of production.

This has manifestly not happened in capitalist industrial societies. The concept of working class has little bearing on the way in which trade unions have developed and work, for instance in Britain, as we shall see in the course of this study. Nor does the simple model of exploiter and exploited fit with the world of negotiation and bargaining of which industrial relations consists. It is of course perfectly possible to have a Marxist view of industrial relations: but that falls far short of the kind of simple yet powerful model which Marx himself set up for industrial society.

Dunlop's system

A much more modest attempt at providing a framework for our thinking was made by J. T. Dunlop, in his *Industrial Relations Systems*.[4] He tried to put industrial relations systems into some kind of order, which at least enables us to marshal our material and make comparisons across industries and countries.

Dunlop sees the industrial relations system as part, a sub-system, of a larger economic-political system. The industrial relations part has the following characteristics. He defines industrial relations as the complex of inter-relationships among managers, workers and government agencies. Groups of actors—the workers and their organisations (trade unions), managers and their organisations, and government agencies concerned with the workplace and the work community—combine to create a complex of rules. For example, this can cover rates of pay, or procedures for handling workers' grievances. In the course of elaborating this web of rules for the workplace and the work community, the actors are of course influenced by their environment. Dunlop sees this in three inter-related contexts:

(*a*) technology;
(*b*) market and/or budget constraints; and
(*c*) the power relationships among the actors.

The system is bound together by an ideology, by understandings which the actors share. These shared common strands could, for instance, cover an acceptance of free enterprise in a mixed economy, free collective bargaining, or some kind of welfare state. Dunlop shows how each of the three environmental contexts helps to shape the complex rules in a system.

The central task of a theory of industrial relations, it then follows, is to explain *why* there are particular rules in industrial relations systems, and *how and why* these change in response to forces bearing on the system. The rules are not ends in themselves, but a way of achieving ends and objectives. The workers may see the main object of the rules as security and stable terms of employment; managers may aim at efficiency in their interaction with the other actors or parties.

Dunlop's "systems approach" has attracted a great deal of interest, favourable comment and also trenchant criticism. It has been criticised as an empty box or, perhaps worse, as a mysterious black box. Inside it the parties busily make rules, but little light is shed on the behaviour, motivations and attitudes of the people inside the hive. What makes them tick? "Social action" critics of Dunlop argue that his approach does not tell us nearly enough about the behaviour of people in the systems. Why, for instance, is the industrial relations mix so varied between countries? Alternatively, is his framework not really a kind of cloakroom, containing pegs on which we may hang industrial relations coats of many colours and cut? Is it really just a labelling or ticketing device?

Critics go on to point out that Dunlop's scheme of things contains no clear analysis of the causal links between parts of the system. It has therefore not been able to predict the development of systems of industrial relations as countries change and develop over time. Dunlop's work does not, for instance, enable us to predict what will happen to the British system of industrial relations as a consequence of new technologies such as microcircuitry, the "chip". Major changes in technology may alter the mix of occupations in a community, and this could obviously affect the standing and vitality of blue and white collar trade unions. But do we know how? Certainly, we do not know in any confident and assured way.

Yet Dunlop's work has proved extremely suggestive. It identified the main pressures of technology, market forces and power which play upon the actors or, to use a less dramatic term, the parties, to industrial relations decisions. We shall be making substantial use of his framework. Best of all, however, his approach has had the merit of stimulating others to propose alternative approaches to building the house of industrial relations. Those who do not think it appropriate or useful to begin from a Grand Design have been stimulated or goaded into undertaking intensive work, shaping particular building blocks. Much fruitful work has been done.

What factors, for example, explain the growth of trade unions? What forces influence workshop bargaining? What is the rationale of employers' organisations? Is the law of industrial relations capable of systematic analysis and exposition in the form of legal principles: or do we simply have pragmatic procedures? This approach, of building upwards, was in fact not at all alien to Dunlop himself. He made explicit cross-cut comparative studies between countries of industrial relations in two major industries, coal mining and construction. Yet building upwards clearly calls for much patient slog and the grind of empirical work.

THE ILO PERSPECTIVE

In an introduction such as this, it would be remiss not to look at the International Labour Organisation, and ask what kind of perspective it can provide on the world of industrial relations. It, if anyone, should have an overview of the variety of national systems and the range of content in industrial relations.

The ILO is a tripartite body with representatives of government, workers and employers taking part in its policy-making and programmes. Since it was set up in 1919, under the aegis of the League of Nations, the ILO has had the continuing remit of improving conditions of work and the general welfare of working people all over the world. It is a challenging and massive task. It now has about 140 member States. Its objective of improving standards is largely promoted through Conventions and Recommendations which the ILO adopts and seeks to have applied throughout the world, as an International Labour Code. So far 153 Conventions and 161 Recommendations have been adopted. Conventions are like international treaties; when a member State ratifies a Convention it pledges itself to apply its terms and provisions. Recommendations are more in the nature of guidelines for national policy on particular topics, frequently amplifying Conventions. They do not require to be ratified. This flexibility is a recognition that countries cannot all be poured into the same industrial relations mould.

The ILO also brings influence to bear in a variety of other ways—through declarations, resolutions, model codes, via the work of its industrial committees, through technical co-operation, surveys, studies, and practical guides, for example on industrial relations procedures like conciliation and the arbitration of disputes. Some themes have been particularly prominent in the work, such as trade union freedom, equality of opportunity, protection against forced labour, the promotion of employment and the development of human resources.

It is important not to be too starry-eyed about the work of the ILO, all the same. Its objectives are noble, its ideals of the highest. Yet the adoption of Conventions and Recommendations is patchy, and adopting these rules of international good conduct is the easy part. It is much more difficult to put them into practice, and also difficult for the ILO to monitor subsequent performance, for instance among the countries of Eastern Europe. Exasperation with the failure of such countries to honour the ideal of tripartitism, that is to say the interplay of trade unions and employers as free agents along with government, led the USA to withdraw from the ILO for a period between 1977 and 1980.

This approach on the part of the ILO explicitly recognises that national industrial relations systems vary hugely. There is no one correct, superior, model system. That is the point to note.

CLASSIFICATION OF SYSTEMS

An ILO scheme

The bewildering variety is well illustrated in the serious attempts which the International Institute for Labour Studies (affiliated to the ILO) launched some years ago in order to advance understanding of industrial relations. A set of nine types of industrial relations systems was suggested, ranging from the peasant–lord to the socialist system. Table I sets out the range. It certainly encompasses a broad sweep.

The lifetime commitment system, for instance, is regarded as a particular Japanese phenomenon. The inspirational ethic, to take another example, is associated with a political élite in a developing society, which tries to mobilise workers and inspire them to dedicate themselves to constructing a new society. The peasant–lord society could, if we are willing to take a historical and biblical view, be expressed via the parable of the labourers in the vineyard (Matthew 20, verses 1 to 16). There, it will be recalled, every labourer received a penny a day, whether he was engaged at the first hour and agreed to work for a penny a day or was taken on at the eleventh hour.

The parable is full of interesting industrial relations questions, and much else. What sort of equitable pay system had the lord devised? What recourse had the first workers against the master for a revision of the rate of pay originally fixed? What would happen the following day, if the master wanted to recruit another, or the same squad? How would he motivate them? Would they be able to refuse to work? What sort of work ethic does the whole episode suggest? Does it not make nonsense of the proposition that the labourer is worthy of his hire?

Apart from such speculations, what the table does bring to our notice is the point that industrial relations do occur in a wide range of societies and economies. The industrial relations subject is not peculiar to private enterprise industrialised economies, not the exclusive vice of capitalism. For our purposes it is of course the bipartite and tripartite groups which have the characteristics that

TABLE I. SUMMARY OF CHARACTERISTICS OF INDUSTRIAL RELATIONS SYSTEMS

Industrial relations system	Worker's choice and mobility	Level of worker organisation	Power of non-state employers	Intervention by state	Ethical nature of labour relations
Peasant–lord	nil	nil	great	nil	paternalistic
Primitive market	small	nil	great	nil	contractual
Small manufacturing	medium	small	great	small	paternalistic/contractual
Lifetime commitment	small	medium	great	small	paternalistic/contractual
Bipartite	great	great	great	medium	contractual
Tripartite	great	great	great	great	contractual
Corporatist–bureaucratic	medium	medium	medium	great	contractual
Mobilising	medium	medium	small	great	inspirational
Socialist	great	great	nil	great	inspirational/contractual

Source: International Institute for Labour Studies Bulletin, No. 8, 1971, p. 149

we associate intuitively with the British and other western-type industrial relations systems. The same ILO source went on to identify various styles of political and social environments in which industrial relations are set, and it lumped together the "industrialised pluralist systems (North America, Western Europe and Australasia)". They were considered to have the following determinants, or conditions, of industrial relations: "Powerful autonomous trade union bargaining with employers to obtain satisfaction and secondarily acting as pressure groups. Variations in degree of state involvement."

So far, so good. Or is it? Have we really bracketed the target? Our table makes the important point that not all industrial relations systems have collective bargaining at their core. Paternalism, for instance, hardly smacks of negotiation. Yet even the "industrialised pluralist" countries in which collective bargaining does feature contain a daunting variety of industrial relations arrangements. Some of the countries (Netherlands, France) have denominational unions, or strongly ideological unions (CGT in France), others (USA) have very pragmatic "business unions"; many, as in Scandinavia and Britain, have trade union movements which are closely allied with social democratic political parties. The structure of trade unionism is very clean cut in Germany (with 16 industrial unions), almost as tidy in Sweden (but with separate blue and white collar union groups), and rather chaotic in Australia and Britain. Employers' organisations are powerful and close-knit in Scandinavia but lack any national standing in the USA. Collective bargaining is typically very decentralised in North America, takes place in a national consensus framework in Scandinavia, and has a concerted action setting in Germany. In Australia, the role of an independent Conciliation and Arbitration Commission is paramount. In Britain, there is a well-known antipathy to giving collective agreements the status of contracts which are binding in law.

Japanese industrial relations hold a particular fascination for the western industrialised countries, mainly because of the phenomenal recovery and economic growth demonstrated by Japan since the Second World War. Like the US system, its centre of gravity lies within the firm or enterprise. Its distinctive feature is, however, a strong permanent attachment on the part of employees to their company. The concept of the internal labour market is a significant one. Unionism is at its strongest within companies.

Variety in the EEC

Even within the EEC there is as yet no clear pattern towards converging industrial relations systems. In his book,[5] Jack

Peel suggested that there are three patterns of industrial relations within the EEC:

> The German system with tight discipline, codetermination, and industrial trade unionism; the British system, strongly emphasising voluntarism but with conflicting rather than cooperative working methods; and the Benelux system of joint consultative committees concentrating on job security, information, and production. Within these mainstream trends are many individual variations.

If variety is the spice of life, there is clearly no lack of it in the industrial relations world, even within western Europe. Once we have explored the main themes of industrial relations, it will be useful to return in the concluding chapter to the idea of "convergence". Can we discern forces at work, for instance within the EEC, which will tend to pull the separate industrial relations systems of the member countries into some kind of standard framework and pattern?

MONISM AND PLURALISM

The reference above in the typologies of industrial relations to "industrialised pluralist" systems leads to another set of insights on the subject, connected with the concept of pluralism and its antithesis, monism, or unitarianism.

A unitary view

Some industrial relations analysts and practitioners see a system of industrial relations as essentially unitary in character. There is a common objective and interest to be worked for, co-operation prevails, and broad harmony reigns among the parties as they pursue an agreed goal. In its most extreme form, a unitary system can come precious close to being a kind of corporate state, in which, to judge by the record of history, the unity is ultimately imposed from above, by the State. This worry about the corporate state was particularly prevalent in the inter-war years, and pluralism accordingly became a rather favoured political doctrine.[6]

Pluralist perspectives

A pluralist view of the political-economic fabric, and of an industrial relations scheme of things within it, stresses instead that there can be more than one ruling principle. There is a variety of groups and pressures, and opposing views and ambitions, that have to be accommodated in a society and system. In industrial relations terms, there is a pragmatic working out of rules and practices governing employee–employer relations. There are checks and balances, organised pressure groups, such as trade unions and employers' organisations, and conflicts that have to be reconciled if not eliminated. On this analysis too, the state, or the government of the day, may be the supreme keeper of the ring, but any particular government is sovereign only as long as it satisfies the groups and individuals making up the society that it is able effectively to sustain a tolerable balance. If it cannot, there will be a change of government, and some alternative approach and balancing act will take the stage.

The idea of equilibrium is central to the pluralist view. The competing interests, actors, parties, reach stable accommodations. The system may not, in a low key version, be going anywhere in particular. Indeed, critics of this kind of analysis see in it the danger of stagnation or, alternatively, a lack of radical spice to keep the system strong and vigorous. But a system tending to equilibrium can of course be on the move; the pluralist point is that the movement is a gradual one, achieved through some kind of consensus, and its course is not guided by a single, unifying principle. It is perfectly possible for trade unions whose long-term objective is radical to take part in the day-to-day adjustment, reform and change of existing arrangements.

It is obvious that the unitary thesis on the one hand and the pluralist outlook on the other can differ sharply in perspective and in programme. The pluralist approach is much more able to deal with the wide variety of disparate groups and social and economic structures in a society, because it is not seeking to push them into one fixed mould. Pluralism also gets away from any temptation to analyse industrial relations in terms of class conflict. This, as in the extreme form of a Marxist analysis, could have only one outcome— the dictatorship of the proletariat. It avoids a rigid position with respect to change or evolution. It accepts that the problems and accommodations that have to be made are too complex to permit a unique analysis or prescription. Progress, if it occurs, is through pressure and counter-pressure, bid and counter-bid, claim and concession, and the resolution of problems on a continuing basis.

There is naturally a danger in making a fetish of pluralism. It can come close to being a ragbag, filled with contending and no doubt contentious groups and individuals. To that extent, Dunlop's analysis is more explicitly structured.

SUMMARY

In any industrial relations system, there are key themes or issues to be handled. First, there are conflicts of interest in relationships at work. The parties involved also depend on one another. They have to develop some orderly arrangements for the conduct of employer–employee relations. They do this by working out rules and practices, codes of conduct, terms and conditions governing the work situation. They engage in transactions about these terms. The process is a continuing one. Action and adjustment are channelled through working arrangements and negotiations, not always without friction and, even, loss of production.

Since these employer–employee relations affect economic and social matters which are at the heart of a society, the Government, the State, has a part to play in at least monitoring the relationships between the parties. As an employer itself, it will, of course, have an interest to look after, but it is likely also to become involved more broadly in setting a national policy framework for the conduct of industrial relations. Even a government which claims to be standing back from the industrial coalface has, by adopting that very detached stance, acquired a policy.

The tests of balance, equilibrium, or stability between labour and management in industrial relations are not easy.

This will emerge very clearly in particular when we examine the role of government in Chapter Three.

Differences between the industrial relations arrangements of different countries then relate in essence to the varying ways in which they handle these key issues. Obviously, there is no merit in embarking upon a Cook's tour, even of the various bipartite and tripartite systems, let alone all the typologies, which were set out in Table I. There is not sufficient scope in this study to make systematic comparative analyses of the national tripartite systems of the western world. We shall focus primarily on the British system. We cannot of course be content simply with taking snapshots. We want to learn how the system fits together and, no less, how it has evolved and is in the process of change. Our theme then becomes the making, operating and administering of the arrangements and rules which govern the world of work in the environment of British industrial relations. In Dunlop's phrase, the actors, or as we prefer, the parties, are workers and managers and their respective representative bodies, and government. Without attempting systematic comparisons with the industrial relations of other countries we shall nevertheless at times stand back from the British scene and look at alternative strategies and policies which other countries have adopted on particular problems or policies. This will prove a useful corrective against an insular outlook.

SEQUENCE OF PRESENTATION

There is no uniquely correct sequence for the treatment of our subject matter, but we shall unfold the drama in the following order. First, we look at some of the main economic and social features which set the framework within which industrial relations are conducted. If industrial relations is a sub-system, we evidently have to look at the wider system of which it is part. We then examine in turn the main parties to the drama—government, management, and unions. To take the main parties in that sequence is unusual, and to some will appear shocking. Most industrial relations texts are impatient to get on with the study of trade unions, warts and all. This is understandable. Trade unions are one of the great social and economic institutions in our society. They are also quite the most interesting of the actors, whether we view them from a historical standpoint or look at them in their many and varied forms at the present time. But they live nevertheless in a wider system of society. Equally, trade unions are frequently viewed as a kind of permanent opposition. We can see them all the more clearly, therefore, if we describe the other parties first, and then bring the unions on stage.

We follow the analysis of the parties by looking at the way they come together in labour markets to determine the "rules of the game" for the groups and individuals in the system. How are terms and conditions determined and observed? In the main, this question can be focused in Britain by examining the workings of collective bargaining, though we must also, if we are to see the system in the round, look at other forms of regulation. We shall not simply take a snapshot of the system, but seek to understand it as it has evolved and as it continues to develop.

Thereafter, we look in turn at particularly important themes in contemporary industrial relations—the growing interest in providing, through legislation and in other ways, for the protection of the individual employee in the world of work; the theme of industrial democracy as an explicit additional element in industrial relations; and the continuing dilemma, not least in a world of collective bargaining, of incomes policies, their pros and cons. A final chapter suggests some emerging themes which students will wish to reflect on as their knowledge of, and interest in, this fascinating subject grows and matures.

SELF-ASSESSMENT QUESTIONS

1. How useful is it to regard the parties of interest in industrial relations as actors? Should there be a place for the consumer in the cast?

2. Does the definition of industrial relations as "social relations in production" suggest too wide a framework for the study of the subject?

3. How far does the classification of industrial relations systems in Table I depend on subjective judgments? How, for instance, would you interpret "inspirational" and "lifetime commitment"? Are these meaningful terms?

4. Is pluralism simply another way of approaching the analysis of power in industrial relations?

5. In what ways, if any, can international organisations such as the ILO and the EEC help to improve national industrial relations systems?

REFERENCES

1. Robert W. Cox, *Approaches to a Futurology of Industrial Relations*, International Institute for Labour Studies, *Bulletin* No. 8, 1971, p. 141.

2. *Royal Commission on Trade Unions and Employers' Associations 1965–1968*, chairman The Rt. Hon. Lord Donovan, *Cmnd. 3623*, 1968.

3. William Brown (ed.), *The Changing Contours of British Industrial Relations*, Blackwell, 1981, and W. W. Daniel and Neil Millward, *Workplace Industrial Relations in Britain*, Heinemann, 1983. *See also* Confederation of British Industry, *Employee Relations Policy and Decision Making*, a survey of manufacturing companies carried out by Arthur Marsh, 1982.

4. J. T. Dunlop, *Industrial Relations Systems*, New York 1958.

5. Jack Peel, *The Real Power Game. A Guide to European Industrial Relations*, McGraw-Hill, 1979.

6. W. Milne-Bailey, *Trade Unions and the State*, London 1934, provides an excellent treatment.

CHAPTER TWO

The Changing Economic and Social Climate

CHAPTER OBJECTIVES

After studying this chapter you should be able to:
* list the main characteristics of British industrial relations in 1914;
* assess the influence of full employment on industrial relations arrangements;
* explain the main changes which have taken place in the labour force in recent years.

The bourgeoisie cannot exist without constantly revolutionising the instruments of production and thereby the relations of production, and with them the whole relations of society.

Karl Marx

If industrialism is the stage on which the drama of industrial relations is played, we ought to endeavour, however briefly, to mark out some of the main features of the industrial society which has taken shape in Britain during the past two hundred years. We can usefully take two vantage points—the early part of the twentieth century, and the decade of the 1960s—from which to survey the scene.

Professor Phelps Brown, writing in 1959,[1] suggested that the system of British industrial relations was then similar in essentials to that prevailing before the First World War. By 1914 it had assumed its main characteristics as part of the institutional framework of Britain. The nineteenth century had brought dramatic developments, though by the end of it concern was being felt that Britain as an industrial power had begun to flag, with the USA and Germany and, later, Japan setting a new surge in train.

INDUSTRIALISM

The widening of the market and associated division of labour, which Adam Smith discerned two hundred years ago as the key to economic growth, the wealth of nations, was only possible because of a profound change in the whole order of society. The old medieval idea of *status* and stability gave way to a new style of society, based on the *freedom of contract*. Established custom and practice were replaced by free enterprise.

It found ample material on which to play. Inventions in coal-based and metallurgical processes, in textile machinery and in the power of the steam engine, provided the means to expand industry and markets, through production and trade. Very quickly, the surge of urban industrial growth brought with it problems of social disruption and economic misery. Nevertheless, the process of in-dustrialisation soon began to spark reforms, such as the admittedly modest Reform Bill of 1832, and the Factory Act the following year. Reforms, extending the franchise and providing protection against exploitation in a free enterprise economy, continued at varying tempos throughout the nineteenth century and into the twentieth. Compulsory education, from the 1870s, was another expression of a more enlightened and progressive society. All of these showed that economic growth was not to have free rein. And the very idea of the free market had soon come under challenge. The era of the Free Trader, after the repeal of the Corn Laws in 1846, was a brief one, ending with the First World War. Even the supposedly self-adjusting monetary system, the Gold Standard, had a comparatively brief reign from the 1840s to 1914, with a nostalgic and disastrous reincarnation between 1925 and 1931.

Trade Unions
By the 1850s British trade unionism had behind it an era of repres-sion and then oppression, and was beginning to acquire its distinc-tive flavour. The engineering industry was the hub of the process of industrial growth in Britain, and typically one of small workshops and varied products. The new unionism of skilled workers focused on this industry, reflecting its fragmentation in the local and district wage bargaining which steadily became established. The British trade union movement was essentially a skilled one until the 1880s, with an emphasis on occupation and on apprenticeship which has persisted. The expansion of transport, trade and commerce, and municipal services provided the impetus for less skilled workers to organise in the 1880s.

After the trade unions acquired their civil immunities in 1906 the movement gathered pace, and industrial bargaining also blossomed. One sees the subtle changes in priorities in industrial relations by looking at the work of various Royal Commissions. The first two, in 1867 and 1874, had been heavily preoccupied with the legal status of the trade unions, particularly with regard to the criminal law. The fourth, appointed after the Taff Vale dispute in 1901 had raised questions about civil liabilities of trade unions, similarly concentrated on the law, this time the civil law. In between, the third Royal Commission majority report led to the Conciliation Act of 1896. This was almost an act of confirmation. The machinery of collective bargaining had become settled, the parties had learned by trial and error the pros and cons of conciliation and arbitration, as well as industrial stoppages, and the state was now providing a supporting service for the parties to use. But it was their show. On a wider canvas, this development showed that governments recognised some kind of balance of social and economic interest as between employers and employees.

Whitleyism, 1916–18
During the First World War another public committee, chaired by the Speaker of the House of Commons, J. H. Whitley, produced five reports which tried to consolidate the industrial relations machinery and point the way forward to the post-war period. The circumstances of the time were admitted on all sides to offer a great opportunity for securing a permanent improvement in the relations between employers and employed. Its comprehensive proposals covered Joint Standing Industrial Councils for well organised trades, the extension of statutory regulation of wages in badly organised trades, joint consultative committees, and the establishment of a permanent Industrial Court (duly set up in 1919). The first two decades of the century had been good growth years for the unions, from a membership of around 2 million to a peak of more than 8 million in 1920. Then came the difficult inter-war years, and the Great Depression, and membership did not regain that level till 1946.

Inter-war years
Yet the machinery of industrial relations appeared stable. What was not stable, or static, was the industrial structure of the economy. Between the wars there were vast shifts in employment as well as dramatic variations in the total employment on offer. Science-based industries gathered momentum, in man-made fibres, chemicals, processing, and in engineering, both mechanical and electrical. Public utilities, not least electrical power, gained. The traditional industries such as mining and textiles went into decline. It is a mistake to think that the inter-war years were an era of stagnation. Nevertheless, unemployment, the stigma of Jarrow, and other social tensions left their mark.

By contrast to Whitley during the First World War, the Second World War produced proposals, not for a new deal in industrial relations, but for the Welfare State. After 1906 there had been a first generation of welfare measures; old age pensions, labour exchanges, and national health insurance were introduced between 1908 and 1911. After 1945 the first majority Labour Government opened up a new vista on a social democratic society.

AFTER THE SECOND WORLD WAR

William Beveridge's *Full Employment in a Free Society* published in 1944, was a sequel to his *Report on Social Insurance and Allied Services*, presented in November 1942. It was also the culmination of a lifetime of passionate concern for people and their well-being. Underlying his first report, and its proposals for children's allowances and comprehensive health and rehabilitation services, was the recognition that the maintenance of employment was a keystone of the whole house of welfare. So his second report elaborated the theme of how to arrive at and maintain full employment. The whole development of the Welfare State followed from this; it gave the government an agenda, and it brought with it freer access to better education and social mobility.

Beveridge produced the dictum that full employment meant not more than 3 per cent unemployment—1 per cent each for seasonal, frictional, and technological unemployment. The economy had to adapt and adjust: but there was no place for "demand deficiency" unemployment. We had learned from Keynes that that could be cured by appropriate "demand management" policies.

In his programme for full employment, Beveridge paid little regard to industrial relations institutions: but he did put his finger on a crucial point. Full employment meant making the labour market generally a seller's rather than a buyer's market, and this would increase permanently and markedly the bargaining strength of labour. Sectional wage bargaining might then lead to a vicious spiral of inflation. The remedy? The TUC should seek to achieve a unified wage policy, and wages ought, secondly, to be determined by reason, with arbitration featuring prominently in the process, replacing the methods of strike and lock-out, "ordeal by battle".

Growth of public sector
There is no doubt that the implementation of full employment policies, which became an international, not just a British objective, was the key feature of the post-war years. It accounted for the growth in the business of the public sector, from welfare and health services to the improved educational opportunity. Somewhat separate from that, but as part of a greater willingness for government to intervene in economic affairs, the command of

strategic basic industries and services led to the establishment of monopoly, nationalised enterprises in coal, gas, electricity, railways and, intermittently, steel. The public sector increased its share of the resources used in the economy quite dramatically. For a time it appeared that full employment policies had unlocked a new door to economic growth as well, for the expansion of the domestic and international economy gathered pace.

Questioning the system of industrial relations

Let us move on now to our second vantage point, the 1960s. In his 1959 assessment already cited, Phelps Brown suggested that the structure, balance and manners of British society had been transformed since 1914. It was these, working on the partners to industrial relations, which had brought improvements in industrial relations, rather than changes in the machinery of industrial relations itself. By contrast to the United States, for instance, where welfare gains, such as sickness and pensions benefit, had to be negotiated through collective bargaining, welfare legislation provided the avenue of advance in Britain. Collective bargaining was under no great pressure to be innovative.

There were, nevertheless, growing anxieties about the machinery of industrial relations. There was suspicion of any co-ordination of wages such as Beveridge had singled out. Proposals for a national wage policy foundered on the determination of the parties to each bargain to maintain their independence. The lack of legal regulation meant there was no *positive code* to distinguish what was permissible in the actions of parties to bargaining. People were worried about the growth in unofficial action, and concerned at the remoteness of industry-wide bargaining from the problems of the company, the shop floor.

THE DONOVAN COMMISSION 1965–1968

Help was at hand, or so it seemed. We shall be referring a great deal throughout this study to the Fifth Royal Commision on Industrial Relations—the Donovan Commission—set up by the Labour Government. It sat from 1965 to 1968, with terms of reference which required it to pay particular attention to the law affecting the activities of unions and employers' associations.

A dual system

The fundamental Donovan thesis was that Britain had two systems of industrial relations. One, formal, was typified by industry-wide collective agreements, embodied in the official institutions. The other, informal, frequently at odds with the formal system, was created by the actual behaviour of trade unions and employers' associations, managers, shop stewards, and workers. The formal system supposedly settled pay, hours and other conditions, the informal generated actual earnings.

Full employment was the key explanation for this dual structure. It gave power to the supply side of the equation, and power on the supply side at the point of the pick, the shop floor. Industry-wide bargaining was out of touch. Employers' associations had lost their authority. The trade union structure of multi-unionism had helped to augment the power of work groups and shop stewards. What was wrong with that? Extreme decentralisation and self-government tended to degenerate into indecision and anarchy, inefficiency, and a reluctance to change.

Economists saw the problem in terms of wage drift, the tendency for pay at the plant level to wander away from the norms set at the industry negotiations, because of the scarcity of labour in a full employment labour market. Students of trade unionism saw the problem as the power of informal groups, the shop steward, and "I'm all right, Jack". Sociologists brooded about the changed nature of organisational behaviour in this new environment in which there had been a major shift of power to the workers. As one observer out it, "The wage drift and the wildcat strike are Siamese twins."[2]

ECONOMIC PERFORMANCE

Donovan concentrated, correctly enough, on the industrial relations machinery. Running alongside it was a more broadly-based critique, which also included industrial relations in its scope, the report by a group of American and Canadian economists on Britain's economic prospects, also published in 1968.[3] Their verdict was that, by its own historical yardsticks, the British economy had experienced lively growth since the war. What concerned us and them was that our performance was poor compared with that of other industrialised societies. The Brookings group found that the key to our *malaise* did not lie primarily in a poor total, or macro, economic policy, or in deficient monetary and fiscal policies. It was more the *qualitative, non-quantifiable factors* that hampered us, such as the quality of management, the competitiveness of markets, the application of pure science to marketable products, and the two-tier system of collective bargaining, which was very deficient in productivity thrust.

This analysis, although on a rather narrower range of themes, was substantially repeated by a further Brookings study published in 1980.[4]

> . . . Britain's economic malaise stems largely from its productivity problem, whose origins lie deep in the social system. This finding points to two policy approaches that could be played in tandem. One approach would strike directly at the productivity problem itself by improving industrial relations (if that were possible), by increasing individual incentives, by improving the allocation of capital (for instance, to small firms), and the like. . . .

(The other approach would be for policy makers to live within the constraint and accept relative impoverishment.)

Self-help solutions

It was the British who invited in the Brooking *rapporteurs*. We have been anxious to be examined, but have also been busy ourselves over the years masterminding improvements in our economic performance, which has been seen as the key to better social well-being. One thinks of the establishment of the National Economic Development Council—NEDDY—in 1962 as a consensus body for great decisions about national priorities. There have been numerous arrangements for economic planning, from the National Plan 1965 to the sector working parties of the late 1970s. Regional development policies have tried to eliminate some of the gross geographical disparities in prosperity and therefore in job opportunities.

From time to time the wage-price problem has been singled out for treatment as a particular key to our difficulties. We shall look at this particular saga in Chapter Eleven. Suffice to say here that, between 1965 and 1970, the Prices and Incomes Board itself made many of the points which Donovan popularised, about the inefficiences of bargaining, the lack of strong company industrial relations policies, and the need to "think productivity". Productivity bargaining had a brief and fashionable reign.

There has been no lack of application to discover solutions. It is generally agreed that the decade of the 1970s brought more experimentation, accompanied by great controversy, in British industrial relations than in any previous period. In particular, the place of the law dominated the debate and the proposals for change. These are examined in the next chapter. More recently, there have been other subtle pressures at work affecting the climate of industrial relations. Massive unemployment in the early 1980s changed the whole environment of the labour markets in which bargaining occurs. Trade union bargaining strength, and trade union membership, were significantly reduced. Employers responded to recession by shedding labour. Another subtle change, not confined to Britain, was the growing recognition that the tempo of technological change called for new attitudes to education and training of the labour force. That too is significant for the future of industrial relations.

THE LABOUR FORCE

Many of the points about the changing nature of our economy and society can be pulled together by looking at some of the changes that have taken place in recent years in the shape of our labour force. It is that labour force, after all, that constitutes the "raw material" of industrial relations. Employers, motivated by the search for profit and efficiency, seek to blend manpower with appropriate technology and raw materials. For their part, the people offering their labour services are seeking income and security.

Labour markets are extremely complicated, and very dynamic. With a total working population of about 26 million, 6 to 7 million jobs are filled each year in Britain, some by new entrants to the labour market, but many through people moving to new jobs, to new areas, to new industries and occupations. Some occupations are fairly self-contained, such as that of civil servants or chemical engineers: others are much more open-ended and accessible to new-comers. Much of the history of trade unionism can be couched in terms of the access to jobs which unions were able to control.

Table II shows the broad movements in the recent past and in prospect with regard to the British labour force. The civilian labour force, which does include those out of work, is expected to grow to nearly 27 million in Britain by the end of the 1980s. Growth was much faster in the 1970s, however, particularly among women. The male labour force was almost static in the 1970s, but will grow in the 1980s, though not by as much as the female labour force. Overall, there is likely to be a static labour force by the end of the 1980s.

These projected movements for the remainder of the 1980s rely heavily on assumptions about unemployment. Despite the recovery in the economy which began in 1983, the numbers out of work in Britain are expected to remain at around 3 million for several years. This high unemployment is likely in turn to affect the activity rate of women in the labour market. The overall growth of women in the labour force in recent years has obviously posed new issues for a variety of industrial relations matters; one thinks of protective legislation of various kinds, equal pay, and the problems which trade unions have in organising women.

TABLE II. ESTIMATES AND PROJECTIONS OF THE CIVILIAN LABOUR FORCE
(GREAT BRITAIN)

	Civilian labour force; thousand			Change since previous year in civilian labour force: male and female	
	Male	*Female*	*Male and female*	*Thousand*	*Per cent*
June 1971	15,548	9,320	24,868	—	—
1972	15,499	9,427	24,926	+58	+0.2
1973	15,503	9,593	25,096	+170	+0.7
1974	15,479	9,734	25,213	+117	+0.5
1975	15,500	9,843	25,343	+130	+0.5
1976	15,457	9,997	25,454	+111	+0.4
1977	15,556	10,299	25,855	+401	+1.6
1978	15,522	10,315	25,837	—	−0.1
1979	15,532	10,338	25,870	+33	+0.1
1980	15,553	10,417	25,970	+100	+0.4
1981	15,627	10,523	26,150	+180	+0.7
1982	15,638	10,512	26,150	0	0.0
1983	15,701	10,582	26,283	+133	+0.5
1984	15,757	10,687	26,444	+161	+0.6
1985	15,775	10,790	26,565	+121	+0.5
1986	15,804	10,881	26,684	+119	+0.4
1987	15,842	10,953	26,795	+111	+0.4
1988	15,867	10,999	26,865	+70	+0.3
1989	15,874	11,028	26,902	+37	+0.1
1990	15,860	11,042	26,901	−1	−0.0
1991	15,834	11,045	26,879	−22	−0.1

Average annual changes in civilian labour force: male and female	*Thousand*	*Per cent*
1971–77	+165	+0.7
1977–81	+74	+0.3
1981–88	+102	+0.4
1988–91	+5	+0.0

Source: Employment Gazette Vol. 92, No. 2, February 1984

TABLE III. EMPLOYMENT BY BROAD OCCUPATIONAL GROUPS, 1971–1990 (MILLIONS)

Year	Higher level service skills	Higher level industrial skills	Management and adminis-tration	Lower level service skills	Craft and supervisory skills	Lower level industrial skills and others	Total
1971	2.32	1.01	1.89	7.49	4.39	7.18	24.28
1990 (est)	3.24	1.37	2.34	8.18	3.39	5.08	23.60
%age change	+40	+36	+24	+9	−23	−30	

Source: Manpower Services Commission, Corporate Plan 1983–1987, p.8

TABLE IV. OCCUPATIONAL SHARES OF TOTAL EMPLOYMENT, 1961 TO 1985

Occupational category	Percentages				Numbers 1978 Thousands
	1961	1971	1978 Estimated	1985 Projected	
Managers and administrators	6.6	7.8	8.7	9.6	2,146
Education professions	2.3	3.1	3.8	4.0	933
Health professions	2.5	3.2	3.8	4.6	942
Other professions	1.9	1.9	2.2	2.5	536
Literary, artistic and sports	1.2	1.4	1.7	2.2	432
Engineers and scientists	1.7	2.1	2.4	2.6	577
Technicians and draughtsmen	1.8	2.1	2.4	2.7	591
Clerical occupations	14.0	15.0	15.9	16.7	3,919
Sales occupations	5.6	5.4	5.5	5.4	1,360
Supervisors and foremen (a)	0.7	0.5	0.4	0.4	106
Engineering craftsmen	9.0	9.5	9.1	8.7	2,250
Other transferable craftsmen	4.5	3.8	3.4	3.1	828
Non-transferable craftsmen	6.2	4.2	3.5	2.6	833
Skilled operatives	3.2	3.1	2.7	2.3	669
Other operatives	22.9	20.4	18.5	16.3	4,553
Security occupations	1.0	1.3	1.2	1.3	297
Personal service occupations	8.9	10.5	11.2	12.1	2,770
Other occupations	6.1	4.8	3.8	2.9	921
Non-manual	37.5	41.9	46.3	50.3	11,435
Manual	62.5	58.1	53.7	49.7	13,228
Whole economy (b)	100	100	100	100	24,663

(a) In engineering and transport only; (b) excluding H. M. Forces.

Source: Manpower Services Commission, Manpower Review 1980, p. 19

Occupational shifts

In addition to the changes in the overall labour force, changes in the employment mix have important implications for industrial relations. Major changes have occurred in employment by sector. Britain has shared in the decline in manufacturing employment and the strong growth of jobs in services which we associate with mature industrial economies. Tables III and IV bring out vividly the dramatic changes that have occurred and are in train in the broad mix of occupations in the economy. These are likely to have enormous significance for the future patterns of industrial relations.

IMPLICATIONS

The major changes in economic and social policy which we have outlined in this chapter are clearly of immense importance for our understanding of industrial relations. One of the recent surveys of change in British industrial relations in the 1970s attributes the change to a number of driving forces reflecting the altering circumstances of the British economy as a whole. Those listed include heavy inflation, a worsening of Britain's foreign trade position, greater overseas ownership of industry, more industrial concentration, and a marked increase in government intervention in industrial relations. It envisaged that the contours of industrial relations would continue to change, not least through the deepening decline of manufacturing industry.[5]

This does not mean that an industrial relations system is passive, the creature of whim and of economic pressures. Much of the controversy surrounding industrial relations legislation and, more broadly, government intervention, has to do with a search for both more efficient arrangements for the conduct of industrial relations and a more equitable balance between the interests of the employer on the one hand and the employee on the other. We see this very vividly in the next chapter, which examines the part government plays in shaping the industrial relations system.

SELF-ASSESSMENT QUESTIONS

1. Consider how the growth of the Welfare State philosophy has affected the climate of industrial relations.

2. How far do you share the judgment of the studies by the Brookings Institution, that industrial relations are an important element in British economic performance? Can this be quantified?

3. What are the main changes that have occurred in recent years

in the mix of occupations in the British labour force? How do you account for these?

4. Are committees and commissions of enquiry, such as Whitley and Donovan, likely to initiate major change in a country's industrial relations machinery?

ASSIGNMENT

List the main changes that have occurred in the industrial and occupational composition of the labour force in Britain in recent years. Check your ideas against the Labour Market Data contained in the *Employment Gazette*. Prepare a forecast which shows how the mix of employment might look by the end of the 1980s.

REFERENCES

1. E. H. Phelps Brown, *The Growth of British Industrial Relations*, 1959, pp. 354 *et seq.*

2. Otto Kahn-Freund, *Labour and the Law*, 1972, p. 13.

3. Richard E. Caves and associates, *Britain's Economic Prospects*, 1968.

4. Richard E. Caves and Lawrence B. Krause (eds.), *Britain's Economic Performance* (esp. Ch. 1, Introduction and summary, p. 19), 1980.

5. William Brown (ed.), *The Changing Contours of British Industrial Relations*, Blackwell, 1981, p. 121.

CHAPTER THREE

The Environment set by Government

CHAPTER OBJECTIVES

After studying this chapter you should be able to:
* account for the recent increase in government intervention in industrial relations;
* understand the main changes that have occurred in the law affecting trade unions;
* explain the usefulness of Codes of Practice as an aid to industrial relations legislation;
* appreciate the nature and function of statutory bodies such as ACAS.

". . . for the law supposes that your wife acts under your direction."
"If the law supposes that," said Mr. Bumble, "the law is a ass—a idiot. If that's the eye of the law, the law's a bachelor. . . ."

Oliver Twist

GOVERNMENT'S GENERAL ROLE

Governments play a pervasive part in national economic policy, pursuing economic growth, price stability, employment and other objectives. Our concern here is with government as one of the actors, parties of interest, on the industrial relations stage. Viewed over the long haul of history, government has interfered more rather than less. The Babylonian Code of Hammurabi, drawn up some 4,000 years ago, saw fit to regulate wages and much else. It is often forgotten how recent the free market economy is; even 200 years ago, Adam Smith railed against the stubbornly surviving restrictions on the working of markets. So government has always been in the action, now fixing prices, now specifying wages, as under the Statute of Apprenticeships in England in the first Elizabethan era. Incomes policies, discussed in Chapter Eleven, are the modern manifestation of this.

Most, though not all, contemporary government involvement takes the form of legislation which either sets a framework of procedures or establishes a standard of some kind, with regard to pay or to terms and conditions. Governments also continue to influence behaviour by issuing Codes of Conduct; these complement the law but may also have a free-standing status in their own right. Government sets up agencies to perform public interest functions in industrial relations.

Government as employer

The Government is also an employer. We can deal briefly with that part of its involvement. Here government has not been an innovator in Britain. The statutes which set up the nationalised industries after the Second World War provided that the corporations should have negotiating and consultative machinery for their industrial relations. It was hoped that they would pioneer new forms of employee involvement. That apart, the corporations simply inherited ongoing collective bargaining arrangements and trade union rights, and the main change was on the employer side. A publicly-owned corporation became the single employer in any one industry. Some modest experimentation with worker directors occurred in the steel industry and the Post Office in the 1970s.

In the more traditional part of the public service, the Civil Service in the narrow sense, the conventional wisdom long was that such employees could not enjoy the same rights as ordinary employees, since they were adjuncts of the state. Their right to strike was always a prickly issue. Trade unionism in the civil service nevertheless has a long history, but a landmark was the introduction of "Whitleyism", Joint Industrial Councils, in 1919. This machinery has endured, and developed. Ironically, when that committee, chaired by the Speaker of the House of Commons, produced its proposals during the 1914–18 war for improving industrial relations, it initially did not include the public service.

Three important points are relevant about the civil service experience in Britain. The first concerns the position of non-industrial civil servants in the trade union movement. The General Strike of 1926 is the landmark. Some civil servants supported it, and in consequence the Trade Disputes and Trade Union Act 1927 prevented such civil servants from belonging to organisations affiliated to the TUC, the Labour Party, and public service international union bodies. The Act was repealed in 1946. Since then the (now nine) non-industrial unions have affiliated to the TUC, and civil service unions are well integrated into mainstream trade unionism, including representation on the General Council of the TUC.

The distinctive position of public employees can still cause concern, however, for instance when national security is held to be important. The British government banned trade unions at a communications headquarters in 1984. Its action did a great deal of harm to relations between it and the trade union movement.

The second point is more interesting in the context of industrial relations developments. In the past, white-collar civil servants tended to be outside the main body of industrial relations legislation, because of their status. However, the bulk of the legislation introduced in recent years has applied to the civil service, directly or through their having the laws applied to them in no less favourable a way. The civil service has not been a major source of new industrial relations techniques or procedures, however; it has largely followed, and benefited from, traditional methods.

A third point is important for the principles of pay policy in the national economy. Since the mid-1950s many public employees have had their pay settled in accordance with the principle of *comparability*, introduced in that year for civil service pay. The policy has not always been popular, particularly when public sector pay appeared to be running ahead of pay in the private sector. Comparability appeared to be a lever. We look at this aspect of government in Chapter Eleven, on Incomes Policies.

GOVERNMENT'S THIRD PARTY FUNCTIONS

In addition to this role as an employer, government has a wider task on behalf of the community. What part should it play as custodian of the public interest in the labour market and industrial relations in that market? Without seeking, at least at this stage, to define "the public interest", it is clear that government has in some sense to represent this. Even a policy of *laissez-faire*, of non-intervention by the Government, is a policy. In fact, however, the growth (or regrowth) of government involvement during the industrial era has long outdistanced the notion that government could, would and should stand back, leaving the machinery to be bipartite rather than tripartite. Keeping the ring is not just a matter of setting procedures, "Queensberry Rules", either; governments have played a part in setting standards, of pay and of performance, e.g., in safeguarding individual rights. One of the curious myths about British industrial relations is that the system is "voluntary", in the sense that the Government opts out and looks the other way. The real situation is much more subtle, and raises challenging questions—in what areas of industrial relations is *voluntarism* to be permitted and encouraged, and in what forms? Another point to notice is that the attitudes of labour and management to government involvement are essentially pragmatic and opportunistic. They are for or against the Government, according as its policies do or do not serve their interests. This interplay has made for a fascinating if turbulent saga in the law of industrial relations in particular.

> The nature and extent of legal regulation has been determined not by some abstract rule-making force, but by the interplay of judicial innovations, public policy controversy, the relative power of management and labour interests, and party politics with a view to electoral advantages.[1]

This can be put another way. The tale of government involvement continually poses the crucial question—What is the balance, the equilibrium, that is being sought? Among what interests? And what are the tests of its success? This runs through all industrial relations systems, not just the British one. It has a number of strands to it, and we look at them in turn, concentrating on British arrangements.

No comprehensive legal code
It would have been helpful if we could at this stage have looked up a single Bible, cataloguing British industrial relations legislation. The Donovan Commission proposed that in due course the English and Scottish Law Commissions should be asked to undertake the task of codifying the law governing labour relations and trade unions and employers' associations, as a matter of urgency. If codification was considered premature, then a comprehensive consolidating measure should be enacted as soon as possible after implementing legislation. This has not been done. The cynic can say that the decade of the 1970s was so taken up with passing and repealing legislation, some broad and some narrow in scope, that consolidation would have called for a modern Moses.

The strands we shall tease out are as follows:

(a) The attitude of the law to trade unions, in particular what they can do within the law.

(b) Protection for the individual employee, e.g., from oppressive factory conditions and arbitrary employers.

(c) The setting of standards, such as minimum rates of pay.

(d) The support for and influence on collective bargaining.

(e) Rules of the game for conducting industrial disputes, including maintaining essential services.

(f) Codes of Practice.

(g) Government agencies servicing public policies, and gathering information and providing intelligence.

The above list excludes one very important area, that of the *internal* government of trade unions, in which the law has been taking an increasing interest in Britain in recent years. The theme of democracy in trade unions, as it may rather grandly be called, raises interesting questions about elections of officers, members' rights, the closed union shop, and the place of the (secret) ballot in union governance. There have been three Acts in Britain in recent years—Employment Act 1980, Employment Act 1982, and Trade Union and Labour Relations Act 1984—which have tackled various aspects of internal union affairs. We simply note that fact at this stage; we shall take up the law's interest in internal union government when we deal in Chapter Five with the whole range of issues relating to the organisation and government of trade unionism. There is still ample to consider in the present chapter.

ATTITUDE OF THE LAW TO TRADE UNIONS

Milne-Bailey, a trade unionist student of trade unions, said of the Trade Disputes Act 1906 that this "drastic and comprehensive statute represents the high-water mark of Trade Union freedom."[2] Others, evidently less familiar with the tides, have seen it rather as an Olympus, "the golden formula of our industrial law". Section 4 was the key one.

> An action against a trade union, whether of workmen or masters, or against any members or officials thereof on behalf of themselves and all other members of the trade union in respect of any tortious act alleged to have been committed by or on behalf of the trade union, shall not be entertained by any court.

Trade unions, as such, were not to be liable for any tort, i.e. civil wrong, alleged to have been committed by them or on their behalf. *Individuals* were equally protected by section 3 if they were acting to induce some other person to break a contract of employment "in contemplation or furtherance of a trade dispute". Section 1 protected *two or more persons*, say trade union officials, in similar fashion.

Legal exemption

It is not the absence of law which is the crucial feature of these provisions, but the exemptions which it conferred. Dicey remarked that it placed unions above the law. If it was a high water mark, the unions had had a very uncomfortable time getting there. They were made illegal in 1799, not only in the wake of fears about subversion being imported from France, but also because freedom of contract was gaining ground and restraint of trade, which combinations of workers could be considered to represent, was frowned upon. Legislation in 1824/25 did give the unions legal standing, but largely prevented them from doing anything with the support of the law,

since they were "in restraint of trade". By 1875, attacks on trade
union activities through the criminal law had been largely stilled,
through the Conspiracy and Protection of Property Act 1875 and
the Employers and Workmen Act of the same year. The ordinary
industrial dispute, peacefully conducted, was thereafter free from
criminal law connotations. There remained, however, the problem
of immunity from liability for tort, i.e., a civil wrong at common
law.

The famous Taff Vale railway case of 1901 involved a union being
successfully sued for breach of contract and for damages caused by a
strike. It left the unions vulnerable and confused. Yet the tide was
running their way. More than anything else, the Taff Vale case gave
the unions an issue with which to press their case for a presence in
Parliament, and the Labour Representation Committee, which the
unions had largely helped to get off the ground in 1900, found here
a Parliamentary issue which it succeeded in pressing through to
the Act of 1906, after the election of that year. An independent
political force for Labour was vindicated; the Labour Party—trade
union alliance was on the march! So the Trade Disputes Act
1906 is a political tide mark, as well as a high water mark in the
exemptions which it conferred on the unions with regard to the
civil law.

The tide stayed in, on this particular question, until 1964, when
the case of *Rookes* v. *Barnard* threw open again what had apparently been a settled question in civil law, the immunity against civil
action for "intimidation" in the context of trade disputes. The
Trade Disputes Act 1965 restored the 1906 position as a holding
operation, pending the report of the Royal Commission, the
Donovan Commission.

One of the interesting features of the 1906 approach was that it
established the position of trade unions through the device of
exemptions from legal action, instead of setting out positive rights,
and obligations, for trade unions and their members. Subsequent,
and controversial, proposals since Donovan reported in 1968 have
ranged much more widely, approaching the topic of union status in
law in a variety of ways.

Donovan's approach
Donovan proposed that the term "trade union" should in law be
reserved for organisations of employees. (It is one of the many
curious features of British law that the 1906 Act, for example,
included employers' associations in the scope of the definition of
unions.) It also proposed that unions should be granted corporate
personality and should register.

The suggested use of the device of registration to put the squeeze on trade unions was interesting. Registration of unions had been available since 1871, and this gave certain advantages for the holding of property and liability to taxation. A majority of the Donovan Commission proposed to confine the traditional immunity under the law to *registered* unions only. This was to be one way of tackling the contemporary problem of unofficial strikes, the worry about which had been one of the main reasons behind the Donovan enquiry. Unofficial strikers could have been liable to prosecution.

The Industrial Relations Act 1971

The Industrial Relations Act 1971 did use the device of registration for this purpose. However, it used registration in another context too, as a way of clarifying the status of unions in law, and presumably of putting pressure on them to tidy up their Rule books. It set standards to which Union rules had to conform with respect to members' rights, finances, and management. The TUC saw this as surveillance of unions by the state, and instructed its affiliates to take advantage of the provisions in the 1971 Act which allowed them not to register. The subsequent history of this use of registration is that first, the Trade Union and Labour Relations Acts of 1974 and 1976 restored the traditional position by which unions are protected against common law actions for certain acts undertaken in contemplation or furtherance of a trade union dispute. Again, this position proved short-lived, however, for the Employment Act 1980 began to make inroads into trade union exemptions by its provisions regarding picketing and secondary action. We consider these later in this chapter, under the heading "rules of the game in industrial disputes".

Certification

As to registration itself, secondly, the Employment Protection Act 1975, section 7, set up a new Certification Office and Officer to replace the traditional Registrar function. The 1975 Act dramatically reduced the inroads into internal union rules which the 1971 Act had made possible. The Certification Officer has only a limited involvement with the content of union rule books. With the exception of the rules governing political funds, unions and employers' associations do not have to submit their rules for approval by a statutory agency. We shall see in Chapter Five how the unions have fared in keeping their own house in order in this respect.

One of the other functions of the Certification Office is to handle procedures for union mergers under the Trade Union (Amalgamations etc.) Act 1964. Again, we shall see this machinery at work in Chapter Five.

Union recognition

The final aspect of union affairs to be looked at in this context is legal support for union recognition. Perhaps because they had made a lot of progress prior to 1906, and were then guaranteed the immunities to which we have referred, the unions have never pressed for legal support on this matter. The unions took the view that they had fought for recognition through their own efforts, whereas legal rights, once given, could be taken away. In their evidence to Donovan the TUC went no further than favouring the reintroduction of arbitration at the request of one party, as a way of pressuring any employer who refused to negotiate, rather than the introduction of legislation on recognition. Donovan, however, did envisage that a new independent body could play a useful part in hearing recognition claims and making proposals for resolving them.

The role of ACAS in union recognition

The 1971 Act contained very explicit provisions for recognition and bargaining rights, including the concepts of sole bargaining agent and bargaining unit. However, none of the arrangements included a full-blooded statement of the case for the right to organise and be recognised. The Employment Protection Act 1975 (sections 11 to 16) laid out procedures involving ACAS (the Advisory, Conciliation and Arbitration Service) if an employer refused to recognise an independent union. ACAS was empowered to try to settle the problem by conciliation, failing which it could make a recommendation, based on appropriate enquiry. These sections of the Act generated a lot of business, and considerable heat, during the period they operated, prior to their repeal in 1980. By the end of 1979, 1,542 references had been received. ACAS itself became increasingly unhappy about its role in recognition disputes. Sometimes it was drawn into abrasive situations and Court proceedings, and disliked the encroaching legalism at the expense of voluntary procedures. It also felt that this involvement was prejudicing its other voluntary advisory and conciliation functions. The provisions of the 1975 Act on recognition were repealed by the Employment Act 1980, in part because ACAS itself stated bluntly that it could not satisfactorily operate the statutory recognition procedures as they stood. One deficiency, which was exposed by the Grunwick dispute in 1977, was that an employer was under no legal obligation to co-operate with ACAS.

Within a decade, then, the union recognition wheel had turned full circle. There is now, once again, no statutory leverage in Britain for obtaining union recognition. The workload which ACAS had been forced to pick up indicated that the references to it on union recognition mainly concerned small and medium-sized companies. The other interesting feature is that, as Chapter Five brings out, the decade of the 1970s saw a brisk boom in union membership in Britain, when the law was certainly involved , and frequently changing. It is a nice question whether union membership expanded in spite of, or because of, the legal involvement, or whether other factors, such as inflation, were critical. We examine this issue in Chapter Five.

PROTECTING THE INDIVIDUAL EMPLOYEE

While the battle raged about trade unions and their industrial activities "in contemplation or furtherance of a trade dispute", a steady procession of protective statutes worked their way through Parliament in the nineteenth century. There was the series of Factory Acts, commencing in 1833, initially assisting juveniles and women directly, but permeating to protection for the male worker as well, not least on hours of work. The 1833 Act introduced the factory inspectorate. The Truck Acts, beginning in 1831, endorsed the principle of paying wages in cash. Employers' liability and workmen's compensation were the subject of legislation late in the century, and the beginnings of the broadly based welfare state were laid in 1911, through the National Health Insurance Act. The culmination of much of the early protective legislation was the Health and Safety at Work etc. Act 1974, which also set up a Health and Safety Executive to monitor and raise the level of workplace health, safety, and environmental provision.

Interestingly, and perhaps significantly, one gap in this protective legislation was the absence of any rules about the individual's contract of employment. That was not the subject of any special provisions, being governed by the ordinary civil law of contract. The employee could take his employer to court, and vice versa. It was only in 1963 that the first of the Contracts of Employment Acts was passed, requiring employers to give written particulars of terms and conditions, and specifying minimum periods of notice. Since then the theme of contractual protection for a wide range of matters has fairly caught fire. A more enlightened view of the security attaching to a job has produced provisions on maternity rights, medical suspension, guaranteed pay etc. Equally significant, protective legislation now recognises that in situations of (a) redundancy and (*b*) dismissal, which may or may not be unfair, protective procedures are needed. The Redundancy Payments Act 1965 and the unfair dismissals provisions of the Industrial Relations Act 1971 are landmarks in this regard. Other legislation, the Race Relations Act 1968 and the Equal Pay Act 1970, for example, cover protection against particular aspects of discrimination. There is no doubt that the law has set the pace on many of these matters, and the whole theme of individual employee rights is now so vast that we shall be returning to it in Chapter Nine, to see it at work.

SETTING STANDARDS

In addition to the protective legislation just discussed, public policy in industrial relations has intervened to ensure minimum or not-less-favourable standards of pay.

Wages Councils

Britain has been reluctant to adopt minimum wage legislation, but has in effect acquired pay floors through Wages Councils. These are the successors to Trade Boards, originally set up in 1909 for four "sweated" low-wage trades, and extended by successive Acts to the present Wages Council Act in 1979, which is a consolidating statute. Wages Councils are tripartite bodies, consisting of equal representation of employers and workers, with three independent members, who if necessary may exercise a casting vote. Their remit is to set statutory minimum remuneration, holidays and holiday remuneration in trades and industries in which organisation among workers or employers, or both, is insufficient for the satisfactory functioning of collective bargaining. The interesting negotiating procedures of Wages Councils are examined in Chapter Eight.

In addition to setting a floor, which may vary from council to council, Wages Councils were intended, from 1919 on, as nurseries for collective bargaining. Councils have been abolished when, in accordance with a stipulated procedure, it could be shown they were no longer needed. In 1983 some $2\frac{3}{4}$ million workers were covered by the 26 councils. There has been some rationalisation in recent years; for instance, the nine councils covering workers employed in retail trade were abolished, and replaced in 1979 by two large separate councils, one for food and one for non-food. A corps of wage inspectors monitors the statutory wage orders which emanate from councils. Other legislation covers minimum wages in agriculture.

Some critics would like to see rationalisation carried further, and would abolish Wages Councils. They argue that when they set wages below market rates the Councils are ineffective; when the rates they set are higher than those that would have occurred in a free market they deprive people of jobs who would have been willing to work at lower rates.

Fair Wages Resolutions

The other approach to setting standards has been through Fair Wages Resolutions. The first of these was passed by the House of Commons in 1891. A revised version, dating from 1946, was abandoned in 1983. The objective of the Resolution was to ensure that employers carrying out government contracts paid fair wages. Fairness was defined by comparing with rates, hours and conditions fixed by negotiation or arbitration, or with the general level observed by comparable employers. Unlike Wages Councils' rates, which aimed at some kind of living minimum, the essence of the Fair Wage Resolution device was that of equity, relative fairness between public and other employers.

Disputes about the observance of the Resolution were settled ultimately by the Central Arbitration Committee. The number of references tended to be high, e.g., 242 awards by the CAC in 1979, when pay restrictions were in force. In 1983 only 21 awards were made.

None of these forms of setting standards was intended to replace collective bargaining. Indeed, as in the intent with Wages Councils, they can lead towards collective bargaining. What then is public policy towards collective bargaining?

SUPPORTING AND INFLUENCING COLLECTIVE BARGAINING

A great many private collective bargaining arrangements, at local, district and ultimately industry or national level, were hammered out in Britain in the nineteenth and early twentieth centuries. There was considerable experimentation, in a pragmatic way, with conciliation and arbitration. The Conciliation Act of 1896 was therefore a kind of confirming enactment when it provided support for collective bargaining through conciliation and arbitration machinery. (The detailed workings of conciliation and arbitration are considered in Chapter Eight.) Compulsory arbitration has been practised in time of war and during the aftermath of war, and in recent times the burning topic of incomes policy has made inroads into "free collective bargaining". Yet the main intent of British industrial relations has been to continue the long-standing practice that collective agreements are voluntary, and binding in honour only. They are not legally enforceable agreements. The Donovan Com-

mission began to nibble at this tradition, when it recognised the
need to develop more comprehensive, sophisticated and govern-
able collective agreements and asked itself how this could be
done, short of making collective agreements legally enforceable. Its
solution was to propose voluntary improvement, but subject to
pressure from a public agency, an Industrial Relations Commission, with the threat that legal enforceability for procedural agreements might have to be contemplated, depending on the progress
made in reforming industrial relations.

Legal presumption
The Industrial Relations Act 1971, section 34, took the very cate-
gorical line that collective agreements should be *conclusively pre-
sumed* to be intended, by the parties to them, to be legally enforceable contracts unless they stated explicitly that the agreement in
whole or part was intended *not* to be legally enforceable. While the
Act was in force, the overwhelming practice was to enter in collective agreements the disclaiming clause "This is not a legally enforceable agreement", until the Trade Union and Labour Relations Act
1974, section 18 reversed the presumption. The tradition thus
persists, that collective agreements are voluntary, non-contractual,
in Britain.
    Strangers to the British scene frequently find this very puzzling.
First, the individual contract of employment has associated with it
the trappings of legal status. Second, it is possible for collective
agreements to bind individual employees, via their contracts of
employment, if their contracts expressly incorporate collective
terms. As the terms of a collective agreement change, so the individual contract of employment linked to it can automatically adjust.

Extension of terms and conditions
A third intriguing point is that, until recently, the law could be used
to extend these "non-legal" collective agreements. Section 8 of the
Terms and Conditions of Employment Act 1959 allowed employers
to be pursued on the grounds that they were not observing recognised terms or conditions in the industry. This provision was carried
forward to section 98 of the Employment Protection Act 1975 and
its supporting "Schedule 11". In addition to the criterion of recognised terms or conditions, the schedule introduced a new criterion
of "general level" where no recognised terms existed. Under this
schedule, The Central Arbitration Committee, the ultimate inter-
preter, had a deluge of claims, not least during the period of
incomes policy guides. In 1978 it made 519 awards, in 1979, 307.
After this brisk round of business the provisions were repealed in

1980. There had been a good deal of disquiet about the way this device operated, in transmitting terms and conditions on the basis of a criterion such as "general level", where "comparators" might be difficult to identify.

The notion of extending terms and conditions has thus passed from the British scene, after a lengthy innings. It is a device used in other countries, for instance West Germany, to extend the frontier of the area within which a collective agreement reigns. Whether the abolition of Schedule 11 will leave a gap remains to be seen. Since the majority of these Schedule 11 awards related to claims for fewer than 100 employees it seems that the abolition of this procedure has done away with a small claims court, rather than being an instrument for destabilising pay setting. In any case, the settlement of pay in Britain since 1980 has been much coloured by recession and very high unemployment, and by a deliberate attempt on the part of government *not* to have a formal incomes policy. So it is difficult to judge what effect the abolition of Schedule 11 has had.

The single most important point to note about the British free collective bargaining system, however, is that the voluntary, non-enforceable agreement has remained remarkably resilient. At times it has come under severe attack from government efforts to operate incomes policies. We take up this enormously important topic in Chapter Eleven.

RULES OF THE GAME IN INDUSTRIAL DISPUTES

The key British rule is that the parties to disputes should resolve their differences themselves. Only after their own procedures have been exhausted does the third party intervention of government aids, such as conciliation and arbitration, come into play. This means of course that the parties are expected to have explicit and effective procedures. This has not always been the case. A good deal of the post-Donovan pressure has been applied to improving procedure agreements. A companion to the Industrial Relations Act 1971 was a Code of Practice, part of which set out guidelines on disputes procedures. For its part, the TUC has preferred to spell out its own guides, most recently in 1979 on Negotiating Arrangements and Disputes Procedures.

Since the Conciliation Act of 1896 the Government has reinforced the third party range of supporting measures, for instance through the Industrial Courts Act 1919, which introduced the idea of tripartite Boards of arbitration to be used *ad hoc*, the "one-off" court of inquiry, and also a permanent industrial court (many of whose functions are now exercised through the Central Arbitration Committee).

Since conciliation cannot force parties to agree, and since voluntary arbitration involves the parties in agreeing to use that device to resolve differences, it follows that disputes between parties can lead to coercive action, such as strikes or lockouts. We have already seen how the position of unions was protected at law in 1906. We have also noticed how at times governments have sought to control unofficial industrial action. In Chapter Seven we shall see how bargaining pressures are deployed in the process of making collective agreements. Here, however, we can single out the following particular themes which have caused problems in recent years in determining the appropriate nature and form of public policy intervention. The problem is to reconcile reasonable freedom on the part of trade unions and employers with the public interest, broadly defined, and with the right of neutral third parties not to be sucked into a dispute. Drawing the boundaries has not proved, and is not, easy.

Maintaining essential services
National industrial relations machinery may have to cope with "national emergencies", threats to "essential services", however these may be defined. Experience shows that definition is not easy. Wartime arrangements are of course exceptional, but in addition to these extraordinary situations, there are interesting features of British arrangements. The Emergency Powers Act 1920 allows government to adopt special powers if the essential services of the community are threatened. This has occurred on occasion, for instance in dock strikes. The *ad hoc* court of inquiry has also assisted in resolving disputes which threatened a national emergency, such as the disruption of electricity supplies during a hard winter, or a winter stoppage by coal miners.

These arrangements have worked satisfactorily in Britain, largely because they have been used sparingly. The national policy was not greatly advanced by two devices which were introduced by the Industrial Relations Act 1971, sections 138 to 145, on emergency procedures. In 1969 the Labour Government had toyed with the possible use of a union membership ballot where a major official strike threatened, and the idea of a ballot was included in the 1971 Act. It also provided for the device of a "cooling-off" period up to 60 days, if this would assist the settlement of the dispute in question. These emergency procedures, of cooling-off period and ballot, were invoked only once under the Act, in the railway dispute of 1972. They may not have had a fair trial, because of the bitter union opposition to the Act. Nevertheless, experience in other countries, such as the USA, where emergency procedures have long been available under the Taft–Hartley Act, does not suggest conclusively that specified procedures are the best answer to the problem. An *ad hoc* approach, relying, where appropriate, on resort to a court of inquiry, may be more flexible, and in tune with British experience. Nevertheless, there has been renewed discussion in Britain in recent years of banning strikes in essential services, possibly in return for some kind of guaranteed pay comparability scheme. This would be intended to ensure that those foregoing the right to bargain backed by the strike weapon would not be disadvantaged in their terms and conditions.

Picketing and secondary action

If coercive action is to succeed it frequently has to be vigorous. But what weapons should be permitted? And against whom may they be aimed? This is one of the most difficult parts of industrial relations terrain. In Chapter Seven we shall be looking at the actual workings of collective bargaining processes, and the range of "weapons", or pressures, which are deployed. They range from overtime bans to all-out stoppages. Some of the most abrasive problems arise with regard to two particular forms of industrial action, (*a*) picketing; and (*b*) secondary action. We look at these in turn here, in the context of public policy.

Peaceful picketing

One of the classic ways in which bargaining pressure can be exercised "in contemplation or furtherance of a trade dispute" is through picketing. Broadly, this involves posting men at an employer's premises, who try to persuade others to desist from working for the employer. This puts pressure on him, by making it difficult for him to fulfil his commercial contracts with others. How far are pickets permitted to persuade without, for example, running foul of the criminal law? Picketing bristles with industrial relations and legal problems.

By 1906 the Trades Disputes Act of that year had codified a consensus. Picketing in contemplation or furtherance of a trade dispute was immune from civil action where the picketing was *peaceful* and aimed to obtain and communicate information and *to persuade* a person to work or not to work. The 1906 Act also contained provisions, now illegal, allowing picketing at a person's home.

In recent years controversy has raged in Britain about the scope of picketing. At what point did the number of pickets become a

crowd? Where was the line between peaceful persuasion and intimidation? Were "flying" pickets legitimate? How widely could a
union cast its net in picketing? The Employment Act 1980 took up a
tight position which drastically limited picketing, by restricting
lawful picketing to a person's *own place of work*. The new definition
of peaceful picketing stated that it is lawful for a person to picket
provided that:

(*a*) he or she is acting in contemplation or furtherance of a trade
dispute, the classic starting point;

(*b*) the sole purpose is *peacefully* to obtain or communicate
information, or *peacefully to persuade* a person to work or not to
work (again the classic criteria);

(*c*) he or she pickets at or near *his or her own place of work*, such
as the entrance or exit of a factory, site, or office.

This was a dramatically new provision.

A trade union official may accompany a member of the union
whom he or she represents and who is picketing in accordance with
the above requirements. A Code of Practice on picketing gives
guidance on both the criminal and civil law as it affects picketing,
and on the proper conduct and organisation of pickets. The TUC
produced its own Code in February 1979.

One important feature of the public code is the suggestion that
the number of pickets reasonably required for peaceful persuasion
need rarely exceed six, and frequently a smaller number will suffice.
This may well help to reduce problems caused by the difficult
boundary between peaceful persuasion and intimidation, particularly when a picketing operation has assumed the scale of a demonstration and physical access to a work site may be impeded. The
demonstration has sometimes, as in the 1977 Grunwick dispute,
embarrassed a union as well as the employer. Equally, this guide
line brings out sharply the pronouncement of the Attorney-General
in 1980, that the picketing immunities "do not diminish the rules
which govern public order". The police have to work with the
Public Order Act in keeping the peace, although it is not their
function to take a view of the merits of a dispute or to enforce the
civil law. The Code gives guidance about the role of the police.

The prolonged stoppage in the coal mining industry in Britain in
1984 threw these provisions into very sharp focus indeed. The scale
on which picketing occurred raised the question whether large
numbers of pickets can be regarded as reasonable in the context of
"peaceful picketing". When the numbers involved become large,
where does peaceful persuasion end and intimidation begin? Who is
to be the judge of this? This raises the sensitive question of the

protection which the police should be expected to provide for workers who wish to continue working, and who might well be deterred from doing so by large numbers of pickets.

Picketing of premises other than one's own place of work was also an issue. Flying pickets were much in evidence, seeking to bring about a stoppage of work at *other* places of work, not only in the mining industry but in other premises, such as steel mills and power stations, which are large users of coal and coke. In principle, this kind of secondary action is illegal under the Act. The police sought on occasion to minimise the risk of confrontation by intercepting pickets en route by coach to other places of employment. This could be defended with reference to the preservation of the public peace.

A final matter concerned the action taken by employers. Experience, not least under the Industrial Relations Act 1971, has demonstrated that law on the statute book is one thing; law as the parties to a dispute, or the public, care to call it into use is quite another. In the coal dispute, the employer chose not to enforce an injunction that had been obtained, in order not to exacerbate a situation already at flash point. In other words, employers may exercise discretion in seeking to use the law. This may put the police in an exposed position, especially when the large numbers of pickets involved make it difficult to manage an exercise in peaceful persuasion in a manner acceptable to those immediately involved, and to the wider, neutral, third party, the public.

Another dispute, between the Stockport Messenger Newspaper group and the National Graphical Association in 1983, demonstrated how speedily pressure *can* be brought to bear when an employer does make determined use of the law. The issue concerned an attempt to enforce a closed shop. An injunction was obtained to stop mass picketing, and the NGA was fined for contempt of the injunction. It refused to pay, and a further fine was imposed, plus sequestration of the assets of the NGA. The matter was resolved when the TUC decided not to back the NGA, in part it appeared because its assessment of the situation was that the Association could not win.

Secondary action

Suppose A initiates an action against B about a question of pay. C then takes strike action against D because he believes that this action will strengthen A's position in his dispute with B. Under the 1906 Act both A and C were protected. This whole issue, of the *spread* of industrial action, or secondary action, has been much in the public eye in Britain in recent years. The 1984 coal strike is a prime example. Two recent cases which were the subject of legal debate also bring out the complexities of the problems. In one case, *Express Newspapers Ltd.* v. *McShane*, the Lords held in 1979 that members of the National Union of Journalists were able to call upon journalists acting for national newspapers to refuse "black" copy coming from the Press Association. Their action was permissible, since it was in furtherance of a trade dispute. Lord Denning had held in the Court of Appeal that the action was *too remote from* the original dispute to be allowed. The Lords disagreed. They also produced the interesting proposition that the expression "in furtherance of a trade dispute" refers to the subjective state of mind of the person doing the act and means that he so acts with the purpose of helping parties to the dispute to achieve their objectives in the honest and reasonable belief that it will do so.[3]

The other dispute which raised questions about the concept of secondary action was *Dupont Steels Ltd. and others* v. *Sirs and others*. In the course of the protracted dispute in the nationalised steel industry in 1980, the union side called out members in the private sector of the steel industry as well, as a means of furthering their trade dispute with the nationalised British Steel Corporation. Again, the Court of Appeal held that the second dispute was not really a trade dispute but was aimed at the Government. The Lords took their stand on the McShane case, and the subjective test of the act having been done in contemplation or furtherance of a trade dispute. Significantly, however, the Lords also made it clear that if the law as interpreted was unacceptable, it was for Parliament to change it, for example by limiting the heads under which immunity at civil law was conferred. If the Parliamentary draftsman was to limit secondary or tertiary "blacking" or picketing, the statute must declare whose premises may, or may not, be picketed, and how far the blacking or picketing may extend.[4]

The Employment Act 1980 responded to this invitation in the provisions which section 17 made for secondary action, defined to cover a broader canvas than secondary picketing alone, and including blacking and sympathetic strikes. The principle is, that secondary action is justifiable only to the extent that it is used to put direct pressure on the employer in dispute, to press for him to settle. The Employment Act 1982 continued this squeeze on the scope of coercive action by allowing employers to sue *unions* that authorise secondary or other unlawful industrial action, and by narrowing the definition of a lawful trade dispute to cover disputes between workers and their own employers.

WHAT IS A TRADE DISPUTE?

We have noticed several times already in this chapter the classic phrase "acts done in contemplation or furtherance of a trade dispute." We have just observed the difficulties of defining and controlling the range of actions done. One recent dispute in Britain brought out vividly the issue of what constitutes a trade dispute. In 1983 the Post Office Engineering Union instructed its members not to connect a privately financed telecommunications system, *Mercury*, to the British Telecom network. Mercury had been granted a licence under the Telecommunications Act 1981 to operate its system. To do this it needed to link into the inter-connection facilities of British Telecom, and this was agreed in 1982.

The Union's action was part of its campaign against the privatisation of British Telecom. When its action was challenged, it argued that it was acting in furtherance of a trade dispute between British Telecom and its employees which related wholly or mainly to job security. When, after the injunction stage, the matter reached the Court of Appeal, it was held that the action of the Union was unlawful because it was motivated by political factors, aimed at maintaining the public monopoly of British Telecom in the face of private competition. It was not a trade dispute. The Appeal Court was influenced by the fact that the Union had a job security agreement with British Telecom. It had made no effort to activate this, nor to seek improvements in it as a safeguard against termination of employment. The Union obeyed the ruling, and called off the action.

CODES OF PRACTICE

The idea of a code of practical guidance for promoting good industrial relations was an innovation in Britain at the time of the Industrial Relations Act 1971. The Conservative 1968 proposals, *Fair Deal at Work*, floated the notion, arguing that while, by analogy, the Highway Code had not made everyone a good driver, it had greatly influenced behaviour in the interests of road safety, and had set standards by which offenders could be judged.

1971 Code

The industrial relations *Code of Practice* was accordingly introduced as an adjunct to the 1971 Act. The code was not a legal document in its own right, but it was to be taken into account by the Industrial Relations Court or tribunal in proceedings under the Act. Although the TUC refused to take up the offer open to it of helping to draft the code, and it was at first regarded accordingly as rather tainted, it has survived. Indeed, it has since been supplemented, through the device of promulgating separate supporting codes, each of which develops particular parts of the original code.

Other Codes

Three Codes were published, on:

(*a*) disciplinary practice and procedures in employment;
(*b*) disclosure of information to trade unions for collective bargaining purposes; and
(*c*) time off for trade union duties and activities.

Additional codes of practice have since been issued dealing with picketing, and the closed shop. The idea of issuing codes has spread to other parts of the industrial relations field, such as health and safety, and race relations.

The advantage of a code is that it can set out, in non-legal language and at length, arrangements which might be difficult to specify in the law. There is no denying that the formulation of industrial relations law in Britain is frequently tortuous, at least to the layman who simply wishes to know what he (and others) can and cannot do. Codes put flesh on the legal structure. The device of making a code an appendage to an Act also ensures that it is taken seriously, since the provisions of a relevant code can be "taken into account" in proceedings under the relevant statute. It is a nice question whether codes of practice on their own would make legislation on the topic unnecessary. Would people pay any attention to them?

Rather different from these codes of conduct are the guidelines drawn up, for instance, by the TUC, to govern picketing, the conduct of affiliates in disputes, and running their union affairs. We shall see these in action in later chapters, particularly Chapter Five. Such Codes have usually been produced as an alternative to some proposed legal intervention, and are more in the nature of house rules.

GOVERNMENT AGENCIES IN INDUSTRIAL RELATIONS

Department of Employment

Until 1917 the Board of Trade was the government department which focused public employment policy, but in that year a Ministry of Labour was created to take over responsibility for public policy, including legislation, regarding employment. In wartime the Ministry of Labour obviously occupied a key position with regard to the allocation of labour resources. Over the "normal" years after the 1939–45 war, however, this department has had a chequered career. It no longer has its role in matters concerning social services, in which other departments have staked a claim. Particularly since 1970, when it acquired its most recent and current title,

Department of Employment, it has not been able to sail a steady course. Indeed, the decade of the 1970s will probably be remembered as the years of the carve-up of the "Ministry of Labour".

The department is still the mainspring of industrial relations policy-making, not least for the public policy as expressed in law, and its minister, the Secretary of State for Employment, is the policy spokesman for the whole gamut of employment policy, from manpower through incomes policies to health and safety. It also provides the central information and intelligence networks on employment statistics. Yet more than any other, the Department of Employment has spawned specialist agencies charged with particular parts of the remits, which formerly were held by divisions of the old ministry.

(*a*) The Manpower Services Commission, set up under the Employment and Training Act 1973, is the "arms-length" operating agency which runs the employment service, dear to the heart of William Beveridge seventy years ago, and which co-ordinates public policy on training.

(*b*) The Health and Safety Executive has assumed responsibility for another traditional function of the Labour Ministry.

(*c*) Perhaps most significant of all, the establishment in 1974 of ACAS, the Advisory Conciliation and Arbitration Service, marked the carving out from the Department of Employment of one of its main historical and historic functions, that of the peacemaker in industrial relations. The department has in consequence lost some of its strategic intelligence functions in major industrial disputes.

In addition, the barrage of legislation which we have been assessing in this chapter has generated its own clutch of institutions, charged with regulating and interpreting the various enactments. One thinks of Industrial Tribunals, and the Central Arbitration Committee, to name but two. There is, then, a somewhat truncated central policy-making Ministry—the Department of Employment. Let us review some of its offspring who have a part to play in industrial relations.

The Advisory, Conciliation and Arbitration Service (ACAS)

We have seen that, in 1896, a Conciliation Act established third-party arrangements for resolving industrial disputes. ACAS was set up in 1974, however, in part because of suspicion that the division of the Department of Employment from which the third-party arrangements were operated could not be trusted to be independent, impartial, neutral, in the matter of official incomes policies. These might have to be interpreted by neutral third agents such as arbitrators, or "kept in mind" by conciliators helping parties to sort out their industrial relations difficulties.

ACAS was put on a statutory footing by the Employment Protection Act 1975 and charged (section 1) with the task of promoting the improvement of industrial relations, and in particular of encouraging the extension of collective bargaining and, where necessary, reform of the machinery of collective bargaining. As its title suggests, its functions cover advice, conciliation, and arbitration, plus certain functions of investigation, such as (between 1975 and 1980) section 11 recognition problems, and investigations into the standing of particular Wages Councils. It is not unusual for a country's conciliation and arbitration service to be contained in a separate agency. It is less usual for the agency to be run, as ACAS is, by a tripartite council, drawn from unions, management and independents, with an independent chairman. This is intended to ensure a broadly based outlook, a consensus, in its activities.

At various stages throughout this book we shall see ACAS in action, providing conciliation services in negotiations and processing claims for unfair dismissal. At this point we simply indicate the scale and range of its work. Precise, year-to-year statistical comparisons of the activities of ACAS are not possible. Changes in legislation and public policy affect its involvement—the climate of incomes policy is important for pay disputes; the specified qualifying period (extended in 1979) for entitlement to make a claim for unfair dismissal obviously affects the workload; and, as we saw on p. 37, the statutory section 11 union recognition arrangements involving ACAS were repealed in 1980. One thing is clear, however; ACAS has a heavy workload.

In 1983, ACAS received 1,789 requests for assistance in collective conciliation, most of the requests relating to pay and other terms and conditions. On rights of individuals, where ACAS has a statutory duty to settle a difference without the need for a hearing before an industrial tribunal, ACAS received some 43,000 cases. Alleged unfair dismissal accounted for 90 per cent. Arbitration and mediation cases totalled 207. ACAS also undertakes a growing volume of long-term advisory work; it estimated that in 1983 over one third of its operational resources were concentrated on preventive advisory work, for instance in 147 joint working parties chaired by ACAS. ACAS also undertakes, on request, *ad hoc* enquiries, for instance, into the future of particular Wages Councils.

Central Arbitration Committee (CAC)

An *ad hoc* arbitration was possible under the 1896 Conciliation Act, but the first standing body, the Industrial Court, was established in 1919. The present Central Arbitration Committee was created by the Employment Protection Act 1975. It replaced the Industrial Arbitration Board which in 1971 had taken over the functions of the 1919 court. (It was necessary in 1971 to rename the Industrial Court because in that year, under the 1971 Industrial Relations Act, a National Industrial Relations Court, with much wider jurisdiction than the 1919 court, was set up. The NIRC was abolished in 1974.)

The CAC carries on the functions of its predecessors—Industrial Court and Industrial Arbitration Board—as a standing national arbitration body in industrial relations. The CAC has a chairman, deputy chairmen, and panels of side members experienced as representatives of employers and workers respectively. The Committee looks to ACAS for the provision of staff, but the CAC is not subject to direction from any minister. It is independent. The links with the conciliation service are, of course, important, and from time to time the committee has subordinated a final arbitration judgment to the desire to seek a voluntary agreement in a dispute. This has evidently been useful in helping parties to tackle difficulties in equal pay cases, and in disclosure of information cases, where, in fact, the CAC is required to refer a complaint to ACAS if it is of the opinion that the complaint is reasonably likely to be settled by conciliation. The links with ACAS conciliation services are then close.

The CAC experienced a boom in business in 1977, largely because of the recourse made to it under section 98 of the Employment Protection Act. We have looked on p. 41 at this device for transmitting equity in pay. Schedule 11 was introduced during a period of incomes policy, and there is strong evidence that the workload of the CAC increases when governments impose restrictions on collective bargaining.

Apart from this Schedule and the Fair Wages Resolution, both dealing with terms and conditions, the main business of the CAC has been concerned with cases about disclosure of information to trade unions for purposes of collective bargaining. That business too has declined. The involvement of the CAC in the Equal Pay Act has naturally subsided, as the adjustment to its requirements is now completed. Perhaps the most interesting contemporary feature of the business of the CAC is that voluntary arbitration through the CAC, which was the main reason for establishing the Industrial Court, its predecessor, in 1919, only accounted for 10 cases in 1983, the same as in 1982. The CAC would clearly like to have a more prominent place in the machinery of arbitration than it currently experiences. It seems unlikely that this will occur, short of a major review of the structure of arbitration arrangements. In the future, as in recent years, the workload of the CAC will vary with (*a*) incomes policy interventions, and (*b*) specific legislative changes, such as the machinery for extending terms and conditions, or new requirements under protective legislation. In the matter of voluntary arbitration, however, the CAC is a pale shadow of the original court, which in its early years after 1919 aspired to establish a body of industrial relations jurisprudence, mainly on wage principles.[5] Voluntary arbitration has never been a major industry in Britain, and the CAC has not been used much for that purpose. This is discussed at greater length in Chapter Eight.

Certification Office

We saw earlier in this chapter, in connection with the attitude of the law to trade unions, that new arrangements were made in 1975 to cover union registration. The Certification Office and officer are responsible for a range of matters covering:

(*a*) listing of trade unions and employers' associations;
(*b*) certification of trade union independence;
(*c*) financial reports of unions and employers' associations via annual returns;
(*d*) their superannuation schemes;
(*e*) transfers of engagements, amalgamations and changes of names under the Trade Union (Amalgamations, etc.) Act 1964, and;
(*f*) political funds established by trade unions under the Trade Union Act 1913.

We see these Certification Office activities at work in various stages of this study.

Industrial Tribunals and the Employment Appeal Tribunal (EAT)

Industrial tribunals

Industrial Tribunals were created under the Industrial Training Act 1964. Their job was to adjudicate on disputes about training levies imposed by Industrial Training Boards. From such a small acorn a large oak tree has now grown. On the swelling tide of legislation with which public policy has flooded industrial relations in recent years, Industrial Tribunals have had their jurisdiction extended. The Redundancy Payments Act 1965, the Contracts of Employment Act 1963 (and later amended versions), Docks and Harbours Act 1966, Selective Employment Payments Act 1966, Equal Pay Act 1970, and the Industrial Relations Act 1971 conferred additional duties. Later legislation, such as the Health and Safety at

Work etc. Act 1974, the Sex Discrimination Act 1975, Employment Protection Act 1975, Race Relations Act 1976, Employment Protection (Consolidation) Act 1978, and the Employment Acts of 1980 and 1982 and the Trade Union Act 1984 have kept up the momentum.

The distinguishing feature of the tribunals is that they deal with statutory rights flowing from legislation dealing with the employment relationship in a speedy, informal and inexpensive manner. Each tribunal consists of a trained lawyer as chairman plus two lay members with relevant experience of industry.

Employment Appeal Tribunal

Obviously, proceedings before tribunals can on occasion throw up problems of interpretation and application of the appropriate statute and, equally, dissatisfied parties may wish to appeal against the findings of a particular tribunal. An *appellate body* is therefore required. Appeals from tribunals on points of law were heard by the High Court until the National Industrial Relations Court was established in 1971. During its three years of life, the Court was particularly active as an appellate body dealing with problems arising from the new provisions governing alleged unfair dismissal. On its abolition, the NIRC's role as appellate body was assumed by the Employment Appeal Tribunal (EAT). This consists of judges of the High Court and lay persons having special knowledge or experience of industrial relations either as representatives of employers or of workers. The EAT normally sits with one judge and two wing members. Beyond and above it any appeals enter the normal legal channels running to the Court of Appeal and, ultimately, the House of Lords. The mixture of legal and industrial relations expertise in industrial tribunals and the Employment Appeal Tribunal appears to work well. We refer to it at work in Chapter Nine.

CONCLUSION

We now draw the threads of this chapter together. It is clear, as we indicated at the outset, that government has not stood back and left industrial relations to be run on a bipartite basis. There have in fact been major "third party" intrusions, mainly by statute, in the procedures of industrial relations in recent years. This has been particularly manifest in two areas, first the added protection provided for the individual employee and, second, the added controls over the scope and nature of industrial action, for example in picketing. A third theme, involving intrusion into internal union government, is now looming large. On the terms and conditions of industrial relations, substantive matters, the law is settled only in the sense that *collective agreements are not legally enforceable*. In one area of terms and conditions, the extension of collective agreements, the present tendency, through the abolition of Schedule 11 claims, is to put a halt to extending the substance of agreements to those not directly covered by them.

The attempt to produce and operate a comprehensive statutory framework under the Industrial Relations Act was short-lived. Nor has the British system distilled the kind of "comprehensive consolidating measure" which Donovan had suggested, though it was not clear how far Donovan intended that to go. Yet the law has obviously become more embracing. Whether it would be easy to codify is another matter. Its impact has, however, been softened by the efforts to establish codes as complements to law, an innovation that has put the TUC in the position of having to produce its own voluntary codes. The growth and extension of the use of conciliation within the enlarged framework of law is also most significant. The agencies, such as industrial tribunals, set up to dispense speedy justice within the law, are also a major development.

Yet we are not in a position to conclude that the spate of legislation has established a fair and balanced framework of rights and responsibilities. In part, this is because the content of an equitable system is not static, but is bound to change as social and economic forces shift. In other countries, equilibrium has not been established without trial and error. In the USA, for instance, the Wagner Act of 1935 swung the balance in favour of the unions; Taft–Hartley, in 1947, was expressly designed to redress the balance. Even countries in which an apparently stable framework had settled down can experience major shifts in the legal environment of industrial relations. Between 1936 and 1970 there was scarcely a ripple of legal change in Swedish industrial relations. Yet in the space of five years legislation on safety at work, employment security and dismissal rules, union representatives at the place of work, employee directors, and the 1976 Act on the Joint Regulation of Working Life had swung the balance in favour of the unions, to the point where on certain matters the management prerogative had instead become a union prerogative.

Taken along with the material of this chapter, this suggests that it is unwise to take a stand on one particular solution to the balance of power in industrial relations. The search continues, and it is part of the political dialogue to argue and press for particular adjustments. Three topics in particular are still sensitive to pressures for change.

(*a*) There is, first, the whole approach to the legal status of trade unions based on the historical golden formula regarding immunities. This has been made the subject of a wide-ranging discussion which included a possible alternative approach. That would be based on a statement of *positive rights*, for example with regard to the right to strike.[6]

(*b*) Secondly, the balance of power in industrial relations is not simply a matter of legal enactment. The topic of employee involvement, industrial democracy, is seen as an attractive and constructive route to good industrial relations. This idea of participation opens up a vast new prospect of power-sharing which is not primarily legal in character, even if it has to be promoted by some legislative framework. We take up this theme in Chapter Ten.

(*c*) Thirdly, the interplay between free collective bargaining and recurring attempts to devise and operate incomes policies raises major questions of public policy towards industrial relations.

The incomes policy theme is the subject of Chapter Eleven. We shall see there that government involvement has sometimes had a strong, sometimes a weak legal underpinning.

One can say with confidence, then, that there is much unfinished business for the third party at the industrial relations table, the government.

SELF-ASSESSMENT QUESTIONS

1. Consider the case for government having a distinctive industrial relations scheme for its own public service employees.

2. Is it possible at the same time to support the voluntary principle in industrial relations and to have legally enforceable collective agreements?

3. Is the case for trade union legal immunities rooted in historical accident rather than the distinctive merits of trade unionism in society?

4. List some tests by which you would assess whether the balance of power among the parties of interest in industrial relations was stable or unstable.

ASSIGNMENT

You are the Secretary of State for Employment and you have to set out in a White Paper the case for a positive framework of law for the conduct of industrial relations. List the main themes which you would include, explaining the concept of "the balance of power" which underlies your thinking about the framework you devise.

REFERENCES

1. Roy Lewis, The Historical Development of Labour Law, *British Journal of Industrial Relations*, Vol. XIV, March 1976, no. 1, p. 1.

2. W. Milne-Bailey, *Trade Unions and the State*, 1934, p. 185.

3. *Industrial Cases Reports 1980*, p. 42 *et seq.*

4. *Ibid.*, p. 161 *et seq.*

5. Lord Amulree, *Industrial Arbitration in Great Britain*, London, 1929; Mary T. Rankin, *Arbitration Principles and the Industrial Court*, London, 1931.

6. *Trade Union Immunities* (green paper), *Cmnd. 8128*, 1981.

CHAPTER FOUR

Employers and Employers' Associations

CHAPTER OBJECTIVES

After studying this chapter you should be able to:
* appraise the role of the CBI as the central employers' body for British industry;
* identify the main reasons which make employers combine in associations;
* explain recent changes which have improved the status of personnel managers in industry.

"We rarely hear, it has been said, of the combinations of masters; though frequently those of workmen. But whoever imagines, upon this account, that masters rarely combine, is as ignorant of the world as of the subject. Masters are always and every where in a sort of tacit, but constant and uniform combination, not to raise the wages of labour above their actual rate. To violate this combination is every where a most unpopular action, and a sort of reproach to a master among his neighbours and equals. . . ."

Adam Smith, Wealth of Nations

THE PROBLEM OF EMPLOYER SOLIDARITY

Of the major interest groups involved in industrial relations, employers have been the least studied and analysed. In part this is because we have assumed, perhaps too readily, that Adam Smith had said it all. Employers appear to have a very simple industrial relations objective, that of holding the line, and it is an objective which is manifestly economic in character. Again, whereas in most countries the unions form a Movement, spurred on by some kind of common identity and aspiration, or solidarity, employers lack any obvious ideology, apart from the profit motive. They seem content to let the trade unions make the running. They react when the unions table demands.

This is of course partly a caricature, and the idea of employers constituting a reactive body sits ill with the kind of positive, indeed aggressive, stance which the Swedish Employers' Confederation adopted soon after its establishment early in the twentieth century. The lockout, backed by a mutual insurance fund, was widely used as a strategic weapon in seeking to impose bargaining structures and procedures on the Swedish trade union movement. There has rarely been the same sustained cohesiveness among British employers, and this is one reason why they are rather difficult to analyse.

This lack of solidarity has been a perpetual problem. One recent publication on trade unions by the Confederation of British Industry—the CBI—continued to lament this. Pleading for the need for greater employer unity and solidarity in industrial relations, the document went on:

> Employers need to act collectively as well as individually to give support to others when not themselves under direct pressure. To date, British employers (though not their European counterparts) have preferred independence to collective action so as to avoid involvement in issues with which they are not immediately concerned, and to retain independence over their affairs. Not only has this been strategically unsound, permitting trade unions to concentrate their limited resources on forcing concessions from vulnerable, key firms or sectors, thus putting pressure on the rest; it also means that employers themselves regard it as acceptable behaviour to take commercial advantage of the plight of others or to create additional pressures to concede.[1]

Why then do employers organise at all? A special study of employers' associations, commissioned for the Donovan enquiry, found that the variations in the scope and influence of employers' associations largely arose as a result of the differing needs and preferences of their member firms. Sometimes, all the members wanted was a common forum, in others a range of services was desired, including a disputes procedure and the settlement of minimum wages for the industry at national level. Very occasionally, effective joint action was desired, including the negotiation of effective rates of pay that did operate throughout the industry. Essentially, therefore, employers' associations could only do what the members wanted as regards the degree of common agreement and purpose among them.[2] The concept of solidarity among employers then becomes fundamentally pragmatic, concerned with a very practical question. On what can they agree, by way of common rules regarding procedures and substantive terms and conditions by which the members are willing to abide? We shall see in Chapter Six that this is quite central to the shape which collective agreements assume.

Basis of organisation

One of the complications with employers' associations is that the boundary lines are not always finely drawn between associations which specialise in industrial relations and those which carry on more comprehensive functions, embracing trade and commercial policy questions. Chambers of Commerce, which have a longer history, tend not to be in the business of industrial relations. This fuzziness makes it difficult to enumerate and classify employers' groups. At the time of Donovan, the then Department of Employment and Productivity reckoned there were 1,350 employers' associations. They ranged in size from the Engineering Employers' Federation, with some 5,200 member establishments in 1983 covering a million employees, out of 2.5 million employees in the engineering industry, to small local and regional associations.

Legal standing

Employers' organisations used to be included in the definition of trade unions, but since the Industrial Relations Act 1971 a separate definition has been provided for employers' groups. The current one is contained in Section 28 of the Trade Union and Labour Relations Act 1974, and makes the point that the "principal purposes of such an association must include the regulation of relations between employers and workers or trade unions". A similar phrase is, however, used about trade unions in defining them. One major difference is the arrangements to which the two groups are subject under the certification rules. Neither unions nor employers' associations are required to be "listed" with the Certification Office (described in Chapter Three), but unions do have to be listed if they are to be eligible to apply for a certificate of independence. Listing also entitles a union to tax relief for expenditure on provident benefits. No such incentive exists for employers' bodies.

The very fact that employers' associations do not need to face up to the need to establish independence is in itself a clear indication of the contrast between a trade union and an employers' body. Nevertheless, employers' associations, whether listed or not, do have to obey the provisions of the 1974 Act, requiring unions and employers' associations to keep accounts and submit annual returns. The Certification Office has fewer than half the known employers' associations on its list. In 1982, 166 were listed and 224 unlisted. As we have already remarked, employers' associations are frequently trade associations as well.

Given this variety of objectives which employers appear to have when they associate, it is hardly surprising that organisation among employers is every bit as devoid of clear principles as that of the trade union movement, discussed in the next chapter. Yet no one criticises employers for their organising mosaic, whereas everyone is, of course, an expert on how the trade union movement should restructure itself!

Historical background

Historically, the following points shed light on the current standing of employers' organisations. First, employers reflected the
preference of unions for organising locally and in trades, by developing similar local arrangements. They were mainly defensive.
Industry-wide organisation, exemplified by the establishment of the
Engineering Employers' Federation, as it is now called, in 1896,
was also defensive. In that particular case the object was to mount
opposition to a claim for an eight-hour day. The lock-out weapon
was used too. Significantly, the Federation was a grouping of
geographical associations, a structure which it has retained to the
present time.[3] Prior to 1914, the industry-wide emphasis, where it
developed, was primarily on procedure agreements. It was the First
World War which brought about industry-wide settlement of substantive terms regarding pay or, more accurately, pay increases.
Industry-wide arrangements could handle simple matters, such as
rates and hours increases. This did not interfere with company pay
structures, but simply lifted the structures together, leaving the.
individual employer some elbow room to work out his own destiny.
This two (and sometimes three) tier arrangement has persisted
under industry-wide bargaining. As Phelps Brown points out, industrial negotiation was also assisted by the fragmentation on
the union side: there was no in-company union co-ordinating
arrangement.[4]

Remarkably enough, this rather recent and wartime development was very much taken for granted by the Whitley Committee,
which proceeded to confirm what it took to be the established
practice of industry-wide joint negotiating arrangements. Donovan
discerned a marked change in the contribution made by employers'
associations to industrial relations since 1914.[5] Up till then, it concluded, they had been innovators, particularly on procedural
matters, with the war bringing government pressure to have industry-wide general movements of pay. Subsequently, innovation
largely passed employers' associations by, leaving them in posses-
sion of the formal system of industrial relations. This, in an era of
full employment, was increasingly out of touch with company and
plant realities. Stressing the need to develop comprehensive company bargaining, Donovan saw employers' associations in a suppor-
tive and advisory role.

Another historical feature, less frequently noticed, is that no
central (nation-wide) employer organisation developed prior to
1914, to bring together the industry federations and match the TUC
on its side of the stage. As with industry-wide bargaining, the First

World War did however provide an impetus, and by the end of it three central bodies had been formed—the Federation of British Industries, concerned with the whole realm of business other than industrial relations, the British Employers' Confederation (originally the National Confederation of Employers' Organisations), which did take industrial relations as its province, and a third body, later known as the National Association of British Manufacturers, which concentrated on small firms. The three separate bodies merged in 1965 in the Confederation of British Industry—the CBI. This took on the whole range of activities, from industrial relations to business policy, and the spectrum of firms and organisations large and small, which had been affiliated to the three groups.

Just as the pressures of wartime had brought the separate groups into existence during the First World War, so the mushrooming of interest in a national economic consensus in the early 1960s made out the case for a unified employer group. The establishment of the National Economic Development Council in 1962 provided an impetus, and the devotion of the 1964 Labour Government to a national plan pulled the threads together. Did it make sense to have separate employer bodies dealing with incomes and with prices and output? Planning helped to show the need to integrate. Additionally, employers needed a single voice to match that of the TUC in these national pow-wows.

FORMATION OF THE CBI

Since 1965 there has been a central focus for employer interests in Britain. The CBI did not find it difficult to carry on the traditional functions of its predecessor central bodies, those of lobbying and making representations to legislators. It is significant, for instance, that the one major study of the CBI which has been published is concerned with its part in the British political system.[6] Political power and influence are important. In addition to pacing the corridors of power, however, the CBI has increasingly[7] broadened its ambitions across a range of activities.

Activities
The CBI's quarterly Industrial Trends Survey is of course well established as an indicator of economic activity. It celebrated its silver jubilee in 1983; in the same year a new survey was launched covering the distributive trades. In recent years, it has also begun to build a systematic economic policy platform, both for purposes of informing and persuading. Various comprehensive publications—
The Road to Recovery (1976), *Britain Means Business* (1977), and

The Challenge to Business (1979)—presented analysis and argument about Britain's economic position, plus policy proposals. It has continued to do this through three regular channels. Its annual conference, introduced in 1977, provides both a forum for discussing policy documents and a platform for projecting the employers' position on national issues. It is also developing as the major mechanism for involving companies. In advance of the annual budget, secondly, the CBI always lobbies the Chancellor of the Exchequer, setting out its priorities on e.g., national insurance taxes, the need for lower interest rates, the case for investment in infra-structure projects, and so on. Thirdly, it always puts before candidates at a General Election a checklist of policies, a business manifesto. In 1983 the theme was *Making Britain Grow*.

On specific themes it promotes policies as the need arises. In recent years it has tried to bridge links with the world of education through its project on Understanding British Industry. Its steering group on unemployment produced plans in 1983 for creating jobs, and a special programmes unit was set up to encourage the provision of employment for young people.

In industrial relations, the CBI has also hammered out policy positions on pay and other matters. It was very much an observer on the sidelines of pay discussions during the reign of the Social Contract between the Labour Government and the trade unions from 1974 to 1978, and it had to develop its own alternative policies. Its strenuous opposition to suggestions, originating in Britain and in the EEC, that legislation is needed to promote employee involvement has led it to develop its own strategy for participation, and it has published guidance, based on good practice, to assist members in their policy-making on employee involvement. We examine this theme in Chapter Ten. In recent years it has also adopted a tougher stance about the 'balance of power' in British industrial relations. Many of its specific suggestions about picketing, the closed shop, and employee protection in small firms found powerful echoes in the Employment Acts of 1980 and 1982 and the Trade Union Act 1984.

CBI and collective bargaining
On the specifics of industrial relations, the CBI continues the tradition of *not* negotiating on behalf of its associations and member companies. It seeks to influence the climate, but not to conduct the day-to-day bargaining. It runs a pay data bank, but not a pay negotiating clinic. It claimed in 1983 that its campaign to hold the line against sustained trade union pressure for a reduction in working time had been very successful. Again, the CBI does not

aspire to interfere in the internal affairs of affiliates. Whether it could in fact do so is doubtful. It has modest resources, with an operating budget in 1983 of £8 million, more than three quarters of which came from membership subscriptions, and it has no formal powers over affiliates. Even the power to expel would be of doubtful use. There was little enthusiasm for a proposal put forward in 1979, for instance, for a mutual insurance fund. The objects would have been to reduce the financial imbalance of strike costs and to compensate affiliates for losses in industrial disputes. This approach is well-established among private employers in a country such as Sweden, but clearly does not commend itself to British employers.

Make-up of membership

The CBI has five categories of membership—industrial companies, commercial firms, public sector enterprises, commercial associations, and employers' organisations and trade associations. Industrial companies account for about three-quarters of the members, and industrial firms with more than 1,000 employees for over half the subscription income. The CBI is sensitive about the charge that it is a big business club, and makes strenuous efforts to be open to individual firms and associations across a wide range of activity. It claims to cover more than 10 million employees through its affiliates.

Government

The CBI's governing body is a council of 400, with a president's committee of 26 as an inner cabinet. The Director-General, the chief executive, oversees ten expert policy directorates. The CBI operates 25 standing committees, covering everything from energy policy to Europe, and taxation to transport. It also has a strong regional network of 13 organisations, and these in turn may have specialist groups on, e.g., industrial relations, and education. A "smaller firms" council of 60 provides a focal point within the CBI for independent small businesses, on matters ranging from the impact of income and capital taxes on succession in small businesses, to the problems which employment protection legislation poses for the small firm. The CBI has a democratic structure and is a loose confederation of individual firms and employers' organisations. The strength of its position with its membership results from its ability to influence, not to compel.[7]

Thus the CBI aspires to be a repository of views, and sees itself as a consensus-making body, but one which is trying to aim high rather than low in identifying an agreed employer position.

Scope of activities

One feature which has caused the CBI little concern is its comprehensive coverage of the whole range of business themes in which employers are interested, from trade and commerce to industrial relations. As we have noticed, not all employers' associations do include trade and industrial matters in their remit, but confine themselves to employee relations. There is no obviously correct definition of the appropriate scope of common interest for employers' organisations. The CBI can claim that its comprehensive overview enables it to assess industrial relations problems in the wider setting of industrial and commercial strategy. This is important when the human factor of production is so central to costs and efficiency. In all probability the CBI could not afford to spread itself so comprehensively, if it actually did have to carry out day-to-day industrial relations discussions and negotiations. Or, if it did, it would require more resources and might then take over the main industrial relations functions of its member firms and federations. Apart from its pay data bank based on survey information, the most the CBI has done in recent years has been to try to find out more about what goes on in bargaining at the grass roots. In 1980 it initiated a survey of the management by companies of their industrial relations among a sample of its member firms in the private sector of manufacturing industry. This was really an information-gathering exercise; it was certainly a long way from being a prelude to some co-ordinated negotiating policy for the CBI membership.

EMPLOYERS' ASSOCIATIONS

Engineering employers

The CBI provides the strategic national overview. In individual sectors and industries employers also find it necessary to come together. Indeed, most employers' associations preceded the founding of the CBI. The largest single-industry organisation of employers in Britain is the Engineering Employers' Federation, the EEF. Founded in 1896, it is a federation of eighteen regional associations. Firms join their regional association. In 1983 the Federation covered some 5,200 establishments, employing about a million people. After substantial growth in affiliations in the 1970s, the early 1980s saw a substantial drop in membership, due to the decline in manufacturing in the recession and ensuing closures and financial stringency.

The EEF has always had a strong industrial relations presence, but it has become increasingly involved in representing the industry's position in commercial, economic and financial as well as employment matters. It is extremely active in European Community affairs, attaching importance to what it sees as the fundamental task of making the Community an economic success, but expressing vigorous opposition to EEC proposals on employee involvement and working time. The Federation had a subscription income of £1.75 million and assets of £2.5 million in 1983. It has recently experimented with an arrangement short of full membership, which provides services for subscribers. About 100 companies with 20,000 employees were involved in this in 1983.

The engineering industry is extremely diverse, with a great variety of products, and companies ranging from conglomerates to small workshops and jobbing contractors. In Dunlop's terms, the technology is extremely diverse (and more sophisticated than the label of 'metal bashing' usually pinned on the industry), and markets also are extremely varied. The EEF has frequently been in the public eye, in connection with the history of trade unionism, in the industry-wide defensive line taken by employers when the Federation was formed in the 1890s, in its key role in armaments supply in time of war, and in its position as a key wage negotiating sector.

It is sufficient to note at this stage that the engineering industry is the classic instance of two-tier bargaining, where a national agreement covers minimum rates and certain general terms, such as hours and holidays, with the "in-fill" of terms and conditions taking place through company, plant and workshop settlements. Its pay system, or lack of it, was the focus of much work on the problem of "wage drift", particularly when full employment labour markets were prevalent. Donavan made the engineering industry the butt of its trenchant criticism of the formal system of industrial relations. In 1983 the EEF did not simply react to a pay claim by the trade unions, but itself tabled, for the first time, counter claims aimed at securing an agreement on working practices appropriate to modern needs. One important development in 1983 which is likely to have profound long-term consequences for the skills mix, and therefore pay, in the industry was the signing of a national agreement on training concluded between the EEF and the Confederation of Shipbuilding and Engineering Unions. Training to achieved standards has now replaced the traditional "time-served" apprenticeship as the foundation of skill training. The system of payment during training has also been changed, from rate for age to rate for stage of training.

Other private sector employers

Other employers' associations in the private sector are similar to the engineering industry in practising two-tier bargaining, though some, as in electrical contracting, work to a standard agreement which sets terms and conditions in a single-tier operation. The geographical element is still extremely strong in many industries. The National Federation of Building Trades Employers has ten regional associations in England and Wales, and the separate Scottish Building Employers' Federation has eight regions. Cotton textiles has ten regional affiliates, eight of them essentially local town groupings in Lancashire. Other parts of textiles, such as woollens, and hosiery and knitted goods, similarly have a marked local geographical make-up. The Brewers' Society continues to reflect the local nature of the brewing industry in the past by having nine regional associations. Frequently, there are separate employer bodies for Scotland, as in plumbing and banking. As one might expect, the National Association of Port Employers has a very strong geographical composition.

Large individual employers

Many of the largest companies, such as ICI, and the main companies operating in the oil and related process industries, such as BP and Shell, are big enough to go their own way and are not federated. Like the motor manufacturing companies, such as Ford and Vauxhall, they have their own company negotiating arrangements with a variety of trade unions. The famous Esso Fawley productivity agreement was an instance of a company "doing its own thing" at one site. In one particular sector, the co-operative movement, which has its distinctive history and philosophy, there is a separate employers' association based in Manchester, the historic centre of that movement.

PUBLIC SECTOR EMPLOYERS

The private and near-private sector is accordingly extremely varied in the response which employers have constructed to trade unionism. The public sector is very different. There the single employer tends to dominate in each part of the sector. By definition, a public activity tends to have a standard technology and a strong, near-monopoly position in the market for a nation-wide product, or products, which it has been established to sell. Dunlop's emphasis on market structure and technology is very relevant to an understanding of the sole employer and his position. Much more so than in the private sector, it appears appropriate and easy to operate a standard, single-tier employer strategy. The nationalised industries are prime examples of the single employer, each being a party to what is essentially a single-company agreement, as in railways, electricity supply, and the Post Office. The National Health Service and local authorities operate across very broad geographical empires, but their activities are uniform and the occupational mix very similar throughout the country, and they work with a single-employer structure. The local authorities, for instance, come together for negotiating purposes in a Conditions of Service Advisory Board, which brings together the separate bodies covering county councils, metropolitan authorities, and districts. Negotiations for the Health Service are covered by Whitley Council arrangements.

The best example of the single public employer is of course the civil service. The Treasury and the Civil Service Department are to all intents and purposes the employer, manning the "official side", from government expenditure estimates through to establishment matters, and negotiating with the civil service unions. Although there are strong departmental involvements in the day-to-day running of industrial relations, through the Whitley machinery, and groups such as the inland revenue have special interests to safeguard, the whole ethos of the civil service is one of standard, service-wide conditions.

THE ISSUE UNITES US

When the Donovan Commission discerned the distinction between the formal and informal systems of industrial relations it was concentrating its analysis very heavily on a heterogeneous industry like engineering. Where there is a single nation-wide employer, as in the public service, and uniform types of work and products, the employer interest can be, and is, organised readily and explictly around a single-tier standard set of terms and conditions. It is a great mistake to think that all employer bodies work to much the same "game plan". The CBI Steering Group asked itself in 1979 what employers could do to help themselves, and discovered that the theme which emerged strongly was "the issue determines the grouping". There was little value in seeking to provide a structure for solidarity or unity without first defining the issue involved.

Furthermore a single company may wish to act in unison with different groupings according to the issue involved. For example, there will be vital legislative issues where an all-industry stance will be called for; there will be issues for individual sectors, very many of them related to sector wage bargaining; there will be issues for large companies only and for small companies only; there will be issues in particular regions and towns. In short, depending on the issue involved, groupings will form and reform naturally. The real problem is whether those groupings can efficiently maintain a line on particular issues and whether the groupings can be effectively administered and supported.[8]

No wonder, then, that employers' associations vary in their aspirations and objectives, at least in the private sector. By contrast, the single-employer situation typical of the public sector provides a firmer and more continuing structure for dealing with the "issues" that arise in the course of industrial relations.

RECENT MAIN DEVELOPMENTS AFFECTING EMPLOYERS' ORGANISATIONS

Let us now round out this chapter on employers by distinguishing some main developments which in recent years have impinged on their side of the industrial relations equation.

Internal government of employers' bodies

The public has never been very interested in the way in which employers' associations run their affairs. The closed shop, internal democracy, members' rights, are meat and drink to discussions of trade unions and their government. Employers are not nearly so much in the public eye. The Industrial Relations Act 1971, Section 69, set out guiding principles for organisations of employers, including the proposition that there must be no exclusion from membership "by way of any arbitrary or unreasonable disciplinary action". The Act also set out requirements about rules, constitution and management, members, and property and finances. This certainly went further than any previous proposals. Donovan had not been particularly concerned about the constitutional arrangements of employers' groups. Its objective was to make them into bodies which gave better and adequate support to effective collective bargaining in companies and plants. The 1974 Act was much less intrusive with regard to the rule books, and employers' associations (like unions) are not required to submit their rules, or changes in them, to a statutory body for approval. As we have seen, they do have to file reports and accounts with the Certification Office.

Industrial action

The main weapon which employers have available when they wish to exert pressure on trade unions is the lockout. In the past, in Britain and other countries, the lockout was used with vigour. It is now almost a thing of the past. Employers' associations tend simply to try to hold a common front and hope that none of the affiliated companies will break it by concluding separate agreements. The CBI welcomed the step towards greater consistency of employer conduct which the Engineering Employers' Federation took in 1979. It published *Guidelines on Collective Bargaining and Response to Industrial Action* which try to point to the things which employers need to do in order to maintain order within the scope of their situation. This is a very low-key document, and the word "lockout" does not even occur in the section on Industrial Action. The main emphasis is on not negotiating where procedure has been breached, and on suspending without pay in the event of go-slows, blacking, and refusal to work normally.

In the absence of economic control over their members, employers' associations can really only use the sanctions of suspension or expulsion. These may be only modest deterrents to companies, if they prefer to settle rather than carry the costs of a shutdown. It is significant that, in the context of the "balance of power" in industrial relations, the CBI has recently been attracted to the legally enforceable agreement. One benefit of this would be to eliminate, or at least reduce, the sporadic stoppage while an agreement is in force.

Professionalism in management

Much of the early work of the National Economic Development Council in the 1960s was taken up with the allegedly poor quality of British management. Management education boomed in consequence. The 1968 Brookings Report, referred to in Chapter Two, criticised management performance, and patterns of management staffing.

> Executives who have come up through the firm lack breadth of view as well as technical training, and have often been apprenticed in the accounting tradition of "the search for the missing shilling". The trouble with the public school and Oxbridge graduates lies not in the "old-boy" network of recruitment but rather in their amateurism and their frequent acceptance of business as second choice when they fail to qualify for a civil service career. They tend to retain the civil service as their model and settle into a trustee role of gentlemanly responsibility that hardly conduces to rapid innovation.[9]

Trenchant stuff, no doubt overdrawn and unfair. For our purposes, however, it is important to notice that there has been an increasing professionalisation of personnel management. In large measure, this has been the evident consequence of the proliferation of legislation referred to in the last chapter. One of the earliest and least controversial enactments in this regard was the Industrial

Training Act 1964. This endeavoured to exert pressure on industry, mainly through a levy-grant arrangement operated by Industrial Training Boards, to improve the quantity and quality of training. The Redundancy Payments Act 1965, and many of the provisions of employment protection legislation, made new demands on the management of company manpower. It is commonplace nowadays to hear labour being described as a fixed asset, involving fixed costs. Put another way, legislation has eroded many management prerogatives, and the "personnel function" has had to acquire new skills and qualities. Pressures for employee involvement, industrial democracy, are adding new challenges as well. All this is reflected in the way the personnel manager has moved up the management pay hierarchy, and the extent to which companies now include professional industrial relations managers on their Boards of Directors.

This assessment of increasing professionalisation on the part of management was confirmed by two of the surveys (Warwick and CBI) of the bargaining scene conducted recently. It also drew indirect endorsement from the 1982 annual report of ACAS, which noted a decline in the numbers and influence of personnel managers in the recession. It has been suggested that in part the personnel manager mirrors the trade union; when union strength wanes, as in the recession, the personnel manager loses standing as well.

The CBI survey also brought out the interesting point that the personnel expert was still mainly an adviser to the production line managers, who were the real decision-makers in matters concerned with manpower.[10]

The small firm
The separation of ownership from management, the managerial revolution, occurred a long time ago, and large companies are managed (with all due respect to Brookings) by professionals and specialists. For the small company, however, general legislation on economic topics has meant severe burdens. The CBI, we noticed, responded to this through its "smaller firms" council. Some of the employment protection legislation was thought to bear too heavily on small firms, for instance in discouraging recruitment. The Employment Act 1980 provided some relief, in the new provision that an employee working for a firm employing 20 people or fewer does not have the right to complain of unfair dismissal during the first two years of service, unlike other employees, for whom one year is the qualifying period. The changes made by the same Act in recognition procedures (Sections 11 to 16 of the Employment Protection Act 1975 were repealed) were more likely to affect small firms, and the

same is true of the abolition of the arrangement for extending terms and conditions (Schedule 11 of the 1975 Act). Perhaps the small business sector will develop an industrial relations lifestyle of its own.

Codes of Practice

We noticed in Chapter Three that much recent labour legislation has been complemented by Codes of Practice. These all put employers (as well as unions) under pressure, and the explicit pressure on employers is quite clear in two of the codes. The code on disclosure of information to trade unions for collective bargaining purposes puts an onus on companies, as does the code on time off for trade union duties and activities. The code on disciplinary practice and procedures in employment is more closely geared to provisions and procedures agreed between the two sides. This is taken up in Chapter Nine.

Union recognition

At the time of the Donovan enquiry, the position of the CBI on white collar unionism was one of waiting and seeing, rather than adopting a positive policy. In practice, as the next chapter brings out, the spread of trade unionism to white collar employees has been one of the most important developments in British industrial relations in the past ten years, particularly in the private sector.

More generally, employer resistance to blue-collar unionism has largely subsided. Nearly a quarter of the labour force is covered by closed shop, union membership, agreements. (These are examined more closely in the next chapter.) There are, nevertheless, three aspects of the employer response to union recognition which still attract attention.

(*a*) First, companies on occasion adopt preventive industrial relations policies, which are intended to "keep the unions out", implicitly or explicitly, by demonstrating to employees that management can look after their interests as well as or better than a union could.

(*b*) Second, there are still cases of outright opposition or hostility to unions. We noted in Chapter Three that ACAS was glad to be rid in 1980 of the responsibility for operating recognition procedures which had sometimes embarrassed it. There is now no strong procedure in being, which a union can use to refer a recognition issue to ACAS for determination. This is unlikely to pose a new major problem, since trade unionism is widely accepted. None the less, occasional outbreaks of confrontation involving maverick

employers are bound to occur, and the abolition of statutory recognition procedures may at least facilitate such happenings.

(c) A third aspect of recognition is much more subtle. What scope
does an employer have for refusing recognition, if he thinks that to
do so would lead to fragmentation in bargaining arrangements?

This could occur, for example, through a group of workers break-
ing away from one union, already recognised by an employer, and
seeking recognition under a new banner. One recent case involved
a small, 1,000 strong Telephone Contract Officers' Association. It
lost its recognition by the Post Office as an "appropriate organisation" with which the Post Office negotiated when these employees
decided to join the large union, ASTMS. The Post Office declined
to recognise this new arrangement, and the Court of Appeal held
that it was undesirable to have a large number of small unions
negotiating on behalf of smallish numbers of members. It accepted
the Post Office contention that it was important that collective
bargaining arrangements should avoid, as far as possible, a multi-
plicity of bargaining units and pay review dates which could lead to
complex and prolonged negotiations and encourage leapfrogging
claims by the various unions. The discretion which the Post Office
had was not absolute, but it was clear that the Post Office could, in
good faith, seek to apply the test of *appropriateness* for the objectives of settling terms and conditions, promoting efficiency, and the
safety, health and welfare of employees, set out in the Post Office
Act, 1969.[11] Employers need not therefore be passive in the face of
recognition claims.

Employee participation

Under the Companies Act 1980 it is now the duty of company
directors to have regard to the interests of employees and not
solely, as in the past, to those of shareholders. This becomes part of
the much wider theme of employee involvement, or industrial
democracy, which will be examined in depth in Chapter Ten. There
is no doubt that one of "the challenges for the 1980s" facing management is its response to this new pervasive pressure in industrial
relations. It has already been argued above that the personnel
management, or manpower, function is becoming a much more
demanding and sophisticated one in British industrial relations.
This is a heartening development for, whatever its origins, it puts
the onus squarely on the employer side to adopt positive policies.
The CBI steering group already cited saw this, even if it put the
point in a negative way:

> Employers have a confusing and disparate system of institutional orga-
> nisation. They have frequently shown an inability or unwillingness to act

cohesively around agreed policies and have only partially succeeded in improving public understanding of economic and industrial reality. They have sometimes acted equivocally and inconsistently, for example in relation to incomes policy, to closed shops and to government subsidies. Sometimes too they have failed to accept their responsibilities as managers, and they have been far too ready to leave them to others.[12]

As our study progresses, we shall have ample opportunity to test how the employer side is responding to this new identification of its roles in industrial relations.

CONCLUSION

One conclusion which is amply evident from this chapter is that "the employer" is not at all a simple interested party to analyse. It is easy to slip in to the habit of thinking of employers as the representatives of capital. Yet the range of economic activity is so great, and organised in so many forms, that we have to pay regard more to the diversities than to the "monolithic" nature of employer organisations. One thread running through the chapter has been the marked diffidence of the CBI to push employers into a particular mould. This is realistic, not least because of the strong geographical anchorage which many employer groups have. But it also means that a consensus form of management leadership in industrial relations is likely to adopt a slower tempo of advance than a strongly centralised employer organisation.

SELF-ASSESSMENT QUESTIONS

1. Why should employers form associations? How would you define "employer solidarity" to an employer whom you were seeking to persuade to join an association?

2. Is the single employer in a nationalised industry in a stronger position for negotiating purposes than an association of numerous companies?

3. What, if any, is the case for separating the industrial relations functions from other activities, such as commercial, trade, and technological functions, in the organisation of employers' bodies?

4. Set out a list of the principal factors which presently shape the industrial relations policies of the Confederation of British Industry.

ASSIGNMENT

Changes in the structure of the economy are likely to bring

increased emphasis on service industries. Select one such industry (e.g. banking, retail trade, hospital service etc.) and identify the main industrial relations issues on which employers in the industry have to develop policies. Are hours of work, the right to strike, lockouts, and problems of organisation likely to be the main problems which such employers would have to face?

REFERENCES

1. *Trade Unions in a changing world: the challenge for management*, CBI 1980, p. 22.
2. Royal Commission on Trade Unions and Employers' Associations 1965–1968, Research Papers, No. 7, *Employers' Associations*, 1968, p. x.
3. Eric Wigham, *The Power to Manage: A History of the Engineering Employers' Federation*, London 1973.
4. E. H. Phelps Brown, *The Growth of British Industrial Relations*, 1959, pp. 362–3.
5. Royal Commission on Trade Unions and Employers' Associations 1965–1968, *Cmnd, 3623*, p. 20.
6. Wyn Grant and David Marsh, *The Confederation of British Industry*, 1977.
7. *Op. cit.*, p. 213.
8. CBI National Conference 1979, *Background Paper, Industrial Relations*, para. 44.
9. Richard E. Caves and associates, *Britain's Economic Prospects*, 1968, p. 303.
10. CBI, *Employee Relations Policy and Decision Making*, a survey of manufacturing companies carried out by Arthur Marsh, 1982.
11. *Times Law Report*, July 23, 1980.
12. CBI National Conference 1979, *op. cit.*, para. 17.

CHAPTER FIVE

Trade Unions—The Worker Organises

CHAPTER OBJECTIVES

After studying this chapter you should be able to:
* explain why trade unions grow;
* state whether there is any obvious principle of organisation for a trade union movement;
* understand the problems which internal trade union government has to resolve;
* judge whether trade unionism is likely to continue to grow in Britain.

"We're gonna roll the union on!"

(*US Steelworkers' song*)

INTRODUCTION

The developing industrial society which we date in Britain from the eighteenth century brought with it one new and frequently chastening experience for the individual worker. Increasingly, he was forced to work in an urban and a factory environment, and he soon discovered that he was at a serious disadvantage to his employer in the crucial matter of negotiating strength. By the same token, however, proximity to other employees in like condition brought recognition of their common problems and the environment in which they could combine and "do something about it". Hence trade unionism. If we are to ask what has been the most profound contribution of trade unions to the status of the individual worker, it lies in the strength which comes from *collective action working through the union*. Sydney and Beatrice Webb, patriarch and matriarch of trade union history, hit the nail firmly on the head when they defined a trade union crisply as "a continuous association of wage-earners for the purpose of maintaining or improving the conditions of their working lives."[1]

This is not a legal definition. That, as the 1974 Trade Union and Labour Relations Act, section 28, brings out, is an altogether drier matter. A trade union is there considered to be *an organisation (whether permanent or temporary) consisting wholly or mainly of workers of one or more descriptions*, and is an organisation *whose principal purposes include the regulation of relations between workers of that description and employers or employers' associations.* To put it more succinctly, the principal, if not the sole activities of trade unions are in the business of looking after the interests of their members and dealing with employers.

In this chapter we have to cover a lot of ground, and we shall treat the following themes in turn:

(a) Theories of trade unionism.
(b) Union membership and growth.
(c) Trade union structure.
(d) Trade union government.
(e) The Trades Union Congress.

THEORIES OF TRADE UNIONISM

The view of the Webbs
The Webbs' definition, robust and incisive, has never been bettered in giving us the feel for trade unions and their objectives as something which is not adequately covered by a juridical concept. Trade unionism, as its colourful and turbulent history demonstrates, is a *movement*; indeed, it is now the largest economic and social group in our society. There are more than 13 million trade union members in Britain; in the 1970s, trade union membership rose by about 2 million. Over half the working population is organised in trade unions.

What are these bodies trying to do? The definition of the Webbs seemed to suggest that trade unions are primarily interested in economic goals, and the Webbs themselves drew attention to typical trade union practices, such as controls over labour supply through *"restriction of numbers"* (apprenticeships, seniority rules and so on), and the "common rule" (minimum wage standards, hours and conditions) which operate as economic pressures on the employer. Yet "the conditions of their working lives" can be given a much broader interpretation, and trade unions have in practice come to widen their range of interest and involvement to include the total economic and social environment. They pay increasing attention, as well, to the quality of working life in the form of wholesome conditions at the place of work, and reasonable standards for those who have reached pensionable age. The "conditions of their working lives" encompass an objective whose content grows and deepens with time.

Over the years, a host of theories has been advanced to explain the driving force impelling trade unions towards certain goals. The theories have invariably been concocted by intellectuals sympathetic to the labour movement, rather than by active trade unionists. It is worth reviewing them none-the-less in order to catch the rich flavour of the trade union as an institution.

Unions as revolutionary bodies

The most radical thesis sees trade unions as part of a revolutionary political process which leads along Marxist lines to the ultimate solution of socialism. There is an inevitable law of social development, and the trade unions are a creature of this process and a means to bringing it about. Historically, this description of trade unionism has held more sway on the Continent than in Britain, where it hardly ever made an impact. Ironically, at about the very time Marx was publishing *The Communist Manifesto* (in 1848), British trade unionism was moving on from its brief flirtation with the idea of one large class union—the Grand National Consolidated Trades Union, formed in 1834, had the briefest of lives—to the New Unionism associated with skilled workers in industries like engineering. The Webbs recognised this occupational rather than class dimension to British trade unionism when they examined *the solidarity of the trade*, in effect, craft consciousness.

Non-materialist ideologies

At the other end of the ideological spectrum from class trade unionism, based on the materialism of Marxism, there is a strong infusion of religion in some trade union movements on the Continent. Denominational unions usually find themselves a minority group in an environment of competing trade unions, some espousing Marxism, others social democracy, and some a religious faith. These last have never made headway in Britain.

Social democratic objectives of unions

Within the broad context of social democratic protest, the British trade union movement has never quite scaled the Marxist heights of class consciousness. A less radical view of unions sees them as economic organisations, concerned with equalising bargaining power in relation to employers. However, they have political manifestations as well, an involvement with social democratic political action. This is aimed broadly at the gradual reform of society, in the direction of greater political and industrial democracy and a more equal status with respect to property and its ownership. It is the trade unions who promoted the Labour Representation Committee at the turn of the century and laid the foundations for the Labour Party, and trade unions continue, through the political levy, to be the main financial provider for the Party. The nearest the British

trade union movement came to espousing fundamental change in
the nature of British society was in the surge of Guild Socialism,
reflected in part in the interest in industrial trade unionism, which
took place around the First World War. Even Guild Socialism,
which saw industry as being controlled ultimately by workers,
through unions organised by industry, was more the theoretical
aspiration of intellectuals such as G. D. H. Cole than the expression
of trade union ambition. The trade unions themselves have been
more pragmatic.

Pragmatic political involvement

A much weaker form of commitment to a political theory of trade
unionism is to be found in American unions. There, the classic
emphasis of trade union leaders on the main objective—"More!"—
has been reinforced by a political involvement which is much more
opportunistic. In political matters, American trade unions seek to
reward their friends and punish their enemies. They support politicians who will advance their interests. The commitment is tactical,
rather than strategic, and it contrasts broadly with the typical European trade union movement's support for a social democratic political party. True, and as one would expect, the US trade union
movement is usually to be found supporting Democratic rather than
Republican politicians; but the ideological commitment is a weak
one.

This type of trade unionism has frequently been labelled "business unionism". The members pay their subscription in order to
purchase services, and it is for the officials to "deliver" through the
economic pressure which they can bring to bear, backed as
appropriate by political lobbying. On occasion, infrequently but
regrettably, business unionism in the USA has spilled over into
corrupt or predatory unionism; but that is an aberration, not a
mainstream development of trade unionism, and legislation such as
the Labor Management Reporting and Disclosure Act (Landrum
Griffin) 1959 has provided a battery of checks against mismanage-
ment of union affairs in the USA.

Scarcity-conscious unionism

One of the most powerful theories of trade unionism is associated
with Selig Perlman, an American professor with an Eastern European background. For Perlman the key element in trade unionism
was *scarcity consciousness*. This, he claimed, is what motivates
unions. They are seeking collective control over available job
opportunities. They do not aspire to control industry, but to ration
jobs, through their collective presence. The primary interest of the

union is in "conserving and enlarging the collective job opportunity, which the union seeks to administer with equity among all legitimate members of the group."[2] This need not be a simple economic model, for social and political factors may be at work within this collective in determining the precise policies of the union as to what is equitable. The union is not simply an aggregation of individuals.

A somewhat similar flavour was provided by Allan Flanders, who considered that the basic social purpose of trade unions is job regulation and control, though the pursuit of that purpose did not stop at the boundaries of an industry. It could, for instance, reach out to include some kind of consensus about incomes policy. The vista is a broader one than job control on the shop floor, complicated as that may also be.[3]

Collective action the key

Perlman's teacher, John R. Commons, doyen of the Wisconsin school of industrial relations fifty years ago, concentrated on the relationship between the individual worker and the group in his analysis of trade unions. In particular, he stressed the social or collective aspects. Collective action was the key. The individual worker was not self-sufficient; more than that, individuals are what they are by taking part in the institutions of which they are members. An institution such as a trade union is then to be regarded as "collective action in control, liberation, and expansion of individual action".[4]

This definition goes furthest in the direction of making the union into an organ which enables the individual to fulfil himself through membership; he can aspire, through the union, to a more complete economic citizenship. This is a bold and exhilarating claim, welding together union aspiration and individual release. The ramifications of this emphasis on the collective group and its significance are enormous. It can provide justification for the kind of wage policy of "solidarity" which the Swedish trade union movement pursues, and for union membership clauses such as the "closed shop". Only through union membership, it can be argued, will the individual worker be liberated. Most fundamentally, then, Commons speaks of the social cohesion, group solidarity and protection of the weak which trade unionism at its best can express.

Politico-economic bodies

We have seen that trade unions are certainly industrial and economic bodies, with in addition a pragmatic or philosophical commitment to some political stance. The industrial and political aspects are complementary, and can be used to reinforce one another. It is this which makes unions so interesting. One debate about the economic/political dimensions of trade unionism has brought out the importance of trade unions as *political institutions* operating in an economic environment. Arthur Ross viewed unions in this way as political organisations. By political he did not mean "party political", but rather that trade unions are institutions which require an internal system of government, and which have pressure groups within them. In determining their goals and bargaining strategies unions go through a political process. The ambitions of the leaders, the development of the union, the welfare of the members have all to be accommodated. In part, Ross's analysis was intended as a counterblast to the heavily economic analysis of trade unions which Dunlop had advanced, stressing the maximising behaviour on which unions were engaged with regard to membership, the wage bill and other economic objectives, not all of which are mutually consistent.[5]

The two perspectives are not diametrically opposed. In pursuing economic objectives the union as an institution has to "deliver" its members and their support, and that undoubtedly involves political activity within the organisation. From a British perspective, Colin Crouch has explored this terrain in a stimulating treatment.[6]

Summary
Where does this review of theorising about trade unions leave us? Perlman counselled that:

> A theory of the labor movement should include a theory of the psychology of the laboring man. The writings of socialists, syndicalists, anarchists, communists, and "welfare" capitalists abound in embroideries on the theme of "what labor wants" or "what labor aspires to." But the safest method is to go to the organizations of labor's own making, shaped and managed by leaders arisen from labor's own ranks, and to attempt to discover "what's really on labor's mind" by using as material the "working rules", customs and practices of these organisations.[7]

That is good advice for the study of unions and their members in action on the ground, in the real world of collective bargaining. Yet our tour of the theory has served to bring out two important points. First, the relationships between members as individuals and the union representing them cannot simply be taken for granted: it has to be studied and appraised. We cannot assume that their interests will always coincide. Secondly, it makes a great deal of difference to our attitude to trade unions whether we see them as "just another business" or as a folk movement. If we regard them as economic organisations we can treat them like a business, subject to industrial and financial legislation and other pressures. If, however, we recognise that they are more than economic institutions, we have a much more complex phenomenon to understand. As we have seen earlier, in Chapter Three, the position in law of trade unions has involved questions of social and political balance, not merely of equilibrium between demand and supply in the markets for labour services.

Probably no one theory is valid for any one country's trade union movement all the time, and at any one time there may be wide differences, particularly in political stance, between unions. The economic/political spectrum of trade unions has to be looked at pragmatically. No one theory has demonstrated that it can predict the behaviour of a trade union movement.

Let us now move from theorising about unions to a study of the British trade union movement in action. We look in turn at the remaining themes: (a) union membership and growth, (b) the structure of unions, (c) their government, and (d) the TUC.

UNION MEMBERSHIP AND GROWTH

What makes unions grow? Is the explanation to be found mainly in economic forces, such as the level of employment and the stage of the business cycle? Can employers obstruct or assist? What part do governments play? As we have seen, governments have certainly adopted a varying stance to trade unionism in the past.

Trade union membership growth
The following figures indicate the broad magnitude of trade unionism within Britain in the twentieth century:

TABLE V. TRADE UNION MEMBERSHIP
UNITED KINGDOM (SELECTED YEARS)

1900	2,022,000
1910	2,565,000
1920	8,348,000
1930	4,842,000
1940	6,613,000
1950	9,289,000
1960	9,835,000
1970	11,179,000
1982	11,445,000

Sources: Henry Pelling, A History of British
Trade Unionism, 3rd ed. 1976, pp. 293–6, and
Department of Employment Gazette

The economic crisis of the 1920s saw sharp declines in union membership, while substantial union growth was experienced in the periods surrounding the two World Wars. For more than ten years after 1950 union membership remained stable, but in the 1970s, as Table VI shows, membership grew steadily by 2 per cent to 3 per cent annually, to a peak of 13,289,000 in 1979. It had grown by over a quarter in ten years. Since then union membership has declined each year, falling faster than the decline in employment during the recession. The largest relative falls occurred in unions with members mainly in manufacturing. Membership held up best in the service industries.

The TUC is *the* national trade union centre. In the 1970s its share of total union membership went up from about 87 per cent to 92 per cent, and has remained at that proportion, despite the fall in total trade union membership.

TABLE VI. TRADE UNIONS—NUMBERS AND MEMBERSHIP 1972–1982

Year	No. of unions at end of year	Total membership at end of year	Percentage change in membership since previous year
1972	507	11,359	+2.0
1973	519	11,456	+0.9
1974	507	11,764	+2.7
1975	501	12,193	+3.6
1975*	470	12,026	—
1976	473	12,386	+3.0
1977	481	12,846	+3.7
1978	462	13,112	+2.1
1979	453	13,289	+1.3
1980	438	12,947	−2.6
1981	414	12,106	−6.5
1982	401	11,445	−5.5

*Thirty-one organisations previously regarded as trade unions are excluded from 1975 onwards because they failed to satisfy the statutory definition of a trade union in section 28 of the Trade Union and Labour Relations Act 1974.

Source: Employment Gazette, Vol. 92, No. 1, January 1984, p. 18

Membership density

Membership data can be expressed another way, as "trade union density", i.e. the proportion of the labour force organised in unions. On that basis, trade union density reached its peak, 54 per cent, in 1978. It was high (45 per cent) in 1920 and in 1943 (40 per cent), 45.2 per cent in 1948, declining to 43.7 per cent in 1967 before it began the steady increase which we have already seen expressed in absolute membership figures. With the decline in trade union membership in the 1980s, it has fallen to about 50 per cent.

Explanations of union membership growth

Various explanations have been advanced for this behaviour of union growth. It has long been observed that trade union membership rose in the course of an economic boom and fell during a recession. Unions can press successfully for improved terms and conditions when the economy is on the rise. They can deliver. As the economy turns down they have, conversely, difficulty in maintaining pressure for higher pay and in resisting layoffs and higher unemployment among their members. The recession in Britain in 1980 made serious inroads into the buoyant growth of the 1970s.

Recent work on British union growth has confirmed the importance of price and wage increases as factors associated positively with union growth, and unemployment as a very significant influence on the aggregate membership of trade unions.[8] More generally, inflation has been stressed as one of the main factors in the boom of union membership which we noticed in the 1970s.[9] Severe and unanticipated changes in inflation have increased the demand for the kinds of collective bargaining services which trade unions can provide. Inflation seems to have been the friend of union growth, though it caused them other problems, particularly those of financing union activity from membership subscriptions.

As to the attitudes of society, which are supposed to be interpreted by governments of the day in their policy towards unions, it is clear from the discussion in Chapter Three that British trade unions had a chequered growth path until their extraordinary position in law was spelled out in 1906. Since then their growth has been affected by particular government policies as well as by the economic climate. In wartime, efforts to promote national unity led to a greater involvement of unions in the national effort. This was particularly pronounced during the Second World War.

In the past decade there has been a persistent involvement of governments in union affairs through a whole barrage of industrial relations legislation. Some of it, such as the Employment Protection Act 1975, was overwhelmingly slanted towards increasing the security of employment of the worker. Even the much-criticised Industrial Relations Act 1971 introduced an enormously favourable element, enhancing the role of the unions, in the protection against unfair dismissal which it introduced. Other protective legislation has also increased the demand for the services of the trade union, as information provider, and representative, for example in proceedings before industrial tribunals. For five years after the Act of 1975, the Advisory Conciliation and Arbitration Service, ACAS, was also involved, under section 11 of the Act, in handling union recognition claims.

One of the most interesting points is that union membership grew most rapidly in 1970, a year in which a Labour government was displaced by a Conservative one. Neither party was in favour with the unions at that time: the Labour party had failed to win support for its proposals, and the unions foresaw trouble from the Conservative ideas set out in *Fair Deal at Work*. After 1974, when Labour returned to power, growth was rapid, probably reflecting the spirit of alliance and collaboration between the Labour Government and the TUC, through the Social Contract. Much of the growth in unionism in the period from 1975 could probably be attributed to that general aura of "togetherness", and to the impetus which inflation gave.

Employer resistance to unions thus had a harder row to hoe in the 1970s, on account of the general *rapport* between the Labour Government and unions, but also because of the numerous and recurring pressures of legislative enactments in industrial relations to which employers had to respond. They found it difficult to opt out. Apart from sporadic and sensational instances, such as the Grunwick recognition dispute in 1977, the spread of unionism, not least among white collar workers, and the steady increase in union membership (closed shop) agreements suggest that employers on the whole have seen the need to come to terms with unions.

No single explanation suffices

There is undoubtedly an element of "chicken-and-egg" reasoning in explanations of union growth which seek to rely on a single factor. There is a complex interplay between unions, employers and government, as we have suggested. This is borne out in other countries too. In the USA, the passage of legislation in the 1930s gave unions access for the first time to organising in basic steel and the motor car industries. In Australia, the Industrial Conciliation and Arbitration Act, 1904, depended for its functioning on the existence of registered organisations. It compelled employers to deal with unions, but also tended to ossify union structure, once a union had acquired recognition rights from the Court. In Sweden, white collar union growth was sharply boosted by the passage in 1936 of an Act governing the right of association and collective bargaining. Blue collar workers did not need it: white collar unions thrived on it. It is naive to imagine that unions are simply passive, bending before the wind that blows from governments and from management. They can pursue active policies to gain recognition.

UNION MIX AND SIZE

By sector and occupation

The picture of aggregate growth in unionism is a vivid one in its own right. But there are important additional points to be made about the mix and the size of unions. As we saw in Chapter Two, there is ongoing change in the industrial and occupation structure of any economy. There have been major shifts away from sectors, such as mining, railways, and textiles, in which unions were densely represented, to service industries which have always tended to be difficult to unionise. The decline in some manual activities has been offset in part by the recent buoyant growth of white collar unionism. In the public sector, which has grown rapidly, the hierarchical nature and standard content of large clusters of jobs have always provided a favourable breeding ground. Yet it seems that, in private industry, white collar workers are becoming more "unionate". Legislation, including statutory and voluntary incomes policies, has helped.

Many unions

The number of trade unions in Britain has been declining steadily. In the ten years to 1982 there was a decline from 507 to 401 unions. Each year there is a steady stream of mergers and transfers. The recent recession has encouraged unions to think of effective size for the conduct of their affairs. In the 1970s the average size of union increased quite sharply, from about 17,000 in 1968 to over 28,000 in 1982.

Such an average is rather meaningless, however. There is a very long tail of unions. Over half have fewer than 1,000 members each, accounting for only 0.5 per cent of total trade union membership.

We have seen that the TUC accounts for over 90 per cent of trade union members, or some 10,500,000.

Large unions

If we concentrate now on the TUC and its 95 affiliates, we find that the twelve largest affiliated unions listed below in Table VII accounted for over 70 per cent of TUC membership. They are a mixed bag, in terms of their history, organising feifdoms, and structure. This is discussed more fully in the next section. It is very evident from the discussion in the present section, however, that unions enjoyed a boom in membership growth in the 1970s, that a process of union rationalisation is in train, and that the TUC enjoyed both an absolute and relative growth in favour. This may explain, at least in part, why the TUC is slowly but surely bringing greater influence to bear on the way the trade union movement runs its affairs. We see this at work in the Sections that follow on union structure and government.

TRADE UNION STRUCTURE

Organising principles, if any

On what principles do unions organise—by craft, occupational groups, by industry, on the basis of the employer's activity, or by pursuing an "open arms" policy? The British trade union movement provides no single answer to this question. There are no clear guidelines, although in the past, for instance in 1924, the TUC has favoured organisation by industry. It was much less positive in a 1964 assessment. Partly because of its long history, but also because of the insistence on autonomy and the lack of any firm policy or plan for trade union organisation, the British trade union movement organises on a variety of principles, if indeed principles is an appropriate term. One of the most frequently heard lamentations about British union structure is that we would now have a nice tidy structure, founded on industrial unionism, if we had had the good sense to follow the example of West Germany, on which we had the gall to impose this principle after the Second World War.

Historically, craft unionism came first in Britain, at first on a local and then a national basis, either in loose or centralised forms. General unions for unskilled workers began to develop from the 1880s, while attempts to form industrial unions, for instance on the railways and in coalmining, occurred later, in the early twentieth century. It is of the utmost significance for British union structure that *general* unions, ranging over a number of industries, were in place before efforts to establish *industrial* unions had been mounted. The general unions have provided an effective roadblock to the industrial principle, whatever its merits in its own right.

Unionism based on the nature of the employer's business, for example in the Civil Service, received a fillip from the introduction of Whitleyism after the First World War. Nationalisation after the Second World War had less effect on union structure, with the exception of the coal industry.

Varied arrangements for largest unions
A list of the 12 largest unions in Britain is in itself an illuminating indication of the variety of organising arrangements under which British unions carry on.

TABLE VII. BRITAIN'S 12 LARGEST TRADE UNIONS, 1982

Union	Membership at 31st Dec (thousands)
Transport and General Workers' Union	1,633
Amalgamated Union of Engineering Workers (all four sections)	1,238
General, Municipal, Boilermakers and Allied Trades Union	940
National and Local Government Officers Association	784
National Union of Public Employees	702
Union of Shop Distributive and Allied Workers	417
Association of Scientific, Technical and Managerial Staffs	415
Electrical, Electronic, Telecommunications Plumbing Union	380
Union of Construction Allied Trades and Technicians	261
National Union of Mineworkers	245
Confederation of Health Service Employees	232
Society of Graphical and Allied Trades '82 (SOGAT '82)	225
Total	7,472

Source: TUC Report, 1983

It is impossible in brief compass to comment on each and all of these. We must be content with making specific points which shed light on the structure of trade unionism in Britain.[10]

Examples of union structure

Some unions which began as craft unions have extended their scope; the prime example is engineering. It took seventy-five years for the skilled engineers to begin admitting semi-skilled workers, in 1926, but since then the AUEW (Amalgamated Union of Engineering Workers) has extended its scope, by skill, or absence of it, by sex, and occupation, so that it now has four sections:

    a) Engineering (1,001,000)
    b) TASS (white collar) Section (172,000)
    c) Foundry Section (43,000)
    d) Constructional Section (22,000).

By no stretch of the imagination can this be regarded as an integrated industrial union. Not only does it have members in other industries; each of the Sections is very autonomous. The AUEW is at most a loose Federation, with strong internal pressures to form breakaways by one or more of the Sections.

There is close approximation to industrial unionism in two of the nationalised industries, coal and railways. Nevertheless, the National Union of Mineworkers has a dominant area element in its make-up, and the geographical areas are in fact registered as separate unions. For negotiating purposes, however, the union seeks to bargain for the industry with the single employer, the National Coal Board. On the railways, where the total manpower employed has been shrinking, the largest union, the National Union of Railwaymen (NUR), with 150,000 members, has aspired for years to lead an industrial union. The persistence of a separate craft union, the Associated Society of Locomotive Engineers and Firemen (ASLEF) with 25,000 members and a self-contained white-collar union, the Transport Salaried Staffs' Association, with 57,000 members has always stood in the way. The NUR and ASLEF formed a Federation in 1983.

Two recent major mergers exemplify the pragmatic approach to union structure. The Boilermakers merged in 1982 with the General and Municipal Workers. The first was a strong craft union with enormous historical power in the shipbuilding industry; the latter essentially an unskilled and semi-skilled union in the public sector. The second merger, which formed SOGAT '82, at least brought together two groups (the Society of Graphical and Allied Trades, and the National Society of Operative Printers, Graphical and Media Personnel) in the same industry.

Public sector unions

Even in the Civil Service, for example, the single employer has not produced a counterpart in the shape of a single industrial-type union. In the industrial civil service, the large private sector unions have stakes. In the non-industrial civil service there are unions with strong occupational, horizontal, almost craft roots. Today's non-industrial unions result from numerous mergers over the years. Most of the original unions or associations were based on small specialist groups which broadened into Service-wide groups through amalgamations. Changes in the class and grade structure of the Civil Service have often facilitated mergers. As recently as 1968 there were 28 unions. The Council of Civil Service Unions could presumably assist the process further towards one non-industrial Union, though the occupational and professional roots of some unions remain extremely strong.

In other parts of the public sector, in education and the hospital service, for instance, there is a very strong persistence of professional or occupational groupings, with teachers frequently organising according to qualification, and doctors and nurses having their own professional organisations which are also powerful trade unions.

General unions, ranging widely, frequently overlap, though their titles usually indicate some core of sectoral groups which are a prime target for their organising capability, e.g. transport, municipal and public employment.

White-collar unions

For white-collar workers, there is considerable confusion, with all the large general unions, plus the AUEW, having white-collar sections, while there are specialist white-collar unions, such as the Association of Scientific, Technical and Managerial Staffs—ASTMS, and APEX —the Association of Professional Executive Clerical and Computer Staff. Competition between the two is strong.

ASTMS is a particularly interesting union, with a remarkable record of growth in the 1970s. Whether out of preference, or necessity, it operates a company bargaining philosophy, and allows its numerous sections—in activities as disparate as insurance staff, pharmacists, and commercial travellers—considerable autonomy.

Federations

Lastly, the device of the Federation is often used by the British unions to tidy up, and achieve some coherence. Such arrangements have, however, no explicit place in the constitution of the TUC. A post-war report on *Trade Union Structure and Closer Unity* (1947) saw a Federation as, in effect, a loose form of industrial unionism; the industrial, craft or general workers' unions concerned in any industry can get together to pursue jointly the problems of the industry with which they are all concerned. It is a half-way house. It is a nice question whether Federations have promoted or impeded further mergers among unions. The largest, the Confederation of Shipbuilding and Engineering Unions, is almost a mini-TUC in its own sector. In 1978 there were forty-four Federations, with a fair number of unions affiliated to more than one Federation.

General conclusions

Some general points are worth pondering as a result of this review. First, the persistence of occupational identity is remarkable. Sociologists would argue that this type of identification with one's professional or craft peers is part of a wider status-consciousness in Britain, though in fact titles which signal a person's occupation have survived longer, for example in Scandinavia. Whatever its rationale, the occupational, or horizontal, group raises problems in an industrial context, of wage differentials, restrictions on access to the skill of the profession or occupation, and so forth. To that extent industrial unionism does not eliminate the problems of blending occupational with industrial interests: the balance of equity within the larger group has still to be struck.

As to industrial unionism itself, the nostalgia for it has been very pervasive. It may be that the growth of process industries and the sharing across industries of technologies based on computers and information processing devices are making the case for industrial unionism less convincing. Probably this is an academic question in Britain, since the general unions already straddle industries. In some industries, such as printing, the industrial union nevertheless would be a more satisfactory arrangement for accommodating the changing technology in that industry than the persistence of craft and other groups organised in separate unions. Recent union mergers in printing suggest that they are getting the point, even if only in a defensive way.

RELATIONS BETWEEN UNIONS

What should trade union and public policy then be towards union structure? We have seen that, in Germany, industrial unionism was imposed as a deliberate act of policy on the part of the occupying Powers, in order to provide a counter to concentration in large firms. Few countries have sought, however, to mastermind the structure of trade unionism from without. For their part, trade union movements have not always made haste to keep the structure of their unions in line with changing production and technological needs. The Swedish trade union movement does have a master organising plan, and that provides a useful framework within which the unions can shape and adapt their coverage. How does the British trade union movement perform in this regard?

Forces making for mergers

It is clear that the number of unions has dropped swiftly in recent years, and the average size of trade union has grown sharply. Despite the lack of an organising plan, there is clearly movement, a continuing ferment. Why should this be so? Unions can frequently identify for themselves sound reasons for merging. Changing technology may lead to loss of members, as in textiles, and to a search for some defensive merger. There may be a genuine recognition that union bailiwicks overlap and compete. Shifts in the structure of production, for example in the direction of service industries, open up new vistas. In recent years, and bearing in mind the financial frugality of most British trade unions, the impact of inflation has frequently made unions vividly aware of economies of scale. The strength which bigness can bring is also important in the hierarchy of the TUC.

Union merger arrangements

When unions do decide to get together, the classic problem which they frequently have difficulty in resolving is the fate of the officers and the allocation of assets. The law tries to help. The Trade Union (Amalgamations etc.) Act 1964 improved upon an earlier enactment of 1917 in setting down the procedures which trade unions have to follow if they wish to merge (amalgamation) or if one union is prepared to be absorbed in another (through the "transfer of engagements" of its members). Procedures are provided for the Certification Officer for Trade Unions and Employers' Associations to monitor proposed mergers or transfers of engagement and to ensure that the membership affected is properly consulted. A transfer of engagements is the simpler alternative. This Act has undoubtedly facilitated the reduction in the number of unions which we have noticed. In 1982, for instance there were eight transfers, and four amalgamations of unions.

Public policy and union structure

There remain none the less problems of inter-union friction and rivalries, concerning the ownership of work and members, access to jobs, and recognition. Is the positive pressure to modernise trade union structure adequate? One of the consequences of the Trade Union Act of 1906 was that it made for a kind of vacuum in public policy towards union affairs. The Donovan Commission, in its 1968

Report, clearly itched to tidy up the structure, but did not quite know how to bring this about, except through union mergers. It attached great importance to the elimination of multi-unionism, competition between unions for members in the same group of workers in a factory, through agreements on representation rights. The Labour Government's 1969 White Paper, *In Place of Strife* (paras. 67–70) was sharply critical, arguing that there was a need for union reform, to eliminate overlap, encourage amalgamations, reduce competition for membership, and rationalise recruitment policies.

What role for the TUC?

The TUC has of course long had its *Disputes Principles and Procedures,* dating from the so-called Bridlington Agreement adopted at its 1939 Congress. This embodies a code of practice and procedural guidelines which are designed to minimise disputes between unions over membership questions. They have been amended from time to time. When it was under pressure to show its capacity to bring about reforms voluntarily, instead of having the kind of changes imposed on it which the 1969 White Paper proposed, the TUC strengthened these procedures, as part of the "solemn and binding undertaking" which it made towards the then Labour Government. Rule 12 of the TUC Constitution was amended to give the TUC considerably enhanced powers in respect of inter-union disputes, official and unofficial. In particular it was laid down that no affiliated union should authorise a stoppage of work in pursuance of an inter-union dispute until the TUC had considered the matter. Indeed, this extended beyond membership disputes to embrace inter-union differences about recognition, demarcations, and wages and conditions. Other changes were made in 1979.

TUC machinery and inter-union relations

Each affiliated union "shall consider" developing joint working agreements with other unions with which they are in frequent contact, in particular, developing procedures for resolving particular issues and specific arrangements for spheres of influence, transfers of members and benefit rights, recognition of cards, and demarcation of work. The TUC stands ready to assist unions in drawing up such agreements and procedures. Behind this arrangement lurks the TUC Disputes Committee, which on an *ad hoc* basis will hear disputes between affiliated organisations. The basic approach is to seek to obtain an agreed settlement, though a Disputes Committee does have power to make an award. The TUC has distinguished four main categories into which disputes between affiliated unions are likely to fall. For two of these: (*a*) membership and (*b*) recognition issues, the Committee makes awards. For two others: (*c*) demarcation and (*d*) wages and conditions, the solution has usually to take account of subsequent agreement with the employer, and the Committee's decisions are therefore more likely to be in the form of recommendations. In 1979, the TUC introduced time limits as firm guidlines for the various stages of the disputes procedures.

Recent TUC experience of inter-union problems

In recent years the TUC has intensified its efforts to conciliate in inter-union disputes. In 1982–3, 68 disputes were reported to the TUC. Of these, 36 were dealt with by the unions after the TUC had advised on procedures. The other 32 were taken to conciliation within the TUC, and 22 were resolved in that way. Disputes Committees had to resolve only eight disputes, relating to the usual categories of organising activities, acceptance into and transfer of membership. These hearings are essentially "one-off" affairs, restricted to the case at issue. Since there is no set of agreed organising principles or blueprint, cases are judged on their merits, within the broad setting of the interests of the trade union movement and the declared policy of the Congress. It is deliberately low key, and the Disputes Committee, as indeed the name implies, is not to be regarded as being in the business of restructuring the trade union movement. That is not its job.[11] Behind the Disputes Committee there is the General Council, which has power to suspend, and ultimately expel, an organisation whose activities are judged to be detrimental to the movement.

It has not proved possible for the TUC to keep all these inter-union matters "in house". The Employment Protection Act 1975, sections 11 to 16 (no longer in effect), enabled an independent trade union to refer recognition issues to ACAS. The position of the TUC was that in cases involving more than one of its affiliates the unions concerned should continue to follow the Bridlington path. It saw the protection under the 1975 Act as being concerned with the extension of recognition, not with the topic of jurisdictional disputes, which it preferred to handle "within the family". On occasion, however, affiliated unions did not abide by this dictum. One celebrated case in 1977–8 involved TASS (The Technical, Administrative and Supervisory Section of the Amalgamated Union of Engineering Workers) and the EMA (Engineers' and Managers' Association), both TUC affiliates, in dispute about organising rights in engineering. Not only ACAS, but the law courts, were drawn into this particular controversy.

Equally, it is not always easy to separate the narrower matters of union structure and inter-union bailiwicks from wider considerations which carry us over into our next theme, trade union government. In essence, any trade union movement has three major themes on which it must seek to conduct a policy.

(*a*) Firstly, it has a whole spectrum of relationships with employers—covering recognition, negotiation arrangements and disputes procedures and the conduct of disputes, including strikes, picketing, attitudes to emergency supplies, and so forth. We look at these systematically in Chapter Seven.

(*b*) Secondly, there are the matters covered in this Section, of trade union structure and, therefore, of inter-union relationships.

(*c*) There is thirdly, a vast terrain which has to be brought into focus through the internal machinery of government of each union. We take up this theme of trade union government in the next Section.

TRADE UNION GOVERNMENT

Trade unions are in many respects like the state in miniature, and it is usual to think of the processes of democracy in the unions by analogy with those operative in the state. Unions have their electorate, legislatures, cabinets and civil service.[12]

The government of trade unions attracts the interest of the political scientist; the constitutional expert is interested in the equity and efficiency of Rules and Constitutions; economists ask how unions function as the agency concerned primarily with the supply side of labour markets; sociologists are interested in union government in terms of group behaviour and power structures. Whatever the approach, union government is an absorbing topic.

Basic arrangements
Part of the reason for this is that, as we have already noticed, the structure of British trade unionism is not cleancut, reflecting some all-wise mastermind. The government of British trade unions has been equally varied, reflecting its topsy-turvy growth. There clearly have to be arrangements for running unions, from the prime mover, the member, up through branches (or union locals), via districts (where appropriate), to the industrial (national) and truly national (TUC) strata. But no unique pattern of government is imposed, for instance by the TUC. Britain has come nowhere near the arrangements which the Swedish Trade Union Confederation—LO—has spelled out in very explicit rules requirements. Sweden is admittedly

exceptional, but the central executive of the Confederation has formidable formal powers over internal disputes, organising plans, wage policy and negotiations, and disputes procedures. It requires affiliates to include in their constitutions rules relating to the open shop, the right and obligation to transfer membership, and a power of veto for the national executive of the union in bargaining matters. In Britain, the TUC has not aspired to such vigorous and explicit requirements. The word from above is modest but, as we shall see, it is not to be underrated, and it is increasing in importance.

Nature of representation arrangements

The problem of union government, said the Webbs, is to combine administrative efficiency and popular control, through *representative institutions*. Rules and Constitutions are intended to solve the problem. Typically, Union rules cover the following themes:

(*a*) objects—these may range from general declarations about socialist objectives and public ownership, to welfare objectives and the advancement of the interests of the membership over an area of economic activity;

(*b*) membership categories and qualifications;

(*c*) subscription rates;

(*d*) arrangements for admission and readmission of members;

(*e*) branches, organised on a geographical or plant basis;

(*f*) area/district/regional or divisional groupings;

(*g*) national executive functions and powers;

(*h*) executive committee, for day-to-day management;

(*i*) financial powers and controls;

(*j*) arrangements for election/appointment of officers;

(*k*) full time officials, e.g. general secretary, method of appointment/election, and duties;

(*l*) staff/employees;

(*m*)(annual) delegate conference;

(*n*) arrangements for ballots of membership;

(*o*) benefit arrangements;

(*p*) industrial disputes procedures;

(*q*) alteration of rules;

(*r*) audit and other financial arrangements;

(*s*) misconduct and appeals;

(*t*) (where appropriate) arrangements for political levy.

Rule books usually conceal as much as they reveal. Nevertheless, there are certain key aspects of union government which we have to bear in mind.

Key aspects

Delegate conference
Firstly, the (annual) delegate conference is the supreme and sovereign policy-making body, the legislature. In fact, however, sovereignty is an intermittent power, and the National Executive will be the continuing repository of power, the "Cabinet".

General Secretary
Secondly, the General Secretary, who is usually elected for a stated period or, more frequently, for life, or "during the pleasure of the Union", is the linchpin of the permanent officials, or Civil Service. In practice, particularly if the President or Chairman of a Union is a lay member with a specified and brief term of office, of one or two years, the General Secretary can be extremely powerful. He may technically be the servant, but he can frequently have all the power he cares to have, particularly if he is wise enough to acquire and use it with discretion. Other officials will have less exalted but significant roles in union government.

Branch
Thirdly, while the intermediate levels of union government such as the area or district may frequently be significant, and often were crucial in the less centralised days of trade union affairs, the *branch* is the basic grass roots organising unit, to which the individual member affiliates. Branches usually have an unpaid elected executive. British unions are often criticised for the persistence of geographically based branches, though the journalist and printing unions' chapel (with its Father) and colliery branch are examples of plant-based unions in two bastions of trade union history and experience, printing and coal mining. Membership participation in union branch government is notoriously patchy and deficient, except on important occasions such as a vote on a pay claim or on industrial action.

The member
Fourthly, the member is the *raison d'être* of unionism, the electorate. As we have noticed, Commons argued that it was only through the Union that the individual "rank-and-file" member really came into his own. Equally, as we have seen, the Donovan Commission was struck by the two industrial relations systems existing in Britain, the formal and the informal, the latter focusing on behaviour of people at the workplace. One of the research studies produced for Donovan commented that few unions troubled to

prescribe for the processes that included election of shop stewards and convening of meetings.[13]

Shop stewards
Here we touch on one of the most important aspects of union government in Britain. The individual union member on the shop floor has to be looked after. If the union branch organisation does not do it the vacuum will be filled, somehow. When in addition there are multi-union situations, a not uncommon position, the problem is accentuated. The shop steward tends to fill the role of link man. Shop stewards have attracted a great deal of attention in the literature and criticism of trade unions. Most carry out well a necessary function as the point of contact between worker (or union member), and union and management. Yet shop floor militancy, mediated through shop stewards, has been an Achilles heel in British industrial relations. Donovan declared that trade unions should provide constitutionally recognised committees to perform many of the functions being carried out by unofficial shop stewards' combine committees. Further, it argued, there was a need to alter the process of union government to accommodate shop stewards and work groups more adequately. Union rules should be revised in relation to such matters as elections, term of office, jurisdictional boundaries of shop stewards, their relations with other union officials and their place in the union's organisation. Quite an indictment.

The evidence from the recent surveys to which we have referred more than once suggests that there has been a substantial improvement in the position in recent years. The growth in bargaining at company level, in joint consultative arrangements and in formal arrangements in general have helped to bring shop stewards more explicitly into procedural structures. The changes reflect the pressures in the 1970s that we have already noted: the growth in trade unionism, the intrusions of law and of a variety of codes of practice, and also a management stance. There appears to have been a strong growth in management support for "the closed shop". This is discussed below.

RELATIONS WITHIN UNIONS

We turn now to a matter which we deferred from Chapter Three, where we looked at government involvement in industrial relations. It was suggested then that the inquisitiveness of governments about union internal management and governance had grown, and that it could best be reviewed in this chapter.

Donovan had found little evidence of abuse of power on the part of unions *vis-à-vis* their members, but nevertheless did recommend tighter union rules, and an Independent Review Body to deal with individual complaints. It is not possible here to trace the tortuous subsequent history of the debate about internal union government. Section 65 of the Industrial Relations Act, 1971, for instance, set out principles as to the conduct of workers' organisations, and the Trade Union and Labour Relations Act 1974, sections 2 to 12, covered the status and regulation of unions and employers' associations. Some of these provisions were ended in 1976. The Employment Act 1980 dealt in particular with the issue of unreasonable exclusion from trade union membership, and secret ballots. The Employment Act of 1982 and the Trade Union Act 1984 have taken the matter further.

Throughout, there has been a running debate as to whether voluntary reform from within the unions was adequate, or whether the law could deal sensitively with controversial internal union affairs. On balance, the law *has* penetrated into union government, but the unions have also been active in developing their own arrangements. If we review the following themes in turn we can see the interplay at work:

(*a*) the closed shop;
(*b*) union disciplinary rules or members' rights;
(*c*) the use of secret ballots, for example in union elections and in decisions about industrial action; and
(*d*) shop stewards

The closed shop

The "union membership agreement", the issue of 100 per cent union organisation, has proved a controversial topic in the industrial relations of many countries. In the USA, "right to work" laws, which are permissible under the Taft-Hartley Act, have been used vigorously in many states to undermine trade unionism. In Sweden, where collectivism is extremely strong, the unions see no need for such a device. In Britain, the unions do wish to have such an arrangement available. The basis of trade unionism is organisation. We have seen how Commons viewed the collective union concept. The requirement to be a union member or to join has been used to spread and defend membership, to ensure negotiating strength, and to try to avoid the problem of the non-unionist, the "free rider", who receives the benefits of trade unionism without paying for them.

Survey finding
A recent survey, covering 84 per cent of people in employment,
shows that in Britain closed-shop practices cover at least 5.2 million
employees, compared to 3.75 in the mid 1960s.[14] The arrangements
are also found over a wider spectrum of industries than in the early
1960s. The older closed-shop industries—coal mining, metal manu-
facture, engineering, shipbuilding and printing—accounted then
for two-thirds of the closed shop population, against two-fifths in
1978. It is now strong in nationalised industries and in multi-
establishment firms. Another survey stresses these features of
ownership and organisational size, rather than industrial sector.[15]
The closed shop has also gained ground in white-collar employment. Nevertheless, it is still more common among blue collar
workers, for at least one-third of blue collar workers are covered,
as against one in ten of white collar employees.

Over 80 per cent of those involved in closed-shop arrangements
are covered by *post-entry* clauses, which require an individual
worker to join an appropriate trade union on taking up employment
or soon thereafter. The remainder are covered by *pre-entry* closed
shops, under which an applicant for a job must possess the
appropriate union card before he or she can be taken on.

Pros and cons
There is no doubting the growth of the closed shop. Employers
sometimes find it convenient: it gives stability, and may avoid the
problem of splintering unions. Yet no topic arouses more industrial
relations emotion. It is not just a matter of internal union government convenience. It raises issues of freedom of access to work, the
liberty of the individual, and the possible threat to efficiency im-
plied in a union controlling the supply of labour. Control by a craft
union does of course have different and deeper connotations, regarding flexibility and deployment of labour, than a situation of
industrial unionism. There is no "correct" solution to such im-
ponderables. A balance has to be struck.

TUC internal review committee
The TUC has tried to develop its own safeguards. In 1976 it established an Independent Review Committee to consider appeals from
individuals who have been dismissed or given notice of dismissal
from their jobs as a result of being expelled from or having been
refused admission to a union in a situation where trade union
membership is a condition of employment.

Before it considers an appeal the Committee has to be satisfied that an individual has exhausted all the internal union procedures. It is possible, however, to provide in the procedures of a collective agreement that the Committee is to be the last arbitral stage for dealing with such matters, and a fair number do. The Committee can conduct hearings, engage in pre-conciliation to try to resolve a matter by agreement, and make recommendations as a result of any hearing it conducts. It sees itself as having to pay regard to not only union rules but to the tests of reasonableness and equity. It has also engaged in "post-hearing" conciliation, with the agreement of all the parties involved in a case, with the object of exploring the possibilities of finding an agreed solution. In its first seven years, the Committee received 53 complaints, 23 of which went to a formal hearing. In 14, the Committee recommended that the union should admit or re-admit the complainant.

This arrangement is rather similar to one which the United Automobile Workers' Union operates in the USA, with an independent Public Review Body established as a court of appeal for rank-and-file members who have grievances against union officials or bodies. The seven-man board operates as a final arbiter in interpreting the Union's constitution and code of ethical practices where disputes arise between it and members.

Adequacy of the internal watchdog
Is this type of internal arrangement sufficient? The unions clearly prefer to handle these matters through machinery which, while independent, is sensitive to the world of trade unionism. Yet the law has taken an explicit interest in the matter since Donovan floated the idea of an independent review body, and the Labour Government of the day proposed that such matters should be referred to a new and independent Industrial Board. Subsequently, the Industrial Relations Act 1971 banned the closed shop, while permitting a version of union membership arrangements termed an agency shop. The Trade Union and Labour Relations Acts of 1974 and 1976 permitted union membership agreements, the closed shop. Provision was made for workers who thought they had been arbitrarily or unreasonably excluded or expelled from a trade union to apply to an Industrial Tribunal. Under the Employment Protection (Consolidation) Act 1978, section 58(3), an employer could dismiss fairly an employee who refused to be or become a member of a trade union under a union membership agreement. The one exception covered the situation where the employee could prove that he or she genuinely objected on the grounds of religious belief to

belonging to any trade union whatsoever. The dismissal is then unfair.

Legal safeguards

The Employment Act 1980, section 4, dealing with unreasonable exclusion or expulsion from a trade union, in effect the closed shop, applies the test of reasonableness "in accordance with equity and the substantial merits of the case." It also widens the objection on the ground of religious belief to comprehend (section 7 (2)) "the grounds of conscience or other deeply-held personal conviction to being a member of any trade union whatsoever or of a particular trade union." As with the previous legislation, complaints can find their way to an industrial tribunal. An official code of practice has been produced to provide practical guidance. Subsequently, the 1982 Employment Act provided that existing closed shop arrangements should be subject to periodic review by ballot, commencing in 1984. Voting arrangements have to be worked out. closed shop agreement, no matter when it took effect, is considered an *approved* agreement only if it has been supported in the previous five years in a secret ballot by 80 per cent of the employees it covers or by 85 per cent of those voting. Between 1982 and 1984 only one such ballot appears to have been held, and it confirmed the closed shop agreement dating from 1976.

Unresolved problems

The trade union movement does not like any of this. Not only does it provide an *entrée* for the law. It also provides more play for eccentrics and "sea-lawyers". It is evident that a stable middle ground has not yet been found, between the preference of the TUC for its own domestic arrangements for monitoring the closed shop and the preference on the part of others for a neutral and public watchdog, able to adjudicate on a range of let-out or conscience clauses. Underlying the controversy is the paradox that, while the debate has raged, union membership agreements have been on the increase, and that obviously has required broad acquiescence from management.

It is a nice question whether the unions could now allow an open shop policy to take over, relying on their strength to "sell their product", and on solidarity to gain adhesion to the Movement. The most likely outcome, however, is that the uneasy balance between self-regulation of the closed shop and attempts to provide legal safeguards will persist, and from time to time flare into controversy.

Union disciplinary rules, or members' rights

General rules
The closed shop problem is the most controversial of internal union governmental arrangements, even though it applies only to a minority. Just as important, however, but on a much broader canvas, is the whole theme of union discipline and members' rights. Union rules generally contain a blanket clause protecting the union from action contrary or detrimental to the aims and interests of the union or its members. The membership has to accept that the collective is extremely important. Specific categories of offence can range from misuse of funds, or assisting an employer during a dispute, to working practices, or working below the union rate.

What rule books contain
Union discipline was also the subject of voluntary guidelines introduced by the TUC in 1969, and covering admission, discipline, expulsion, and electoral procedures. A recent survey of the rule books of 79 unions, covering 99 per cent of TUC membership, proved rather unsensational.[16] It endorsed the view of the Donovan Commission that there was little evidence to suggest widespread abuse of power by unions over their members or would-be-members. There were probably few instances of injustice to individual members. "Natural justice", in the eyes of the TUC, involves the opportunity to be heard, a fair hearing, and a *bona fide* decision. The survey also concluded, however, that admission and disciplinary standards did not reach those suggested by the TUC in 1969, or those required under the Industrial Relations Act 1971. The latter, of course, had little opportunity to make an impact. With the exception of the closed shop problem, the law seems, temporarily at any rate, to be leaving this matter to the slow tempo of internal adjustment to the TUC Guidelines.

Secret ballots
Secret ballots are altogether a more emotional subject. Unions employ a wide range of voting systems in relation to elections, rule changes, and the calling and ending of industrial action, including postal ballots and secret ballots at the workplace. In 1969 the TUC resisted firmly government proposals that, when a major official strike was threatened, a ballot of the union membership concerned could be advised or required. In its 1979 Guides on the conduct of

disputes, the TUC considered that unions needed very clear procedures. In particular, it strongly recommended the following principles to unions to incorporate in their rules as the basis for procedures to be followed in disputes.

Strike procedures. These should state clearly the procedures to be followed, and which bodies have the authority to call or approve or terminate a strike.
Strike ballots. These should:

(*a*) provide for ballots before or during a strike, with the appropriate body of a union having discretion about holding such ballots;
(*b*) specify the size of the majority required;
(*c*) lay down a strictly defined procedure for the conduct of strike ballots, and sanctions for breach of such procedure;
(*d*) set out machinery for dealing with complaints about the conduct of the ballot.

Employment Legislation and secret ballots
These principles were enunciated after TUC—Labour Government discussions in February 1979 about the economy, the Government, and trade union responsibilities. They were clearly an attempt to forestall any further intrusion of the law into trade union affairs. The Employment Act 1980, sections 1 and 2, passed by a Conservative government, however, proceeded to set out various purposes for which public funds could be made available towards the expenditure incurred by trade unions in respect of secret ballots. These purposes are:

(*a*) obtaining a decision or ascertaining the views of members of a trade union as to the calling or ending of a strike or other industrial action;
(*b*) carrying out an election provided for by the rules of a trade union;
(*c*) electing a worker who is a member of a trade union to be a representative of other members also employed by his employer;
(*d*) amending the rules of a trade union;
(*e*) obtaining a decision about union mergers or amalgamations under the Trade Union (Amalgamations etc.) Act 1964;
(*f*) other specified purposes.

The intention is clear, to encourage an environment in which individual union members may make their own decisions unhampered by the atmosphere of the mass vote, or the show of hands. Equally, the opposition by most trade unions to the scheme is clear; to them it smacks of Danegeld, the thin end of the wedge, another attempt to infiltrate the law into union government. Public funds would inexorably involve public accountability. The scheme would not of course have been necessary if union rules had uniformly provided for clear and equitable procedures. The TUC Guides of 1979 were clearly a move towards standardisation, and should have helped to reassure the public. But perhaps they came too late. The government has kept up the legislative pressure, at any rate. For example, on two of the matters on which the Employment Act 1980 encouraged secret ballots, the 1984 legislation introduced requirements. First, in the context of the question who leads a union, the governing body of every trade union has to be elected by individual secret ballot of the members. Second, on industrial action, a union can lose its legal immunity if there has been no secret ballot of the members concerned before industrial action is taken. One recent study casts doubt on this approach to reforming the internal affairs of unions.[17]

Shop stewards

The Donovan Commission argued the case for reform and clarification of union rules in general, including specifying rules relating to shop stewards. It argued, too, for official multi-union committees within the framework of union rules, rather than unofficial combine committees of stewards. After the initial post-Donovan flurry, it is astonishing to see how little explicit attention this crucial problem received. The industrial relations Code of Practice set out guidelines for employee representation at the place of work, including shop steward functions. But there is little evidence of changes in union rules to meet the Donovan case. True, proposals by the TUC for tighter strike control and dispute procedures can assist in identifying authorised individuals or bodies within a union, and the recent legislation facilitating ballots could help to regularise internal voting procedures. The TUC has also recognised that some unofficial action may arise because of faulty communications within the union, and that unions need periodically to review their internal machinery. This could obviously include the status of the shop stewards. Union mergers also help to eliminate overlap through multi-unionism, and tidy the structure. As we noticed earlier in this chapter, procedures are becoming more explicit, and that must improve the standing of stewards in the formal structure.

THE TRADES UNION CONGRESS

What now of the TUC, the Fourth Estate, the central focal point of the trade union movement in Britain? Is it, as one General Secretary described it, a tabby cat, or a powerhouse, a paper tiger, or an effective central policy agency for the unions? There is no doubting the pre-eminence of the TUC as the single central organisation of unions in Britain. It has no rival, for blue or for white collar worker affiliation. Nor is there any denying its recent rapid growth. Yet it remains an elusive body, very much in the public eye, but curiously unknown with regard to its power, if not its influence.

General powers

The TUC was formed in 1868, a Parliament of Labour. It has never had Draconian powers over its affiliates. We have noticed that in:

(a) inter-union disputes;
(b) problems about closed shop agreements; and
(c) strike procedures

the TUC has recently been enhancing its formal status, and the strength of the advice which it gives. Its most recent Guides, from February 1979, traverse a broad range of union activity embracing negotiating procedures, the conduct of disputes, and union organisation.

Its main control over the affiliated member unions is the sanction cf solidarity. Formally, under Rule 13 the General Council of the TUC has power to investigate the conduct of any affiliated organisation across the very broad terrain covered by the phrase "on the ground that the activities of such organisations may be detrimental to the interests of the trade union Movement or contrary to the declared principles or declared policy of the Congress." This could, for instance, relate to recalcitrant unions disregarding the awards or recommendations of a Disputes Committee, or disregarding official policy towards legislation of which the TUC disapproved. The TUC took a tough line with affiliates who did not abide by the policy which opposed registration under the Industrial Relations Act 1971, and the available sanctions of (a) suspension and, ultimately, (b) exclusion (expulsion) were used.

The prominent position occupied by industrial relations legislation in recent years has brought the TUC into the centre of the stage. It was extremely active in 1969 in opposing proposed legal intervention, based on the Labour Government's White Paper, *In Place of Strife*, and was adroit enough to put forward its own alternative programme based on voluntarism. It has continued to do this whenever it saw proposed legislation as a threat, as in 1980, 1982, and 1984. During the era of the Social Contract with the Labour Government, from 1974 to 1978, its involvement with law was much more positive, for the TUC pressed hard for the kinds of *protective* legislation embodied in the The Employment Protection

Act 1975 and the Trade Union and Labour Relations Acts of 1974 and 1976. Attitudes to legislation have been pragmatic; based on the criterion of what the TUC saw as "good for the unions".

Policy on pay negotiations
In one area of important social and economic experiment since the Second World War, that of wages or incomes policy, the TUC has been equally pragmatic. Rule 11 (*b*) sets out the general policy of the General Council on industrial disputes, i.e., not to intervene unless requested to do so, so long as there is a prospect of the negotiating machinery in the trades in question generating an amicable settlement. It can, however, intervene if it looks as though other groups of members are becoming involved, or their situation imperilled, and it can then apply its positive influence, with the backing of its formal powers. Under this arrangement it can, if it wishes, find an *entrée* to co-ordination of union attitudes towards wages policies. It was committed to observance of the "twelve-month rule" as part of the Social Contract pay policy. Yet the TUC has been very circumspect about lending itself to any policies which put it in the position of a policeman *vis-à-vis* its affiliates. It does not see itself telling affiliates what their negotiating policy should be, though it can, through the General Secretary, advise and counsel.

Influence of TUC on public policy
Formal powers are one thing: influence is another. Both within the TUC and outside it, *influence* is the main characteristic which the TUC displays. Its internal power and influence have been discussed throughout this chapter. Externally, the TUC is now extremely influential, part of the economic and social Establishment. Prior to the era of full employment following the Second World War, the involvement of the TUC in "running the country" was sporadic, tending to be sustained only in wartime. The spread of:

(*a*) macro economic and social policies;
(*b*) the search for consensus on national economic goals;
(*c*) the establishment of bodies such as the National Economic Development Council;
(*d*) the plans for an industrial strategy;
(*e*) sector working parties

have all drawn the TUC into permanent involvement. The additional industrial relations legislation, where accepted, and involvement in the Social Contract have also required it to be represented in public agencies. Increasingly, too, the TUC has been willing to range widely in offering alternative economic and social policy strategies as platforms for its affiliates to support. It is woven into national policy-making, warp and weft.

Organisation and government

Organisationally, the TUC conducts its business via a General Council. This was enlarged in 1983 from 42 to 54 members. In 1981 and 1982 the TUC reviewed the make-up of the General Council, with a view to ensuring that it was representative and could act for the affiliates between the annual Congresses. The outcome of the review was that the composition of the General Council was changed. The affiliated unions used to be grouped into 19 trade groups, each with a number of seats on the Council, depending on the membership covered by the group. From 1983 the Council has been composed of three Sections. Section A provides automatic membership, weighted by size, for all unions with 100,000 members or more (a union with 1,500,000 members or more has five representatives); Section B provides for eleven places for unions with membership of less than 100,000, elected on a single list from these unions; Section C provides six places for women, elected by the full Congress.

Much of the work of the TUC is undertaken through the Standing Committees, e.g., on Education, Employment Policy and Organisation, with the Finance and General Purposes Committee acting as an inner Cabinet.

The General Secretary is in a key position, as a member of the General Council and also head of the Departments into which the secretariat of the TUC is grouped. He is, effectively, the recognised spokesman for the TUC, and therefore for the British trade union movement, on national policy matters of common interest to the affiliated unions.

As with individual unions, the *Congress*, held annually, is the supreme policy-making body. The *regional councils* of the TUC are gradually being strengthened by the appointment of full-time administrative and research officers. The TUC also operates eleven Industry Committees, covering sectors such as Fuel and Power, Construction, and Steel. There are also *Joint Committees* for e.g., Nationalised Industries, Women's Affairs, and the very important TUC Labour Party Liaison Committee.

Finance

Financially, the TUC is not an affluent body. Total affiliation fees in 1983 were £4.5 million, and this made up over 95 per cent of total income. The financial centre of gravity of British unions lies in the member unions. For a number of years the TUC has conducted a

TABLE VIII. TRADE UNION INCOME AND EXPENDITURE, 1973–1982

	1973	1974	1975	1976	1977	1978	1979	1980	1981	1982
Membership covered (thousands)	8,837	9,204	9,984	10,499	11,048	11,889	11,968	11,415	10,019	10,227
Income per member										
Contributions	£6.60	£6.99	£8.25	£10.10	£11.56	£12.68	£14.26	£17.34	£21.22	£24.48
Investments	0.55	0.74	0.86	0.81	1.09	1.13	1.31	1.53	1.51	1.73
Other sources	0.26	0.45	0.41	0.40	0.23	0.28	0.54	0.56	1.01	0.84
Total income	7.41	8.18	9.52	11.31	12.88	14.09	16.11	19.41	23.74	27.05
Expenditure per member										
Services and administration	£4.42	£4.98	£6.60	£7.72	£8.66	£9.72	£11.52	£14.99	£18.05	£21.17
Benefits	1.16	1.24	1.15	0.97	1.51	2.11	2.46	2.47	3.12	2.59
Total expenditure	5.58	6.22	7.75	8.69	10.17	11.83	13.98	17.46	21.17	23.76
Weekly contribution income and average earnings										
Contribution income	£0.13	£0.13	£0.16	£0.20	£0.22	£0.24	£0.27	£0.33	£0.41	£0.47
Average earnings	35.90	41.10	53.40	63.40	69.30	78.10	88.40	108.70	123.10	134.50
Contribution income as percentage of earnings	0.4	0.3	0.3	0.3	0.3	0.3	0.3	0.3	0.3	0.3

Source: TUC (to be published in Report for 1984)

survey of the income and expenditure of its affiliated unions. Table VIII sets out the position for 1982. It hardly conveys the impression of financial robustness. Put another way, the average trade unionist contributes 0.3 per cent of his or her earnings in support of the union. To the TUC the per capita annual affiliation fee is 60p (from 1985).

Review of TUC strategy

In 1979, the TUC initiated an internal review of its organisation, structure and services. This led in 1981 to a *Development Programme*, and to the changes in the size and composition of the General Council referred to earlier. In 1984 it returned to its affiliated unions, asking them to agree the basis on which they should set about a critical examination of their functions in achieving trade union objectives in the light of the rapidly changing and increasingly hostile environment. The 1983 Congress provided the impetus, with a discussion on TUC strategy and membership services. A consultative document, *TUC Strategy*, invited the unions to range widely in their thinking and suggestions. A unified approach to change was needed. Organisational development and changing approaches to industrial relations has to respond to the changes taking place in employment, industrial and corporate structures. It was necessary to build upon and deepen the representative capacity of trade unions.

> While the changes that have taken place in the past in union organisation and union methods have been substantial and far-reaching, they have occurred as fragmented and uncoordinated responses to gradually changing circumstances. The pace of current changes will not afford the luxury of gradualism. Unions must, as far as is possible, plan change. The task for each union is to build a sensible, flexible strategy to enable it to adapt to the changing economic and industrial environment.[18]

It remains to be seen how major an overhaul this will produce. One thing is certain, however. Trade union officials and representatives are now extremely important and influential members of the decision-making bodies in our society. The work of officials has developed and changed dramatically, with involvement in the work of:

(*a*) industrial tribunals and other bodies;
(*b*) industrial training boards;
(*c*) sector working parties;
(*d*) regional and industrial planning machinery;
(*e*) pensions schemes; and
(*f*) public committees of enquiry.

Negotiations remain important, but are becoming more sophisticated. Employee involvement, industrial democracy, is opening up new vistas. Rapidly changing technology is forcing the tempo of adjustment. It is imperative that the unions should be well organised and well led. Their contribution to national well-being has the inestimable value of being grounded in practical experience. Trade union government is a hard and effective school. The opportunities open to a brisk and efficient TUC are dramatic, but also demanding. The internal review mentioned above faces a serious challenge.

SELF-ASSESSMENT QUESTIONS

1. Which theory of trade unionism fits British experience best?
2. Assess the likely implications of technological, occupational and industrial change for the structure of trade unionism.
3. How far can the functions of shop stewards be separated from the structural problems of trade unionism in Britain? Would industrial unionism make shop stewards redundant?
4. Is the appeal to solidarity a more important aid to the TUC in its activities than any formal powers under its Rules?
5. Is the attachment to the union membership (closed shop) policy a sign of trade union weakness rather than trade union strength?

ASSIGNMENT

Consult one of the TUC's recent Annual Reports. List the range of activities which the TUC has undertaken with a view to improving relationships between member unions. What problems seem to be the most difficult to resolve?

REFERENCES

1. S. and B. Webb, *History of Trade Unionism*, 1896, p. 1.
2. S. Perlman, *A Theory of the Labor Movement*, 1959 ed., p. 299.
3. Allan Flanders, *Industrial Relations: What is Wrong with the System?*, 1965.
4. John R. Commons, *The Economics of Collective Action*, 1950, p. 21.
5. Arthur M. Ross, *Trade Union Wage Policy*, 1948; and J. T. Dunlop, *Wage Determination under Trade Unions*, 1944.
6. Colin Crouch, *Trade Unions: The Logic of Collective Action*, 1982.
7. Perlman, *op. cit.*, p. 237.
8. George Sayers Bain and Farouk Elsheikh, *Unions and the Business Cycle*, 1976.
9. David C. Smith, "Trade Union Growth and Industrial Disputes", in

Richard E. Caves and Lawrence B. Krause (eds.), *Britain's Economic Performance*, 1980, pp. 81 et seq.

10. Arthur Marsh, *Trade Union Handbook*, 3rd ed., 1984.

11. Peter J. Kalis, "The Effectiveness and Utility of the Disputes Committee of the Trades Union Congress", in *British Journal of Industrial Relations*, Vol. XVI, March 1978, pp. 41–51.

12. B. C. Roberts, *Trade Union Government and Administration in Great Britain*, 1956, p. 243.

13. John Hughes, *Trade Union Structure and Government* (two parts), Research Papers 5, Royal Commission on Trade Unions and Employers' Associations, 1967.

14. John Gennard, Stephen Dunn and Michael Wright, "The Content of British Closed Shop Agreements", in *Department of Employment Gazette*, November 1979, p. 1088 et seq.

15. Daniel and Millward, *op. cit.*, Ch. III.

16. John Gennard, Mark Gregory and Stephen Dunn, "Throwing the book. Trade union rules on admission, discipline and expulsion", in *Department of Employment Gazette*, June 1980, p. 591 et seq.

17. R. Undy and R. Martin, *Ballots and Trade Union Democracy*, 1984.

18. *TUC Strategy*, Consultative Document, March 1984.

CHAPTER SIX

Collective Agreements and Rules

CHAPTER OBJECTIVES

After studying this chapter you should be able to:
* know why collective bargaining is the most commonly used method for determining terms and conditions;
* understand what the case is for industry-wide agreements;
* explain in what way the scope of collective bargaining can reflect changing aspirations on the part of workers;
* say whether legally enforceable collective agreements could improve collective bargaining.

> Eight hours' work,
> Eight hours' play,
> Eight hours' sleep,
> And eight bob a day.
>
> *Traditional song*

INTRODUCTION

The main, though not the only way in which terms and conditions of employment are set in Britain is through collective bargaining. In 1978 the New Earnings Survey found that about thirty per cent of full-time employees were not affected directly or indirectly by any collective agreements. Nevertheless, that is simply another way of saying that the majority of employees are covered by collective bargaining. In this chapter we shall look at the content of terms and conditions, with particular reference to collective agreements. That gives us a good awareness of the stuff of agreements. In Chapter Seven we can then investigate how the parties go about determining these agreements first through negotiations and bargaining techniques, and thereafter living with them.

FEATURES OF COLLECTIVE AGREEMENTS

We have already noticed a number of important features which affect the nature of collective agreements in Britain, directly or indirectly. The Government supports the voluntary settlement of terms and conditions through the provision it has long made for conciliation and voluntary arbitration machinery. There has never been strong support for the legal settlement of minimum rates of pay, and Wages Councils, the findings of which are the nearest proxy for a legal minimum, are tending to decline in importance. We have also noticed how employers come together in various ways to negotiate on terms, and that there is great variety in the degree of common purpose to which they adhere. Obviously, that variety is bound to affect the precision with which terms and conditions are set at different strata of the labour market. Trade unions also have their historical, occupational and industrial priorities in selecting, if they can, the focal points for their bargaining. All these forces help to shape the content of the deals which trade unions and employers conclude with one another. In Dunlop's phrase, "the actors determine a complex of rules".

Collective agreements can be viewed from a number of standpoints, not least by the student of industrial relations. The economist looks at an agreement primarily as an economic trade-off, which settles the employers' costs and the incomes and job security of the employees. Wage tariffs can be regarded as a set of prices, balancing demand and supply of labour services. A political scientist may view an agreement as a statement of power-sharing, a peace treaty, a form of industrial self-government. Sociologists scrutinise agreements for patterns of group behaviour which become visible in the form of norms for occupational pay, stratification of the terms of settlement by groups, and the community of work which the clauses of the agreement govern.

Agreements can also be viewed as a form of industrial or economic democracy. As we saw in Chapter Five in considering trade union objectives, an agreement may represent the triumph of the collective action of the employees, not only in relation to the weakness of the worker in isolation, but with regard to the prerogatives of management. Many of the "social relations at production" will be organised through the terms of an agreement.

Just as the industrial relations of countries vary in their approaches to social relations in production, so the whole flavour and content of collective agreements in a particular country may be quite distinctive. The reasons are obvious. Agreements embody the accumulated experience of employers and employees dealing with one another, frequently over lengthy periods. Let us set the scene by identifying some of the main characteristics of agreements in Britain.

Agreements in Britain

Voluntary

Notice, first, that the principle of free collective bargaining is not sanctified in Britain by any statement of legal support. Obviously, the "third party" arrangements for conciliation and arbitration testify to the idea of voluntary collective bargaining. The Whitley proposals for Joint Industrial Councils presupposed a voluntary approach. Section 1 of the Industrial Relations Act 1971 included among its general principles that of "collective bargaining freely conducted on behalf of workers and employers and with due regard to the general interests of the community". Since its repeal in 1974 there has been no legal expression of the arrangements which now typify the settlement of terms and conditions in Britain.

Not legally binding

Second, collective agreements in Britain are not legally binding documents. Chapter Three brought out the point that there has not been sustained support for regarding them in this way, though it should be added that the British stance on this is not typical. British agreements are also open-ended, in the sense that it may be possible for the parties to raise any matter for re-negotiation, at any time. The parties are not bound "hand and foot" for a fixed period. True, this general rule has at times been modified, when parties entered into agreements for a fixed term. This was popular, e.g., in engineering, in the 1960s, with three-year agreements. The prevalence of some form of incomes policy in recent years tended to prevent pay being re-negotiated at intervals shorter than twelve months. That particular door is only open once a year, and the annual round is now a well-established routine.

Rights and interests

A more subtle way of expressing this tendency to treat agreements in an open-ended way, is to say that Britain does not draw a clear distinction in collective agreements between (a) matters of right (i.e. existing agreements) and (b) matters of interest (i.e. claims; see Ch. 7, p. 140). In some countries, there is very close regulation of matters arising out of an agreement. It is considered that the clauses of the agreement confer rights and obligations on the parties, and the parties may be required by law to settle disputes as to rights under a peace obligation, while their agreement is in force. Disputes of interest usually relate to matters about which the parties are negotiating in the course of revising an agreement which has expired, negotiating new terms, and they may then not be constrained in the same way.

The distinction between "rights" and "interest" disputes is frequently more complicated than has been suggested above. It is obvious that in the course of an agreement matters may arise betwen the parties which are not covered by the agreement, but raise new issues of interest. Parties can often experience great difficulty in determining whether such a matter is a rights dispute or an unresolved interest dispute. We shall examine this problem more fully in the next chapter, when we look at bargaining in action. For our purposes, at this stage it is important to notice that in Britain agreements are not tightly drawn on the basis of such a distinction between rights and interests.

Open-ended bargaining

It follows that British bargaining can be a bit like the war-time boast of the Windmill Theatre in London's West End—"We never close"! Donovan in effect said this, and appeared to applaud it.

> . . . Collective bargaining is not in this country a series of easily distinguishable transactions comparable to the making of a number of contracts by two commercial firms. It is in fact a continuous process in which differences concerning the interpretation of an agreement merge imperceptibly into differences concerning claims to change its effect. Moreover, even at industry level, a great deal of collective bargaining takes place through standing bodies, such as joint industrial councils and national or regional negotiating boards, and the agreement appears as a "resolution" or "decision" of that body, variable at its will, and variable in particular in the light of such difficulties of interpretation as may arise. Such "bargaining" does not fit into the categories of the law of contract.[1]

Since agreements in Britain are likely to be the subject of a continuous process of review, it is neither necessary nor common to ensure that an agreement is as comprehensive as the parties care to make it "for the duration". This contrasts vividly with the comprehensive agreements which are concluded in the USA for a clearly specified period of time.

British bargaining tends to be incremental, and clauses are reviewed whenever the parties care to take them up for scrutiny. All the same, there is a broad contrast between the regular review of pay clauses and less frequent consideration of more general terms and conditions. To put the matter another way, bargaining in Britain can be fairly continuous, not only for the above reasons, but also because an employer may have a number of agreements, with particular unions, with groups of unions, and with all the unions who have interests in his labour force.

A final, and very powerful, force in British agreements is the vague but potent rule of "custom and practice". These rules may not even be set down in writing, but are simply an ongoing, informal and frequently oral arrangement. Changing such custom and practice can frequently be a delicate, time-consuming and costly matter.

THE PATTERN OF AGREEMENTS IN BRITAIN

In its evidence to the Donovan Commission, the TUC estimated that the pattern of wage and salary determination in Britain could be classified in the five broad categories included in Table IX below. The estimates of the numbers of employees in each category were admitted to be only a rough guide, and the line of demarcation between one category and another is difficult to draw. Nevertheless the classification and its distribution are suggestive. The TUC has not repeated these estimates since, though one or two differences are obvious from other information which we have about the more recent pattern. The numbers covered by Wages Councils had dropped to 2¾ million in 1983.

TABLE IX. THE PATTERN OF COLLECTIVE BARGAINING

Type of negotiation	Employees (millions)
National machinery making the main agreement on an industry basis, which is closely adhered to at company and local level	7
National machinery making the main agreement, but coupled with bargaining within a company, which has a big influence on actual earnings	6
Company machinery making the main agreement	1
Wages Councils	4
Employees not covered by any joint negotiating machinery	5
Total	23

Source: Trade Unionism, TUC 1966, p. 86

Table X gives more recent evidence about the mix, from the annual New Earnings Survey.[2] The data here are for men.

One obvious broad distinction suggested by Table X is between the high proportion (40.5 per cent) of non-manual workers not covered by a collective agreement and the much smaller proportion

TABLE X. INDUSTRIAL ANALYSIS OF COLLECTIVE AGREEMENTS, 1978

Industry	Full-time manual men: Percentage affected by					Full-time non-manual men: Percentage affected by				
SIC order (1968)	Number in sample	National and Supplementary/ Company, etc agreements	National agreement only	Company, district or local agreement only	No collective agreement	Number in sample	National and Supplementary/ Company, etc agreements	National agreement only	Company, district or local agreement only	No collective agreement
All industries and services	57,268	29.3	36.4	12.6	21.7	36,775	11.7	38.5	9.4	40.5
All Index of Production industries	38,333	34.9	32.0	14.4	18.6	13,124	14.3	19.5	15.5	50.5
All manufacturing industries	28,328	41.0	19.4	18.8	20.9	10,071	15.8	10.6	19.0	54.7
All non-manufacturing industries	28,940	17.8	53.0	6.6	22.5	26,704	10.1	49.0	5.8	35.2

Note: Percentages of full-time adult men reported to be affected by various types of collective agreements, by industry, April 1978. Full-time men aged 21 and over, including those who received no pay for the Survey Pay-period April 1978.

Source: ACAS Industrial Relations Handbook, 1980, p. 296

(21.7 per cent) of manual workers in this category. Collective bargaining still is less widespread among white-collar than blue-collar workers. There is an interesting contrast for manual workers between the high proportion (53 per cent) in the non-manufacturing sector whose terms and conditions are settled by national agreements only, and the dominance (41.0 per cent) of two-tier (national plus company) agreements in manufacturing industries. This last certainly reflects the importance of engineering. Company agreements have gained in importance, particularly in manufacturing industry. The recent Warwick survey of manufacturing industry, relating to the position in 1977–8, suggested that there had been a major shift in the centre of gravity since Donovan. For two-thirds of manual and three-quarters of non-manual employees the formal structure of bargaining had become one of single-employer agreements covering one or more factories within a company. A more broadly-based survey confirmed this conclusion for manufacturing. However, it also stressed, as this chapter seeks to do, the rich diversity of the British system of pay determination when national and local government, nationalised industries, construction and private services are added to the picture.[3] In general, it is the variety that is the main distinguishing feature of British agreements.

What, then, are the main characteristics of agreements in these various categories?[4]

National agreements
National negotiations are usually conducted through standing machinery in the form of a joint industrial council (JIC), a national joint industrial council (NJIC), or a national joint council or committee (NJC). Many of these bodies have constitutions modelled on proposals set out in the Whitley reports. Engineering is an important exception, with no standing JIC, but with established machinery involving the Engineering Employers' Federation (EEF) and the Confederation of Shipbuilding and Engineering Unions. Two main types of national agreement exist.

National agreements closely adhered to
The public sector—central and local government, education, and health services—has agreements concluded nationally which set standard terms and conditions that operate throughout the territory covered by the agreement. There may be more than one pay agreement, as in the non-industrial civil service and the Post Office. Depending on the number of grades and unions, distinctive pay agreements operate. This may make it difficult to establish and

maintain a "pay spine", and groups may seek to leapfrog one another. Non-wage provisions tend to be standard throughout, though local flexibility may be permitted, e.g., in operating a national agreement on flexitime, or in introducing bonus schemes within a nationally agreed set of principles. In the non-industrial civil service, the prevailing pay principle has been comparability with outside, comparable jobs, and this is expressed through pay scales negotiated with particular unions. There are nine unions involved. In the Post Office, internal comparability tends to be the principle to which the unions look in negotiating their separate pay agreements. Thus, the prevalence of a number of unions can shape the make-up of the total pay structure. Once set, however, pay scales are standard throughout the national territory in which the agency or department operates. More so than in central government, local authority central bargaining allows provincial and local negotiation, on some general terms and on productivity schemes. There can accordingly be many agreements. The National Health Service operates eight functional national councils for main groups of employees.

Nationalised industries similarly have agreements which set standard terms and conditions, these being almost in the nature of nation-wide company agreements. There may be some local flexibility, e.g., at pit level, in dealing with the implementation of an agreement to take account of local conditions.

The single-employer concept mentioned in Chapter Four (p. 67) is the main factor behind the setting of standards at national level, which then apply throughout the function or occupational group covered. Local circumstances may allow some flexibility within nationally determined guidelines, and the existence of a number of unions can mean more fragmentation than the employer may regard as ideal, particularly with regard to separate pay agreements for certain grades. Yet the contrast between this group and the following one is still striking.

National agreements coupled with local bargaining
In this type of structure the national agreement is not intended to set a very rigid framework. It may simply set, or raise, the "floor", and local bargaining is expected to improve upon the terms set in the national agreement. Engineering is the most widespread example of this kind of two-tier arrangement. Much of the supplementation at company and plant level occurs through payment-by-results schemes, complemented, in cases where piecework is not operated, by time rates which are enhanced "in lieu of" payment-by-results. Historically, national bargaining has concentrated on

setting minimum time and piecework standard rates, and, since 1964, minimum earnings levels, premiums for shiftwork and overtime, normal hours of work, and holidays. Such bargaining is typical of an industry with a very varied product mix, and with a multi-union situation. The industry bargaining can only deal with broad aggregates. As Donovan and others stressed, the imponderable in this type of tier bargaining is plant autonomy, not just in the sense of separate company or plant agreements supplementing the national agreement, but agreements *within* plants covering autonomous groups. In effect, this constituted a *third* tier. The surveys already referred to suggest that in the 1970s there was movement from workshop to plant level in the focus, single-employer bargaining at plant and company level becoming the prime locus for settling pay. So the position is by no means a static one.

Company agreements

Such agreements typically cover large employers prepared to "go it alone". Company agreements occur, to put the point another way, when a company is a market leader. Foreign companies in Britain, particularly those with an American or Japanese background, are also accustomed to company bargaining, and this too has added its weight to the company level as a stronger focal point in bargaining. There may be a company master agreement, and company-wide policy on terms and conditions such as hours and holidays. Yet plant supplementation may be substantial, allowing varying degrees of flexibility on pay, productivity and bonuses. Equally, there may be separate company and plant agreements for craftsmen and for general workers, depending on the union situation.

Wages Councils

Wages Councils set minimum remuneration, holidays and holiday pay in sectors where pay is low and organisation poor. Wages are, almost by definition, paid at or near the minimum, and the arrangement produces a kind of multi-employer minimum agreement. In Chapter Three we noticed how they originated as standard-setting bodies, that they are tripartite bodies, and that they have a very explicit remit in trades and industries where there is not adequate organisation to ensure satisfactory collective bargaining. As collective bargaining develops, Wages Councils can and do "wither away". The Road Haulage Wages Council, for example, was abolished in 1978. It was no longer needed as a prop to ensure a reasonable standard of pay for the workers it covered. Most were by then covered by voluntary agreements and the unions were strong enough to negotiate on their own. It may happen, however, that the pattern of earnings in an industry is very patchy, with some groups earning much more than the wages council minimum and others faring less well. Recent surveys in the Laundry Wages Council sector have shown a widely varied pattern of earnings. This makes it difficult to move from the Wages Council to a collective bargaining envrionment for settling terms and conditions, though there has, as we also saw in Chapter Three, been some movement of this nature in recent years.

Other arrangements

Many sectors and companies may not be covered explicitly by collective agreements, but may nevertheless follow them. Until recently, in addition, it was possible for an employer to have prevailing terms and conditions imposed on him through the extension of terms, under section 8 of the Terms and Conditions of Employment Act 1959 and, more recently, Schedule 11 of the 1975 Employment Protection Act. We discussed these in Chapter Three. Other groups, such as the Armed Forces, who are not allowed access to free collective bargaining, have their terms and conditions set through a standing review body on armed forces pay. Doctors and dentists have separate review machinery, as do the judiciary, senior civil servants, and board members of nationalised industries.

CONTENT OF A TYPICAL AGREEMENT

What, then, in this undulating terrain, can we discern by way of content in a "typical" collective agreement? The following list suggests the kind of framework which one can distill from the vast range of agreements in operation in Britain. The list is bound to be skeletal, but it at least gives some feel for the range and content of agreements.

Clauses in collective agreements
 (a) Basic clauses on pay, arranged by occupational categories:
     (i)   skilled;
     (ii) semi-skilled;
     (iii) unskilled.

These crude occupational categories may be replaced by explicit job grading structures, occupational titles being allocated to the grade considered appropriate. Age and length of service scales may be set for white-collar occupations. Other clauses will cover piecework bonus arrangements, shift and overtime provisions, Sunday work, holiday work. Earnings targets may be specified for "normal" performance.

(*b*) Hours of work.

(*c*) Holiday arrangements.

(*d*) Non-wage provisions (which do involve costs to the employer):

    (*i*) allowances, for clothing, tools, dirty conditions;

    (*ii*) flexitime arrangements;

    (*iii*) sickness and pension benefits;

    (*iv*) safety and health at work.

(*e*) Apprenticeship arrangements, including pay progression.

(*f*) Job security: principles governing redundancy, seniority clauses, supplementation of legal minimum scheme.

(*g*) Arrangements for adult training and retraining, and relaxation of existing customs; manpower utilisation.

(*h*) Facilities for worker and trade union representatives, including time off for union duties; union membership, and deduction of dues.

(*i*) Consultative arrangements.

(*j*) Procedures for avoiding and resolving disputes, and disciplinary code, including unfair dismissal.

Job grading, pay systems, procedures

Underpinning the various clauses there may be a wealth of experience, and also of sustained work and negotiation. Three themes can be mentioned, by way of illustration. Firstly, a systematic job grading scheme may be used to provide the hierarchy of jobs to which a pay structure is then fitted. The development of such grading schemes, which may be intended to replace the more crude division of jobs into categories such as skilled, semi-skilled, and unskilled, can require very searching analysis of jobs, and the use of sophisticated *job evaluation* techniques.

Secondly, pay systems can range from simple time rates to very complicated incentive schemes based on work measurement and method study. It is significant that, amid its barrage of reports, the Prices and Incomes Board produced general guideline reports on:

(*a*) job evaluation;

(*b*) payment by results schemes; and

(*c*) productivity bargaining.[5]

These were intended to assist parties to review and modernise systems of job groupings and pay which had often become encrusted with irrelevant and historical anomalies.

Thirdly, the legislation to protect the individual employee, plus associated codes of practice, frequently works through to provisions in agreements, e.g., on supplementary redundancy pay, and on codes of discipline at work. There is interaction between the collective agreement and the surrounding environment set by public industrial relations policy.

Company agreements

Donovan attached great weight to reforming British industrial relations through developing comprehensive company agreements and, at a lower level, factory agreements. "The basis of reform must therefore be a combination of company and factory agreements".[6] The latter could, it argued, cover:

(a) effective and orderly bargaining over the control of incentive schemes, regulation of hours actually worked, the use of job evaluation, work practices, the linking of pay and performance, facilities for shop stewards and disciplinary rules and appeals;

(b) methods of production, distribution of overtime;

(c) detailed methods for timing jobs for systems of payment by results, with realistic conversion factors from time to money;

(d) differential rates of pay, and merit pay, with criteria for deciding merit;

(e) grievance procedures and factory negotiating arrangements;

(f) redundancy and discipline procedures.

Suggested principles

Following Donovan, the 1969 government White Paper, *In Place of Strife*, set out the principles which should inform a satisfactory set of agreements:

> So far as possible agreements should be clear and precise. They should assist the negotiation of pay structures that are comprehensive, fair, and conducive to efficiency. They should also provide a link between pay and the improvement of performance or results within the individual plant or company. The introduction of such agreements will often provide a suitable opportunity for negotiations over restrictive practices. Employers should also develop, and discuss with employees' representatives, clear policies on such matters as recruitment, promotion, training and retraining.[7]

The White Paper then went on to set out principles for procedural agreements; we shall be looking in the next chapter at such arrangements.

The whole tenor of these assessments was clearly critical, suggesting that the British mix for determining pay and conditions was rather a confusing one. Collective agreements presented a bewildering picture, and perhaps no clear pattern. Yet Britain is by no means unique in this regard. The complexities in Britain have tended to be exposed when bodies such as the Donovan Commission have looked critically at the whole bargaining scene, or when national incomes policies have sought to control and manipulate the tempo of pay increases. We shall be examining the particular problem of incomes policy in Chapter Eleven. At this stage, however, it is useful to single out certain themes which help to consolidate our understandings of the make-up of British agreements. Three themes are taken up:

(a) wage drift;
(b) job evaluation; and
(c) productivity bargaining.

ADDITIONAL ASPECTS OF COLLECTIVE AGREEMENTS

Wage drift

Wage drift, in crude terms, is "paying over the odds". More precisely, wage drift occurs when "the effective rate of pay per unit of labour input is raised by arrangements that lie outside the control of the recognised procedures for scheduling wage rates".[8] In the past, trade unions found that industry-wide bargaining helped to maintain a "floor" on pay when the labour market was slack and individual employers might be tempted to apply pressure to reduce their pay bills. In an era of full employment, such as that which prevailed in the period from 1945 to about 1970, both unions and management experienced the opposite problem, that of wages tending, in tight labour markets, to drift away from (i.e. above) the rates set in an agreement. Drift could form a very substantial proportion of the actual increases in pay that occurred. The problem seemed particularly vivid in situations of two-tier bargaining, where the national or industry structure had, by definition, to be *generally* operative and did not settle the detail at company or plant level. Obviously, the more the effective scheduling of rates takes place locally the less scope there is for this "topping up" via wage drift.

Thousands of articles about the nature and causes of wage drift have been written, in Britain and elsewhere. On the positive side, wage drift has been regarded as a phenomenon rooted in demand and supply, which simply helps the labour market to work efficiently by the use of the wage, and wage flexibility, to allocate and reallocate labour.

Flexible payment systems, particularly payment-by-results schemes, facilitate this process. The negative side of wage drift, however, is that it often represents a response to the demands of groups of workers who are simply exploiting their bargaining strength. This can be viewed as additionally ungovernable when, as Donovan and others argued, autonomous work groups use unofficial action to obtain pay increases. They are bought off, through employers paying "over the odds". There then follows a secondary problem in the murky world of pay differentials, when workers who are not able to benefit from slack payment systems find their pay is lagging, and insist on compensation. This can, and does, in a number of countries, produce serious tensions between different types of agreement and in successive pay rounds. The pay structure becomes very volatile. We give further consideration to the dynamics of wage structures in Chapter Eleven.

The paradox in all this is that industry-wide bargaining cannot control wage drift, and, equally, grass roots bargaining within plants cannot be controlled either. Hence Donovan's search for the middle ground, company agreements. Two other problems associated with wage drift have frequently been overlooked. First, incremental pay scales for white-collar workers can be utilised to provide accelerated pay progression, incremental drift. Secondly, jobs can be regraded—the "grade creep"—in order to move particular jobs into higher pay brackets. Obviously, these two phenomena occur more commonly in the type of job and pay schemes associated with white-collar workers.

Wage drift, then, has been a persistent problem which has drawn attention to the phenomenon of multi-tier agreements and agreements which do, or do not, facilitate control over movements in pay. The problem appears particularly vexatious when attempts are being made, for instance via a pay policy, to moderate the tempo and size of pay increases.

Job evaluation

A great deal of the work of collective bargaining concerns the classification and evaluation of jobs. The outcome may be expressed in crude job and pay categories (the skilled rate, the craftsman's rate). Sometimes, however, there may be a very explicit grading of jobs with a pay structure married to it. Once a system is established, however, the preservation of traditional differentials can become a running sore, particularly in a situation of multi-unionism. Job evaluation may then appear to offer a handy tool for bringing order into a job and pay hierarchy. It is no accident that much of the interest in job evaluation, at the time when the writ of the Prices and Incomes Board ran large in Britain, from 1965 to 1970, stemmed from the stresses caused by fragmented bargaining, arguments about anomalies and differentials, and leapfrogging between groups of workers.[9]

Job evaluation involves the comparison, ranking and evaluation of jobs by the use of specific procedures. Some methods use ranking or grading of jobs in a qualitative way, others use "factor comparison" or "points rating" to arrive at the valuations. In the factor comparison method, for example, jobs may be broken up into the factors which are thought to distinguish them—e.g., mental, physical, skill, responsibility and working conditions factors. Jobs are then examined and appraised within that framework. Note that it is the *jobs*, not the people doing them, which are evaluated, and note too that job evaluation is not an objective science. It involves elements of judgment. For that reason alone it is frequently said that the best and most acceptable job evaluation schemes are those which have been the outcome of joint study by the management and employees concerned. After a job evaluation study has been completed and agreed, there follows the separate task of marrying the job hierarchy to a pay structure. In itself, job evaluation does *not* produce a pay system, but it is a tool which can assist in arriving at and monitoring an orderly pay system.

There is no reason in principle why a job evaluation scheme should not seek to cover a whole industry as well as an establishment, a plant or a group of jobs within a plant. Even a nation-wide job evaluation scheme is possible, and indeed the Netherlands used such a national scheme in the early post-war phases of the Dutch national incomes policy. Yet there is no doubt that job evaluation has to be seen by the interested parties to be relevant if it is to serve its purpose, and this is more likely to be the case if the scheme is local, backed perhaps by framework agreements on job evaluation concluded by industry-wide organisations. Increased management professionalism, exemplified by the use of job evaluation techniques, has been a factor in the growth of company agreements.

While the high fashion for job evaluation appears to have passed, steady progress continues to be made with job evaluation schemes devised to bring about more orderly arrangements for appraising and remunerating jobs. In that sense, they are helpful to a more rational structure of collective agreements, in Britain as elsewhere. As Phelps Brown has brought out, however, the theme of inequality of pay is one which goes far beyond the technique of job and pay setting, to include social, psychological and economic factors which differentiate the capacities of individuals to earn.[10] Social and economic differentiation, inherited and acquired, has a great deal to do with differences in pay. Collective agreements may often be the waves on the surface of a deep and strong stream of social and economic forces.

Productivity bargaining

On the face of it, productivity should always be at the heart of collective agreements, at any rate in those sectors of the economy in which some form of measurable output is being produced. The employer is interested in obtaining a fair day's work, and the union in ensuring that the pay is also fair in relation to the performance. Productivity bargaining nevertheless enjoyed a particular vogue in the 1960s. Initially, and certainly in the context of the Fawley refinery project, it represented a genuine effort to break with the traditional bargaining that had existed even in a non-federated company, unhampered by a national agreement. What happened was that the company offered its employees significant increases in rates of pay in return for the consent by the unions to specific changes in working practices. These included a drastic reduction in overtime, relaxation of job demarcations, and redeployment.[11] There were very explicit "trade-offs".

Subsequently, productivity bargaining became widespread, as one more-or-less legitimate method of justifying higher pay during a period of severe pay restraint, in 1967. By a productivity agreement, the Prices and Incomes Board meant "one in which workers agree to make a change, or a number of changes, in working practice that will lead in itself—leaving out any compensating pay increase—to more economical working; and in return the employer agrees to a higher level of pay and other benefits".[12] For a productivity agreement there had to be a contribution by the workers by way of more exacting work or a major change in working practices. The significance of productivity deals was that they could be sharply distinguished from conventional wage agreements. Conventional bargaining tended to relate general pay increases to matters external to a firm, such as the cost of living, and movements in comparable wages. Productivity agreements related pay increases to changes in working practices. They came nearer to the hard core of efficiency.

This is an enormously significant distinction, for it speaks volumes about the nature of traditional bargaining in Britain. Pay negotiations have frequently been kept apart from discussions about the organisation of work and the "trade off" between efficiency and pay. The merit of productivity bargaining is that it widens out the perspectives on the terms of the agreement, and draws attention to the benefits to both sides that can be gained from positive deals geared to improvements in efficiency. It emphasises the activity of production as well as the general factors produced via the collective agreement.

Productivity bargaining made it fashionable in Britain to look at the whole interplay between the use of labour and its remuneration. The fashion may have passed, yet a good deal of work undoubtedly continues in a low key, on sensitive matters such as manning levels, work reorganisation, method improvement, and efficient utilisation of labour. Many of these matters lend themselves better to longer-term solutions, based on employee involvement, than some of the get-rich-quick productivity deals which were pushed through at a time of pay restraint. They have also lent their weight to the increased emphasis on company bargaining.

Mention should be made in conclusion of the rapid increases in productivity achieved in the course of the recession in the early 1980s. There is no doubt that many of the dramatic gains reflected the shedding of labour, though the recession also concentrated action on using the remaining cadre of employees in more cost-effective ways.

QUESTIONS POSED BY BRITISH ARRANGEMENTS

What does this analysis suggest about British collective agreements? Some questions spring to mind.

Need for modernisation?

How progressive/modern is the British collective agreement? We have seen that agreements are of infinite variety. This is hardly surprising, given the way in which agreements have "just growed" over a very lengthy period. In itself, that can provide a capacity to change to meet developing requirements. The growth of interest in job evaluation and, despite its associations with incomes policy, the device of productivity bargaining, also suggest flexibility. In certain substantive matters, such as standard hours of work and holidays with pay, there have in addition been major improvements since the war, hammered out slowly and persistently, agreement by agreement, rather than by some central accord or a comprehensive statutory provision.

Donovan was not at all sanguine about the capacity of the system to adapt quickly. After pleading the case for comprehensive company agreements, it envisaged that some outside pressure would be required to promote progress towards that objective. The main suggested solution was that companies with at least 5,000 employees should be required to register collective agreements with the Department of Employment. This was to serve the dual purpose of highlighting the strategic importance to companies of their industrial relations and drawing attention to the matters which should be covered by clear and firm company agreements. They were to be placed in a public goldfish bowl.[13] Not much happened. The CBI, for instance, has complained recently about the bargaining system and structure.

> The situation is made worse by the fragmented nature of our bargaining system. It is fragmented vertically in that collective agreements can be made at industry level, company level and the plant—groups of employees may bargain at all three levels. It is fragmented horizontally, since employees in the same company or industry who normally make comparisons with each other may be split into several bargaining units. Frequently, each bargaining level or unit has a distinct settlement date to itself. So an employee may be covered by two or three separate agreements each with a separate date of implementation, while employees working side by side may settle pay awards at different times of the year. Fragmented bargaining is characteristic of the pay determination system in many parts of the private sector.[14]

Almost at the same time (February 1979), the TUC sounded off about the need to review negotiating arrangements, paying particular attention to such matters as:

> whether the industry-wide agreement is relevant to current circumstances, particularly to the determination of wages and the development, where appropriate, of comprehensive and authoritative collective bargaining machinery at company or factory level.[15]

After stressing the importance of disputes and grievance procedures (discussed in the next chapter), the TUC concluded:

> How best to answer these questions must be decided by those concerned in each case: circumstances vary too much to allow a universal formula to be prepared. The objective in all industries and services should be to establish arrangements whereby matters of common interest to employers and workpeople can be discussed and negotiated at the appropriate level. Some issues, such as basic wage rates and general terms and conditions of service, may be appropriate for industry-wide collective bargaining. Others, such as the general principles on which job evaluation, for example, is to be used, may be best carried out at company level, while a large number of issues (including the application of company and industry agreements) need effective collective bargaining at establishment level.[16]

Both the central organisations concerned with industrial relations have thus identified some of the problems brought out in this chapter, and have suggested solutions. The evidence of the surveys already cited in this chapter suggests that there may have been greater movement in the 1970s than these respective views from Olympus have allowed, at least in the manufacturing industry. The range of pressures from government in the 1970s, through legislation, codes of practice, and incomes policies, provided pressures for change. The emphasis on more participation of employees in shaping their own destiny "in-house" also drew attention to arrangements at and within companies. Greater concentration, and an influx of foreign companies, acted as a leaven. Collective bargaining arrangements in Britain may be more dynamic than has been recognised, at least until recently.

Fixed-term agreements?
The environment of inflation and annual incomes policy pronouncements just mentioned have militated against any willingness to enter into longer-term agreements. Even in more tranquil times, however, there has been no great zest in Britain for agreements which bound parties to them for a period of (say) two or three years. The reasons are not far to seek, given what was said earlier in this chapter. British bargaining is traditionally open-ended. The fixed-term agreement seemed to suggest stagnation and inflexibility. There has been much less willingness in Britain than in other countries, such as the USA, to endeavour to design agreements which carry the parties through time, providing, for instance, for (*a*) phased pay increases (annual improvement factors), and (*b*) cost-of-living escalator clauses. For their part, employers have seen the advantages which longer-term agreements could provide in planning payroll costs. Yet there has been no strong drive to adopt fixed-term agreements. It is of course a mistake to imagine that a fixed-term agreement means absolute rigidity, and equally it is erroneous to imagine that problems do not arise during the life of such agreements. In addition, fixed-term agreements often involve a build-up of claims which are presented *en masse* at the conclusion of the agreement's lifetime. What such agreements do require is very explicit grievance machinery for handling the problems that are bound to arise as the agreement is worked through. This point is taken up in the next chapter.

Legally enforceable agreements?
Complementary to the British scepticism regarding fixed-term agreements is the fear that fixed-term agreements may mean legislation. Donovan was willing to contemplate the registration of certain collective agreements—the "goldfish bowl" argument. It was equally willing to contemplate that at some future date procedural agreements might have to be made legally enforceable. But

Donovan opposed making collective agreements into legally binding documents. Why? Few collective agreements were in a form
suitable for legal enforcement. Anyway, employers would not seek
to enforce them. Official stoppages in breach of collective agreements were rare. And how would unions control their members?
Donovan pinned its faith instead on the development of *comprehensive company agreements* and on the *reform of procedural
agreements*, in the latter case backed in due course by the law, if this
should prove necessary.

One member of the Donovan Commission, Andrew Shonfield,
entered a dissenting note in favour of binding agreements. They
would encourage management to innovate and broaden the scope
of collective bargaining, and benefit union members accordingly.[17]
In recent years the CBI has, though not unanimously, reopened the
argument in favour of legally enforceable agreements. Meantime,
as we saw in Chapter Three, the legal position is one in which parties
to an agreement have to "contract in" to legal enforceability.
Meantime, too, Britain remains exceptional in not treating collective agreements as legally enforceable contracts.

CONCLUSION

Collective agreements are not an end in themselves. They represent
a joint effort on the part of management, unions and workers to
regulate terms and conditions. They are neither a management
support-system nor a blank cheque for the employees. Equally,
they are imperfect instruments of industrial relations self-
government. It is important to remember that agreements are
frequently concluded under stress and may therefore not be formu-
lated in a way which meets every eventuality. By the same token, a
party to an agreement may not wish the agreement to be crystal-
clear as to its intent, if there is some possibility of his getting away
with interpreting it in a way that favours his side. Agreements
contain bargains, trade-offs, and there is no point in pretending
otherwise.

Yet, to be realistic is not the same as being cynical about the
capacity for improvement in the structure of British agreements.
There are genuine dilemmas in the problems of two- and three-tier
arrangements and their harmonisation. Even the strong emphasis
in the USA on company agreements does not prevent pattern
bargaining from occurring, and differences between plants from
emerging. In their efforts to design and operate national framework
agreements, the central union and employer negotiating bodies in
Sweden have over the years wrestled with enormous technical

problems of designing agreements. The quotations from the CBI and the TUC set out earlier in this chapter suggest there is a desire for change, for modernisation, in Britain. The surveys cited suggest also that change has been occurring in manufacturing industry through a growth in company agreements.

This chapter has deliberately focused first on the substantive matters of British collective bargaining about terms and conditions. Obviously this cannot be divorced from bargaining power and from the procedures which the parties adopt to arrive at and operate agreements. Accordingly, in the next chapter we take up the related questions of negotiating techniques and dispute procedures. These form another key part of any industrial relations system.

SELF-ASSESSMENT QUESTIONS

1. Is it sensible to regard a collective agreement as a peace treaty, a code of government, and an economic package?

2. In what ways could fixed-term collective agreements affect the content and the negotiation of agreements?

3. What principal wage and non-wage clauses would you insist upon including in a comprehensive company agreement which you were negotiating?

4. Indicate ways in which you would wish to modernise British collective agreements, and suggest ways of bringing this about.

ASSIGNMENT

Obtain a copy of a collective agreement from a local factory or union office and examine the clauses on pay. Are they clear enough to make it easy for the employer to calculate his hourly and weekly wage costs? Are they flexible enough to enable the workers to ensure increases in their pay keep up with changes in the cost of living? Suggest ways in which improvements might be made.

REFERENCES

1. Royal Commission on Trade Unions and Employers' Associations, *Cmnd. 3623*, 1968, para. 471.
2. *Industrial Relations Handbook*, ACAS 1980, Appendix 1, p. 292 *et seq*, gives greater detail.
3. William Brown (ed.), *The Changing Contours of British Industrial Relations*, London, 1981; W. W. Daniel and Neil Millward, *Workplace*

Industrial Relations in Britain, London 1983; ACAS, *Collective bargaining in Britain: Its extent and level*, Discussion Paper No. 2, 1983.

4. The *Industrial Relations Handbook* mentioned above gives extensive descriptions of collective bargaining arrangements in a wide range of activities.

5. Prices and Incomes Board, reports on: *Job Evaluation* (*Cmnd. 3772*, 1968, No. 83, with supplement; *Payment by Results Systems* (*Cmnd. 3627*, 1968, No. 65, with supplement; *Productivity Agreements* (*Cmnd. 3167*, 1966, No. 23, and *Cmnd. 3311*, 1967, No. 36).

6. Royal Commission (Donovan), *op. cit.*, para. 170.

7. *In Place of Strife*, *Cmnd. 3888*, 1969, para. 30.

8. E. H. Phelps Brown, "On Wage Drift", *Economica*, Vol. XXIX, No. 116, Nov. 1962, p. 340.

9. Prices and Incomes Board, *Job Evaluation*, *Cmnd. 3772*, 1968, Report No. 83.

10. Henry Phelps Brown, *The Inequality of Pay*, 1977.

11. Allan Flanders, *The Fawley Productivity Agreements*, 1964.

12. Prices and Incomes Board, *Productivity Agreements, Cmnd. 3311*, Report No. 36, 1967.

13. Royal Commission (Donovan), *op. cit.*, para. 191.

14. Confederation of British Industry, *Pay: the choice ahead*, 1979, p. 8.

15. Trades Union Congress, *TUC Guides*, 1979, p. 4.

16. *Ibid.*, p. 5.

17. Royal Commission (Donovan), *op. cit.*, pp. 288–302.

CHAPTER SEVEN

The Bargaining Process and Pressures

CHAPTER OBJECTIVES

After studying this chapter you should be able to:
* understand the nature of procedural agreements as an aid to bargaining;
* the role of the strike in industrial disputes;
* the problems of distinguishing between interpretation (rights) and interest disputes.

The golden rule is that there are no golden rules.

Bernard Shaw

IMPORTANCE OF PROCEDURES

This chapter is concerned with negotiating or bargaining arrangements and with the procedures and practices which the "parties of interest" may invoke in arriving at, and living with, their agreements. It covers a wide spectrum, from model negotiating arrangements to the use of coercive sanctions such as industrial action.

The concept and practice of collective bargaining are extremely well established in Britain. We have had a long time to develop them. However, "free collective bargaining" is an empty slogan until it is given some content with respect to its aims, its procedures and its achievements, both good and bad. We have already noticed that collective bargaining is not static. The discussion in Chapter Three of the changing involvement of government as the third party at the bargaining table has already disproved any such notion.

Nevertheless, there are some fundamental aspects about negotiating and disputes procedures which can be summarised at the outset. Collective bargaining occupies the middle ground between the aims of management on the one hand and the needs of the individual employee on the other. It is concerned with balancing management and employee interests, with trade unions acting as the principal agent on behalf of the workers. The scope of bargaining about these respective interests is not fixed. It is likely to change and also to expand with the passage of time, and it is itself an obvious subject for negotiation.

Continuing relationships

Negotiating and disputes arrangements are also concerned with the *continuity* of the employment relationship. This may not always be harmonious. A good case can be made for the part which "creative tension" can play in industrial relations. Yet the parties are much closer to the married estate than to the divorce courts in their relationships. Where there is conflict, negotiations under the banner of procedures seek to contain and resolve differences, even if conflict cannot be finally eliminated. The trade-offs which work their way through to the agreements which we scrutinised in the previous chapter may be simple, or immensely sophisticated. All of them relate to the balance between labour and management which has to be struck somewhere in the middle ground of give-and-take. Procedures are a means-to-an-end of bringing about a workable, sustained accommodation between management's objectives and the aspirations of workers.

BARGAINING IN GOOD FAITH

Not explicit in Britain

While the British are fond of speaking about "free" and "voluntary" collective bargaining they have on the whole avoided exhortations to the parties, such as the requirement that they should bargain "in good faith". The Whitley Committee clearly regarded voluntary joint machinery as desirable whenever practicable. The Industrial Relations Act 1971 set out the general principles of free collective bargaining and orderly procedures with due regard to the general interest of the community, while the companion Code of Practice covered a host of matters which were considered to be relevant to the practice of bargaining and disputes settlement. As we have seen, the framework of law within which this should take place can be a subject of controversy. In the USA however, the requirement to bargain "in good faith" is very explicit. It is not an easy concept to interpret, and a great deal of industrial relations jurisprudence in the USA has been generated on such matters as what subjects are to be considered negotiable, those which are optional, and topics which one party may seek to have excluded, while still bargaining in good faith. The approach in Britain has been a good deal more pragmatic, and less philosophical.[1]

Canada, so close to the USA in many matters, nevertheless reflects a British rather than an American outlook on the tenor of collective bargaining:

We do not think it useful to industrial relations in Canada to put the issue of good faith bargaining into such an elaborate jurisprudential container. The duty to bargain is not a duty to agree; nor does the right to bargain grant a right to a particular bargain. We see no reason why the subject matter of bargaining should not include anything that is not contrary to law. As to tactics, the highest duty that should reasonably be placed on either party to a bargaining situation, in which each has a claim to preserve its freedom respecting its bargaining position, is to state its position on matters put in issue. But we cannot envisage such a duty being amenable to legal enforcement, except perhaps to the extent of an obligation to meet and exchange positions. We wish to make it clear that we do not condone minimal adherence to the standards of good faith bargaining. Our concern is to avoid writing into law standards that are unenforceable or that could encourage either minimum bargaining or litigation.[2]

Admirably put. The sentiment chimes well with the practical but positive outlook on guidelines in collective bargaining which the Engineering Employers' Federation recently adopted in Britain. The Federation's position is that collective bargaining should take place against the background of a continuous and positive programme of fostering employee involvement in a company through the best practice of communication of information and of consultation over possible change. It should be the employer's objective to create conditions in which both sides engaged in the collective bargaining process work from the common premise of jointly wishing to further the prosperity of the company and the well-being and security of its employees.[3] Matching practice to such precepts is of course much the more difficult problem.

The sequence of presentation in this chapter is to look first at negotiating procedures developed for the purpose of handling claims, what in other countries would be termed *interest* disputes. Then we consider grievance machinery, which is established for the purpose of resolving differences about what agreements mean and how they are to be applied. In essence this means rights disputes. These may be collective in character or can involve individual grievances.

PROCEDURES FOR PROCESSING CLAIMS

By definition, negotiating procedures presuppose union recognition. The Code of Practice speaks of collective bargaining being carried out in a reasonable and constructive manner between employers and strong representative trade unions. One can put flesh on this by looking at the kind of model constitution and functions which Whitley envisaged for a joint industrial council in Britain. The object was to secure the largest possible measure of joint action between employers and workpeople for the development of the industry as a part of national life and for the improvement of the conditions of all engaged in that industry. In addition to detailing specific objects, such as the regular consideration of wages and working conditions, the consideration of the existing machinery for settling differences, and its establishment where it did not already exist, the model did, however, offer the practical advice that "No hard and fast policy is suggested as to what should constitute the functions of an Industrial Council. This is a question which the employers and workpeople in each industry must settle for themselves."[4]

Perhaps it is because of this emphasis on "doing one's own thing" that the official Industrial Relations Handbook has ceased to include the Model Constitution for a JIC as an appendix. The arrangements vary, not unexpectedly, to suit the needs of the parties. All the same, it is possible to distil the essentials of collective procedural arrangements for the conduct of industrial relations. These may sometimes be set out in a self-contained procedural agreement, or may be included as part of a substantive collective agreement. Many matters may be covered—procedures for processing pay claims, for dealing with redundancies, facilities for shop stewards, and the handling of individual grievances. Some procedures may derive from, and be closely geared to, the separate public codes of practice promulgated on discipline, time off for trade union duties, and the provision of information for collective bargaining purposes.

Outline procedure

Let us concentrate at this stage on procedures for handling claims. An agreement for negotiating purposes might then cover the following:

(a) constitution and composition of the joint body, with a statement of the specific parties to it. (The matter may be treated much more informally, as in engineering, on a regular but informal and *ad hoc* basis);

(b) a written statement of matters that are negotiable. This in itself may be a negotiable matter;

(c) a statement of the matters that are negotiable at different levels, e.g., the industry, the company, the establishment. Problems can arise when matters overlap between bargaining levels, or when a matter reserved for one stratum is taken up at another.

Particular subjects, such as payment-by-results, may be reserved for local negotiation;

(*d*) re-negotiation—a statement may be given of the circumstances in which a party may serve notice of a wish to re-negotiate, and at what level, with a time scale. National policies, for example on incomes, may sometimes circumscribe "normal" arrangements here by stipulating intervals between negotiations, the treatment of incremental scales etc., and by setting norms for earnings increases;

(*e*) facilities for union negotiators, from stewards to union officers, should be specified;

(*f*) the provision of information for bargaining purposes is now blessed by a code of practice on the subject. This can be crucial for the conduct of negotiations in a constructive way;

(*g*) an indication, for instance by stating a sequence of negotiating meetings, of the stage when the parties recognise that they have "failed to agree". This is no mechanical ritual. As Singleton points out, "The management of time is always an important part of negotiating tactics."[5] It is a mistake to prescribe too precise a timetable. (This is less evident in grievance procedures, discussed below, where "steps", with accompanying deadlines, may be specified);

(*h*) the use, if any, to be made of third parties once the parties seem to be finding it difficult to agree. Some agreed procedures may incorporate a neutral third party as independent chairman from the start. More probably the parties will leave themselves the option to call in an outsider, perhaps through the good offices of ACAS, to conciliate or mediate. ACAS itself has noticed a growing tendency for the availability of its services to be mentioned in procedure agreements. In some procedures, as in that for the co-operative movement, a National Conciliation Board with a stated composition and an independent chairman may be the next stage. In Canada, the device of compulsory conciliation has been used to interpose a third party function before any stoppage may be called arising out of a failure to agree;

(*i*) whatever the formal final stage of procedure, the "golden rule" is that *disputes procedures should be exhausted* before any coercive action is taken. It is for this reason that stoppages, such as strikes, which take place before all stages of procedures have been utilised are labelled unconstitutional.

Implications

Two other points should be stressed here.

(*a*) First, procedures are an "enabling device", and the outline given above is no more than a suggestion of an orderly structure and sequence.

(b) Second, trade unions may have to insist that any joint procedure takes account of their rules, if for instance these require union negotiators to have provisional agreements ratified by the union members in (say) a secret ballot.

Obviously, the practice referred to in (b) is a mixed blessing. It tempts the employer to hold back from going "the last mile" if there is a prospect that union members may overturn a recommendation made by their negotiators. For their part, the union members may feel that there is nothing to be lost by rejecting the preliminary agreement. The whole art of bargaining on both sides may be to sense the "sticking point", since there is no uniquely "correct" settlement of a pay claim. Bargaining is, in the jargon, indeterminate.

If both sides can reach agreement, with or without a third party and with or without a ratification vote by the union membership, well and good, at least until the next time. If not, the parties have then to assess the pros and cons of exercising additional pressure on one another, to the point where they may employ coercive action. The dimensions of such industrial action are discussed below.

GRIEVANCE PROCEDURES FOR RIGHTS DISPUTES

So far our treatment of negotiating arrangements has been couched in terms of an "interest" dispute. Coercive action is usually regarded as a legitimate weapon in bringing about a resolution of such a dispute. We saw in the previous chapter, however, that disputes can be categorised broadly into disputes of interest and disputes of rights (*see* p. 115). The distinction is not clearly observed in British industrial relations. If it had been, we could then have proceeded to examine procedures for resolving them in their British habitat. Instead, we have to cast our net wider. *Rights disputes can be defined as disputes which relate to the application or interpretation of existing agreements or, in the case of individuals, contracts of employment.* Rights disputes procedures are frequently more clearly structured than procedures governing differences of interest, for the very good reason that an agreement or contract is in existence. It has to be administered, interpreted and, above all, observed. Countries, such as the USA, in which collective agreements are legally binding, have an extraordinarily well developed set of mainly private procedures for this purpose. Whatever the country, the broad procedural principles are the same:

Main features

(a) seek to resolve a rights dispute locally, and speedily;

(b) do so as near to the action as possible, and between the individual or group involved and the immediate supervisor, with the union representative being called in as appropriate;

(c) specify "steps" (stages) in the procedure through which a rights dispute can be progressed up the hierarchy. Such steps may have time intervals assigned to them, to obviate delay;

(d) settle the dispute peaceably. This may be a requirement in law, and labour courts may be to hand to act as the final stage if required. Alternatively, arbitration may be prescribed as the final recourse. In the USA this latter procedure has led to arbitration of interpretation disputes becoming a major private industry.

Such arrangements do not provide a cast-iron guarantee against stoppages occurring, even when they are banned; but they do provide orderly procedures. Procedures of this kind do actually operate in British industrial relations, though it is doubtful whether they could be accorded the accolade of "rights disputes procedures". They may, in fact, be part of a mainstream procedural agreement, and form the channel through which an individual processes his grievances. It is important always to bear in mind that an individual grievance may contain the seeds of a dispute involving others, and disputes and grievance procedures should at least be in harmony and not at odds with each other.

Rights-interest grey area

The rights-interest dichotomy is a fascinating one in the environment of British industrial relations. Donovan was not averse to moving in the direction of the practice, common in other countries, by which a labour court or arbitration is used to settle all unresolved differences relating to the application of an agreement. However, it judged that this could only be feasible *after* collective bargaining had been reformed and comprehensive and effective agreements were in force. In the meantime, it concluded, shopfloor agreements were so closely linked with customs and practices that were not set down in any agreement that no clear distinction existed at that level between disputes of right and disputes of interest.[6] The Code of Practice (para. 129) accompanying the Industrial Relations Act 1971 happily stated that arbitration was particularly suitable for settling disputes of rights. Where it was used, the parties should undertake to be bound by the award.

The feel for the British attitude is well summed up in the following comment by an authority on procedures:

It is sometimes suggested that an appropriate field for greater use of arbitration could be established by distinguishing differences of right from differences of interest on lines familiar in the United States. On this approach terms and conditions of employment would be settled in negotiations by the parties but any disputes regarding the interpretation of agreements between the parties would be determined by arbitration. In general this is not a distinction which is clearly present in the minds and practice of negotiators in this country as reflected in the agreements they make. Substantive consequences of some importance may turn on questions of interpretation and the intentions of the parties on any disputed matter are seen by the parties as a further question of interest for discussion and settlement by them rather than as matters of construction of the terms of the written agreement. To use the distinction between questions of right and questions of interest as a general basis for defining arbitrable issues would require fundamental changes in the nature and status of collective agreements. It is however a distinction which may be useful to parties who are seeking to identify and define arbitrable issues within their own agreement.[7]

Once more this raises the spectre of the questionable quality of British collective agreements. One can get at the dilemma another way. Take the problem of "management prerogatives". The most famous, or infamous, example of this creed was paragraph 23 of the Constitution of the Swedish Employers' Confederation, which declared management's prerogative to hire and fire in unequivocal terms. It no longer has quite the defiant air of supreme sovereignty about it; indeed, it has almost given way to the opposite, that of preferential interpretation in favour of the employee, who broadly gets the benefit of the doubt under the Swedish Act of 1976 on the Joint Regulation of Working Life. On the face of it, the problem is a simple one. Frequently it is referred to in Britain as the *status quo* issue; it was for some years a bone of contention in the engineering industry. Suppose management wishes to make a change in working arrangements while an agreement is in force, and unions and their members judge that the proposed change affects their interests. Can management proceed? A *status quo* clause along the following lines could checkmate any such managerial prerogative: "It is agreed that in the event of any difference arising which cannot immediately be disposed of, then whatever practice or agreement existed prior to the difference shall continue to operate pending a settlement or until the agreed procedure has been exhausted."[8]

The matter in dispute could be an interpretation issue, susceptible in principle to treatment by peaceful adjudication, if necessary by arbitration or a labour court. On the other hand, it could be a new matter not covered by an agreement, in effect an unresolved interest dispute. As the above formulation, culled from the TUC, implies, the problem could also be part of the mysterious world of "custom and practice". Once again, this demonstrates the predicament in which Donovan found itself. Agreements in Britain may not be couched in a form which readily lends itself to interpretation. Until they are, the world of rights and interest disputes will continue to be even more of a grey area than is necessary.

Having said that, there is evidence of growth in, and formalisation of, industrial relations procedures in Britain since the late 1960s.[9] This is hardly surprising; law, codes of practice, the establishment of ACAS, and the pressure, e.g., from the TUC, have all built up a momentum in favour of regularised arrangements of the kind discussed in this chapter. The evidence from the 1980 CBI survey of company employee relations and decision making stressed the importance of the legislation in the 1970s as a particularly powerful pressure.

Canadian approach to technological change problems

The "rights–interest" dilemma is well exemplified by Canadian experience. The practice there is to ban any coercive action whatsoever while an agreement is running. Collective agreements traditionally had to contain a provision for the final settlement, without stoppage of work, by arbitration or otherwise, of all differences between the parties to, or employees bound by, a collective agreement, as to its interpretation and application. The equity of the rule was evaluated some years ago, in the context of rapid technological change. The task force which reviewed Canadian labour relations recommended that the ban on stoppages should be partially lifted. Parties should, it argued, be free to resort to economic sanctions when disputes arose about the permanent displacement of employees as a consequence of industrial conversion (technological change) occurring during the life of an agreement.

The proposal was a controversial one, but eventually an enactment passed in 1972 did provide a let-out from an absolute prohibition on stoppages while an agreement is in force. Now the Canada Labour Code provides that an employer, bound by a collective agreement, who proposes to make a change in technology which is likely to affect the terms and conditions and employment security of a significant number of his workforce covered by that agreement, is required to give notice of the change to the bargaining agent (trade union). The union may then seek to serve notice to bargain, for the purpose of revising the existing provisions, or concluding new ones, aimed at helping the employees to adjust to the effects of changing technology. It is essentially a "contract reopening" device, permitting the use of the industrial action which may follow. The important and suggestive point about this development is that industrial change may certainly occur while an agreement is in force. The employment relationship continues and develops. The real question is whether procedures can be devised which facilitate orderly adjustment in the labour–management relationship.[10]

Conclusion

We can conclude this section by repeating that in Britain any disputed matter can, after the exhaustion of procedure, go further. What then happens if "my patience is exhausted", if procedures do not solve the matter at issue? Two avenues are open. First, the parties can invoke the third party good offices of conciliation, mediation and arbitration. Indeed, this stage of third party involvement can, as we have already seen, be built in to procedures. Alternatively, it can be *ad hoc*. These third party facilities are such a large subject that we shall devote the next chapter to them. The other avenue, which we explore in the remainder of this chapter, is that which takes the parties towards sanctions, aimed at persuading the other side to see, or do it "my way".

COERCIVE ACTION

Lockouts

No party to industrial relations in a free society can be compelled to agree on terms and conditions. Negotiation implies and involves the right to reject the terms of the other side. The coercive action to which parties resort in negotiations can take a number of forms. The most dramatic weapon on the part of employers is the lockout. This has almost vanished from the industrial relations scene, though it still occurs with sufficient frequency for us to be reminded, now and again, that employers sometimes wish to "hold the line", if necessary by an agreed common front, through the shut-down which a lockout involves. Much more common is the threat to close down, permanently or temporarily. Layoffs provide another form of pressure.

Pressures from employee side

Undoubtedly, however, it is on the employee side of the account that we see most frequent recourse to industrial action. This, too, can take a rich variety of forms—working-to-rule, go-slows, bans on overtime or Sunday working, are all pressures which may be applied short of an "all-out strike". Demonstrations, or lightning stoppages of short duration, are also deployed. The French seem particularly fond of the "quickie" stoppage. The most full-blooded form of coercion from the side of the employees is, however, the strike. Strikes may be official, that is to say they have the approval of the appropriate union authority; they may lack this approval, and be unofficial; however, unofficial stoppages may also be unconstitutional, occurring before the disputes procedures have been fully utilised.

Strikes

A great deal of nonsense is written and spoken about strikes. The purpose of the analysis here is to set the strike weapon in context.

The right to strike

In a famous case, *Crofter Harris Tweed* v. *Veitch*, Lord Wright pronounced in 1942 that "the right of workmen to strike is an essential element in the principle of collective bargaining". An American authority writes about strikes as follows:

> But a strike is more than a test of strength over a particular issue. It is also a release from the humdrum existence of everyday industrial life, a proving ground for union leaders, a moment of excitement, glory, and perhaps of disillusionment in a battle against an opponent who usually holds the upper hand, a sharing of hardship which may weld the union together, and a high-level poker game at which plays and counterplays are expected.[11]

Dimensions in Britain

We are able to identify the main dimensions of "the strike problem" in Britain by reference to the official information about them which we have from the Department of Employment. Table XI shows how Britain fares in an international league table of eighteen countries. The crude statistics suggest Britain is not unduly strike-prone, for she lies broadly in the middle, with six countries above and nine below her (Belgium and Portugal are omitted). This is of course broad brush; while it helps to put international information in context, it appears that variations in strike-proneness between firms and plants *within* countries are likely to be much greater than total differences *between* countries.

Interpretation of statistics

There are enormous pitfalls in studying strike data. Working days lost per 1,000 employees tell us about the *incidence* of strikes, but not about their *frequency*. Strike statistics are riddled with other problems as well; they do not cover other forms of industrial action, such as work-to-rule, for instance. British official statistics also exclude "quickie" stoppages lasting less than one day and those

TABLE XI. INDUSTRIAL STOPPAGES: WORKING DAYS LOST PER THOUSAND EMPLOYEES IN ALL INDUSTRIES AND SERVICES: 1973–82

	1973	1974	1975	1976	1977	1978	1979	1980	1981	1982	Average† 1973–77	1978–82	1973–82
United Kingdom	318	647	265	146	448	413	1,276	523	197	250‡	365	532	448
Australia	550	1,274	715	771	335	357	656	530	660	340	729	509	619
Belgium	281	183	195	290	215	325	197	69	..	..	233	(197)	(219)
Canada	732	1,121	1,303	1,367	381	741	756	842	812	548	981	740	860
Denmark	2,007	96	53	107	116	63	83	93	315	45	476	120	298
Finland	1,436	226	155	725	1,313	64	114	729	294	91	771	258	514
France	233	198	228	292	211	126	209	95	86	133	232	130	181
Germany (FR)	25	48	3	19	1	115	18	3	3	1	19	28	24
Irish Republic	280	732	390	1,032	571	765	1,752	479	509	511	601	803	702
Italy	1,549	1,251	1,722	1,588	1,017	625	1,602	920	589	1,108	1,425	969	1,197
Japan	127	266	220	88	40	36	24	26	14	13	148	23	85
Netherlands	14	2	—	3	57	5	73	13	5	50	15	29	22
New Zealand	210	137	158	355	431	306	303	284	194	259	258	269	264
Norway	8	228	9	90	15	34	4	54	15	144	70	51	61
Portugal	..	..	..	..	128	..	138	136	189*	..	..	(155)*	..
Spain	125	199	205	1,438	1,907	955	1,598	549	472	255‡	775	766‡	770‡
Sweden	3	16	96	7	32	6	—	1,047	48	—§	31	220	126
United States	364	613	406	479	435	384	352	355	246	..§	459	(334)§	(404)§
European Community (9 countries)	..	..	409	386	348	286	673	319	..	..	(381)	(426)	(404)

‡ Provisional.
† Annual average for those years within each period for which data are available, not weighted for employment. Brackets indicate incomplete data.
* Includes only 85 per cent of strikes in 1981.
§ The threshold was revised in 1981; see text for further discussion. On the new threshold, numbers of working days lost per thousand employers were as follows: 1978, 273; 1979, 207; 1980, 210; 1981, 168; 1982, 91; annual average 1978 to 1982, 190.

Source: Employment Gazette, Vol. 92, No. 3, March 1984, p. 102

involving fewer than ten workers unless more than 100 days are lost. In fact, the short stoppage is the dominant form of strike. In 1982 stoppages lasting one to three days in Britain accounted for 60 per cent of the *number* of strikes, though for only 13.5 per cent of days lost. In addition, strike statistics do not throw up the secondary effects they cause through workers in other establishments being laid off as a consequence of strike action. Strikes data therefore can only give a very crude and incomplete indicator of their economic impact. Donovan concluded (para. 410) that ". . . it would be seriously misleading to base one's assessment of the economic significance of these stoppages merely on the tally of working days lost on their account."

It is the *character* of strikes that makes the most significant points about the state of our industrial relations in general, and the peace-keeping machinery in particular. The following points emerge from a recent major study of the official data covering lockouts (sparse as they are) as well as strikes, mainly for the period from 1966 to 1973.[12]

Concentration of strikes
There is a high degree of concentration of strike activity by industry. There was a fairly stable ranking of industries in terms of strike frequency and incidence, with five industries—coal mining, docks, motor vehicle manufacturing, shipbuilding, and iron and steel—accounting for a quarter of the strikes and one-third of the days lost, although in total these industries accounted for only 6 per cent of employees. Differences in "the inter-industry propensity to strike" have long been a subject of interest to students of industrial relations. One study found that inter-industry differences in the incidence of man-days lost through industrial disputes were very similar in eleven countries.[13] Along the same lines, Dunlop found, in his work for the book on industrial relations systems which we examined in Chapter One, that certain work rules in coal-mining and construction were basically similar in a number of countries, while others were more strongly shaped by their national industrial relations systems. Dunlop's points about technology and market structure may be very instructive for understanding this evidence about concentration of strike activity by industry.

The ILO bases its reporting of strikes on four selected industries—mining and quarrying, manufacturing, construction and transport, storage and communications—since these sectors tend to account for a large proportion of the days lost in all countries. There can of course be sharp differences from year to year. In Britain in 1982 the three national rail stoppages plus the dispute in the National Health Service (which ran from April to December), together with the sympathetic action shown by other groups in the health service dispute, accounted for about half the total (5.3 million days) of days lost through stoppages. The sympathetic actions alone accounted for 13 per cent of all days lost.

The official data on British stoppages also throw up the point that large stoppages, defined as involving a loss of 200,000 working days or more, are less frequent than popular mythology imagines. They accounted for 64 stoppages in the two decades from 1960 to 1979, the annual average being higher, at four or five stoppages, in the early 1970s than previously. With such small numbers, however, the numbers in any one year can be influenced, as they were in the early 1970s, by pay and legislative controversies. This is not to minimise the importance of the "big bang" strike. These 64 stoppages did account for 46 per cent of working days lost. In 1982, 15 stoppages involving 10,000 workers or over accounted for 61 per cent of all days lost.

Another interesting feature to emerge from the data is that, in manufacturing industry, there were in the years 1971–3 on average strikes in only 2 per cent of establishments, and the incidence of strikes was concentrated in a small number of large establishments. This suggests that it is large units in particular that may have to pay attention to the "alienation" problem and, in practical terms, ensure that their procedures are explicit and relevant. Certain occupations (and this point cannot be entirely separated from the industrial concentration of strikes referred to above) emerged as important focal points for stoppages—dockers and stevedores, drivers, fitters, labourers, welders, electricians, mining power loaders, and machinists featured in a high proportion of stoppages (some 30 per cent) in the period 1966–73.

Causes of strikes
As to the cause of strikes, pay disputes accounted in 1966–76 for over half of all stoppages and four-fifths of days lost. (In 1982, disputes over pay accounted for 43 per cent of stoppages and two-thirds of days lost.) Almost 80 per cent of strikes and 90 per cent of working days lost were over basic economic issues of pay and job security. This lends support to those theories of the labour movement, discussed in Chapter Five, which stress the economic nature of union behaviour. Among the other reasons, trade union issues accounted for eight per cent of all strikes. Within that group, about one-third concerned the status of worker representatives, and more than one in ten were disputes between unions. Disputes

about job demarcation ("who-does-what" disputes) accounted for about one in a hundred of all strikes in that period, 1966 to 1976. Work done on the association between the number of strikes and economic variables suggested the strongest associations were between strike frequency and the rate of increase of money wages, the rate of price inflation, changes in real wages, and unionisation. Changes in the level of unemployment and strike frequency did not provide any simple picture of the association between them.

Official-unofficial stoppages
As to official and unofficial stoppages, the analysis brought out that fewer than 5 per cent of all strikes were official, though these accounted for over 40 per cent of all days lost. This emphasis on the frequency of unofficial stoppages very much endorses the conclusion of Donovan and the subsequent White Paper, *In Place of Strife*, that the worrying problem in Britain with regard to strikes has been unofficial stoppages, called in breach of procedure. It is their unpredictability which is so troublesome, even though their economic impact is difficult to evaluate. But the analysis certainly underscores the relevance of procedures, the theme of this chapter, to the avoidance of coercive action and the settlement of differences without recourse to stoppages.

When all is said and done, however, overt stoppages are a narrow indicator of the quality of industrial relations. In this respect, the survey of workplace industrial relations in Britain covering the "cross-section" of 1979–80 threw up some interesting information. Even allowing for the fact that the year was one of high strike activity, two points in particular are worth highlighting. First, trade union density was a strong characteristic in the proportion of the workforce involved in a stoppage. Secondly, the study suggested that, for many levels of employee and sectors, strikes are *not* an adequate measure of the collective action which employees take against employers. Non-manual workers generally and workers in local and national government were much more likely to resort to overtime bans, working to rule, and going slow, than they were to go on strike.

In view of the growing proportion of non-manual workers in the national labour force, the results suggest that the incidence of strikes is no longer an adequate measure of the level of overt industrial conflict.[14]

PUBLIC POLICY ASPECTS OF COERCIVE SANCTIONS

In Chapter Three we examined the role of government as keeper of the industrial relations ring, and included in that discussion an exposition of the rules of the game in industrial disputes. There is no need to repeat that presentation here, but we can now draw some threads together in the light of our present theme of bargaining and disputes procedures.

Government involvement

However much government is seeking to support and assist collective bargaining, and develop acceptable rules, some key public policy issues arise when the parties of interest in industrial relations resort to direct action.

Strikes and picketing

The strike raises problems about picketing, closing-off the employer's premises by peaceful persuasion. This was discussed fully in Chapter Three, and we saw there how the Employment Act 1980 sought to draw a tight line round the legitimate domain for pickets.

Other secondary action

The scope of industrial action poses problems not only with respect to picketing, but with regard to blacking, and the pressure on neutral third parties through secondary action. Again, we saw in Chapter Three how the Employment Acts of 1980 and 1982 have sought to confine such pressures to the employer in dispute.

Particular types of dispute

Should *major official strikes* be preceded by a ballot of the membership? Is a "conciliation pause" an appropriate device for getting to grips with *unofficial stoppages*? When is the public interest threatened by an *emergency dispute*? In Chapter Three in particular, but also elsewhere in this book, we have seen how the government, unions and employers have had to think about the appropriate mechanisms for handling this range of types of dispute. Coercive action has many facets, and there has been no lack of concern for containing and channelling industrial action, either via legal provisions or through voluntary codes designed by the TUC. Private procedures have not sealed off industrial relations differences from the wider public, and successive governments have therefore had to develop policies, often controversial. They have not been able to stand aside.

Employment protection

In the same way, the individual employee has not always been fully safeguarded by private arrangements for handling grievances.

Legislation concerning redundancy provisions, unfair dismissal criteria, and the Code of Practice on discipline have sought to raise standards of industrial relations conduct. They have all had to be worked into the practical arrangements for disputes procedures. Legal requirements have often provided the minimum framework, on to which parties have grafted their own additions. There has been much rationalisation of grievance matters and machinery in consequence, and areas of potential conflict have been reduced, or at least contained.

Unofficial action

The Achilles heel of much British industrial relations continues to be the unofficial strike. Breaches of procedure have not noticeably diminished as a result of the various codes of practice and changes in law which we have noted throughout this book. By a curious irony, major disputes are not the running sore of British industrial relations. As we saw in the previous chapter, agreements are open-ended, and custom and practice are difficult to channel into explicit codes of procedure. Yet this turns out to have certain advantages, for we manage to avoid the blockbuster disputes that can sometimes arise in an environment of fixed-term agreements with strong procedures for keeping the peace while they are in force. Donovan recognised this: "Our problem is the short spontaneous outburst, not the planned protracted industrial action of long duration which is the main problem, for example, in the United States and Canada."[15]

ALTERNATIVES TO LEGAL PROVISIONS

A joint CBI-TUC procedural code?

Despite the barrage of legislation and counter-legislation, and dialogue between the major parties of interest and the government, there has only been a flicker of interest in Britain in the top organisations, the TUC and CBI, about entering into a joint comprehensive procedural agreement. In his last book, the late Sir Otto Kahn-Freund floated the idea, rather tentatively, that a basic agreement, to use the Swedish term, could cover many procedural matters, such as those we have pursued through this chapter.[16]

Is it because, as we saw earlier, the TUC and CBI have such modest ambitions for directing the affairs of their constituents that so much of the initiative on procedural matters has come from the side of government, or has been channelled by the parties *towards government* rather than to one another? There was some promise of such a consensual agreement in 1980 on precisely the theme which caused Canada such a headache—the handling of technological change—but that failed to be confirmed. It is one of the paradoxes of British industrial relations that, while insisting on the so-called voluntary principle, the parties of interest have frequently done their best to undermine it by rushing to government for assistance rather than to one another. The possible scope and content of a central procedural agreement between the CBI and TUC offers an interesting agenda item for the practitioner and for the student of industrial relations.

Joint consultation

We have deliberately neglected consultative procedures in this chapter, since the prime objective was to follow through the bargaining power game. Obviously, procedures for joint consultation, employee involvement, and industrial democracy have an important, and potentially very constructive, role to play in industrial relations. We shall explore these aspects fully in Chapter Ten, noting in the meantime that we have not covered the full panoply of procedures until that more creative dimension has been opened up.

Advice from ACAS

It has already been suggested that legislation and Codes have provided added thrust towards a more orderly structure of industrial relations procedures. To that one must add the additional drive which is generated through the advisory work of ACAS. Grievance, disciplinary, disputes and redundancy procedures feature prominently in the in-depth work which ACAS undertakes. It is not dramatic; but here at least may be one answer to the question that has run throughout this chapter: If procedures are deficient, how are improvements to be brought about? ACAS can and does assist.

We now move on to the theme which we introduced earlier in this chapter. Strikes and coercive action in a variety of forms provide one avenue along which the parties can move to resolve differences; the alternative of "third party facilities" will now be considered.

SELF-ASSESSMENT QUESTIONS

1. What principal negotiating stages would you keep firmly in mind in bargaining about a claim for a substantial increase in pay and a reduction in working hours?

2. Check your understanding of steps in a grievance procedure. Is arbitration the appropriate final stage in such a procedure?

3. Examine the proposition that strikes are not a general problem of industrial relations, but a very special problem caused by such factors as unconstitutional action, industrial technology, and inadequate wages.

4. Is the strike only one of several means by which workers can bring pressure to bear in negotiations? Evaluate the alternatives.

ASSIGNMENT

Management in a printing firm want to introduce new technology, with the full co-operation of the trade unions. The trade unions are prepared to co-operate but they want a two-year "no redundancy" clause in exchange. Management wants to retain the right to dismiss workers. Draft an agreement which will satisfy union and management aspirations in balancing job security with labour flexibility.

REFERENCES

1. See Howard F. Gospel, "Trade Unions and the Legal Obligation to Bargain: An American, Swedish and British Comparison", in *British Journal of Industrial Relations*, Vol. XXI, no. 3, November 1983, pp. 343 et seq.

2. *Canadian Industrial Relations*. The Report of the Task Force on Labour Relations, Ottawa 1968, p. 163.

3. Engineering Employers' Federation, *Guidelines on Collective Bargaining and Response to Industrial Action*, 1979, 1.4 a.

4. *Industrial Relations Handbook*, Ministry of Labour, 1961, ed., p. 209.

5. Norman Singleton, *Industrial Relations Procedures*, Department of Employment, Manpower Paper No. 14, 1975, p. 13, para. 33.

6. Royal Commission on Trade Unions and Employers' Associations, *Cmnd. 3623*, 1968, paras. 455–7.

7. Norman Singleton, *op. cit.*, p. 58, para. 184.

8. Trades Union Congress, *TUC Guidelines*, 1979, p. 6 d.

9. W. W. Daniel and Neil Millward, *Workplace Industrial Relations in Britain*, London, 1983, ch. VII.

10. The exposition here is based on T. L. Johnston, "Arbitrating Industrial Change", in K. J. W. Alexander, ed., *The Political Economy of Change*, 1975, pp. 87–8.

11. R. W. Fleming, *The Labor Arbitration Process*, 1965, p. 203.

12. *Strikes in Britain*, HMSO 1980. See also articles in *Department of Employment Gazette*, Volume 86, 1978, No. 11, pp. 1255–8; Volume 88, 1980, No. 3, pp. 237–9; and No. 9, pp. 994–9, and Volume 91, No. 7, p. 297 et seq. and J. W. Durcan, W. E. J. McCarthy, G. P. Redman, *Strikes in Postwar Britain*. A study of stoppages of work due to industrial disputes 1946–73, London, 1983.

13. C. Kerr and A. Siegel, "The Interindustry Propensity to Strike—an International Comparison", in Kornhauser, Dublin and Ross, *Industrial Conflict*, New York, 1954, ch. 14.

14. Daniel and Millward, *op. cit.*, p. 292

15. Royal Commission, *op. cit.*, para. 462.

16. Otto Kahn-Freund, *Labour Relations. Heritage and Adjustment*, 1979, pp. 86–7.

CHAPTER EIGHT

Conciliation and Arbitration

CHAPTER OBJECTIVES

After studying this chapter you should be able to:
* comprehend the differences between conciliation, mediation and arbitration;
* understand the role of the arbitration and other third-party functions in British industrial relations;
* appreciate the need to think creatively about methods of assisting parties to resolve their differences.

". . . so far from being the crown of industrial organisation, the reference of disputes to an impartial outsider is a mark of its imperfection."

Sidney and Beatrice Webb, Industrial Democracy

INTRODUCTION

It is well to commence this chapter with the kind of cold douche which the above quotation from the Webbs provides. Human nature being what it is, some outside assistance may be helpful, and occasionally necessary, to resolve industrial relations complexities. But there is no point in making too much virtue out of necessity. Third parties are not gods, or even Solomons.

BACKGROUND OF THIRD PARTY INVOLVEMENT

We noted in Chapter Three that, by 1896, the State was confident enough to confirm the experience which parties to industrial disputes in Britain had acquired for themselves, that third party intervention could be useful. The Conciliation Act 1896 gave powers to government to inquire into causes and circumstances of a dispute, to take steps towards bringing the parties together, to appoint a conciliator or board of conciliation on the application of employers or workers, and to appoint an arbitrator on the application of both parties (voluntary arbitration, in other words).

Following Whitley, The Industrial Courts Act 1919 extended the arbitration arrangement in two ways, first, by adding a board of arbitration to the single arbitrator arrangement and, second, by establishing a permanent, independent Industrial Court as a kind of high-level judicial instance, but still concerned with *voluntary* arbitration. (That Court has suffered two changes of title, to Industrial Arbitration Board in 1971, and then to Central Arbitration Committee in 1975. We outlined its nature and contemporary remit in Chapter Three.) The 1919 Act also made it possible for a Court of Inquiry to be appointed into a particular (serious) dispute. Already the provision of the 1896 Act for inquiring into the causes and circumstances of a dispute had allowed a committee of investigation, or a single person, to be appointed as a kind of mini-court of inquiry. Individual conciliation has subsequently become an important activity under various aspects of protective employment legislation. Mediation is rather recent as a separate activity, at least in Britain.

With the exception of wartime and periods of reconstruction, it has never been national policy in Britain to provide for compulsory arbitration; and it is exceptional for unilateral arbitration to be included in procedures.

Range of third party facilities
The spectrum of third party intervention in Britain can accordingly be set out as in Table XII, with some indication of the relative importance of the various forms this takes.

Table XII covers only the third party activity channelled through

TABLE XII. THIRD PARTY INVOLVEMENT (ACAS ONLY)

Type of involvement	1978	1983
Collective conciliation completed cases	2,706	1,621
Individual conciliation cases dealt with	43,545	42,960
Single mediator	28	20
Board of mediation	1	—
Single arbitrator	346	151
Board of arbitration	39	25
Courts and committees of inquiry/panels of investigation	1	1
Central arbitration committee	5	10

Source: ACAS Annual Reports, 1978 and 1983

ACAS. It gives only a partial view, moreover, of the workload of the Central Arbitration Committee. It also takes no account of particular types of arbitration machinery in which ACAS may play a part, such as servicing the Post Office Arbitration Tribunal and panels on teachers' pay. We shall discuss the activities covered by the Table as we proceed, by particular reference to the *functions* they perform. The first task, however, is to be quite clear in our minds what we understand by conciliation, mediation, and arbitration, as third-party functions.

Types and definitions of third party involvement

(*a*) *Conciliation* encourages parties to examine their differences and helps them to develop their own proposed solutions.

(*b*) *Mediation* offers the parties proposals or recommendations for the settlement of their differences.

(*c*) *Arbitration* determines a solution of the problem referred to it by the parties.

These functions of conciliation, mediation, and arbitration make up a spectrum or continuum. At one end is conciliation, seeking to help parties to work out their own salvation; in the middle is mediation, going beyond suggestions and making recommendations; at the other end, arbitration is decision-making by the outside party.

Along the spectrum may also be clustered inquiries of various kinds. These come closest to mediation, particularly through the general capacity which they enjoy to make recommendations. All of these stations on the continuum have sometimes been viewed as gravestones, marking the failure of free collective bargaining. This is a very simple view. Third party functions may be included explicitly by the parties in their procedural agreements. Arbitration may appear to be an abject abandonment of the right to determine one's own destiny; but arbitration is typically voluntary; and parties to it are careful to delimit the role of the arbitration office by specifying terms of reference. Finally, none of the third party functions is likely to begin to operate via the good offices of an impartial official agency, such as ACAS in Britain or the US Federal Mediation and Conciliation Service, until the parties have exhausted their own negotiating machinery.

TYPES OF CONCILIATION

Collective conciliation

The involvement of a neutral third party to assist parties towards the peaceful resolution of conflicts between them is long-established. It is an extremely flexible facility. What does it involve? As a neutral, a conciliator can assist parties to understand and clarify their differences, by identifying common ground, sticking points, and by suggesting possible approaches to a solution. He might say, "Have you thought of X, or Y?" He builds bridges. It is a function which requires the capacity to listen, to reason, and gently to persuade. The ILO guide to conciliation lists the following topics under the heading of conciliation techniques:

(*a*) conciliation as an art;
(*b*) personal style;
(*c*) listening, asking questions and timing;
(*d*) persuasion—understanding the parties, moral authority of the conciliator, marshalling pressures;
(*e*) the many sides of the conciliator—from discussion leader, alternative target or safety valve, communication link, prober, source of information and ideas, sounding board, protector, fail-safe device, stimulator, sympathiser, assessor or adviser, advocate, face-saver, to coach or trainer.[1]

No wonder conciliation is described as an art!

In somewhat lower key, ACAS itself has summed up the activity in the following way:

> The Service pays due regard to established and recognised procedures for dealing with disputes so that normally ACAS will not seek to concili- ate unless and until any such procedures have been exhausted or have broken down. On the occasions where the employer or the union would prefer ACAS not to assist, the Service does not impose its intervention. Each stage of the conciliation process is voluntary. The conciliation officer aims to provide a calm and informal atmosphere, a patient under- standing of difficulties and a knowledge and experience of industrial relations. He probes and identifies the areas of agreement and disagree- ment, and acts as an intermediary between parties in dispute conveying proposals without the formal commitment that direct negotiations some- times require. He makes suggestions at appropriate times on how to make progress towards a settlement. In conciliation the Service seeks to be impartial. Responsibility for the settlement lies with the parties and the Service does not exert pressure on either party in order to achieve a settlement.[2]

The technique

As to technique, a conciliator may meet the sides together, com- municate with them as a go-between as they sit in separate rooms, and deal with the leaders on each side. As one senior conciliator expressed it, he may begin by shuttling between the parties but end up shuffling, as the flesh weakens! Officers of the public conciliation service, such as ACAS, normally perform the conciliation function, though there is nothing to prevent parties from making their own arrangements. Conciliation boards, made up of a neutral chairman plus two "wingmen", who may, respectively, represent an employer's and a union's perspective, are not commonly used in Britain.

Range of business
Conciliation is utilised for a wide range of industrial disputes in Britain, and Table XIII shows the mix of ACAS *collective* conciliation business in 1983.

TABLE XIII. COMPLETED CONCILIATION CASES IN 1983 ANALYSED BY CAUSE AND SOURCE

	Union	Employer	Joint	ACAS	Total
Pay, terms and conditions of employment	297	119	510	40	966
Recognition	175	15	24	2	216
Demarcation	1	2	10	—	13
Other trade union matters	32	2	22	1	57
Redundancy	41	14	45	3	103
Dismissal and discipline	60	23	86	9	178
Others	33	14	38	3	88
Total	639	189	735	58	1621

Source: ACAS Annual Report, 1983

One country which has for many years made use of compulsory conciliation is Canada. There the services of a conciliation officer are mandatory before parties are permitted to engage in direct action in the form of a strike or lockout. The procedure evidently works satisfactorily, which is no doubt an excellent reason for retaining it. Other arguments advanced in support of the device are that under voluntary conciliation a request by one party for the services of a conciliation officer can be construed as a mark of weakness and, again, that compulsion avoids any hint of one party bringing pressure to bear on the public agency operating the conciliation facility. As the quotation above from ACAS brought out, a public agency does have to be sensitive about the need for impartiality, and the Canadian arrangement resolves any dilemma by its mandatory provision.

In 1969 the Labour Government in Britain proposed in its White Paper, *In Place of Strife*, to reinforce the machinery of conciliation which already existed by giving the Secretary of State for Employment a discretionary reserve power to secure a "conciliation pause" in unconstitutional strikes and in strikes where, because there was no agreed procedure or for other reasons, adequate joint discussions had not taken place. It was intended that the power would be used only when the stoppage, if continued, would be likely to have serious effects. An Order requiring a return to work for a period of 28 days was envisaged, during which time the dispute could be investigated. This device of a breathing space as an extra arm of conciliation did not command support. Interestingly, however, there is now mandatory involvement of conciliation officers in Britain, but only with regard to *individual* conciliation. Let us consider it.

Individual conciliation

Section 146 of the Industrial Relations Act 1971 introduced "the conciliation officer" into the procedures for dealing with claims alleging unfair dismissal which could be made under section 22 of the Act. Where a complaint had been filed with an industrial tribunal and a copy sent to the conciliation officer, it was his duty if requested by the parties, or if he considered he could act with a reasonable prospect of success, "to endeavour to promote a settlement of the complaint without its being determined by an industrial tribunal". The main types of settlement open to the conciliation officer were to seek to promote the re-engagement of the employee or an agreement between the parties about financial compensation to be paid by the employer to the employee.

Scale

This new departure in conciliation has led to a great boom in the use of *individual* conciliation. The original remit concerning complaints of alleged unfair dismissal still accounts for the great majority of cases dealt with by individual conciliation.

The provisions have subsequently been extended also to other statutory rights which individuals have in the world of work, e.g., with regard to equal pay, and sex discrimination. Table XIV shows the mix of individual conciliation business.

Table XIV also shows that through the intervention of individual conciliation officers about two thirds of the cases were screened out (settled by ACAS, settled privately, or withdrawn), while about one third went on to hearings before an industrial tribunal. As ACAS itself states, successful ACAS intervention saves the parties the time, trouble and expense of a tribunal hearing and also saves the cost of providing the tribunal from public funds.

Procedure
The mechanics of this involvement by conciliation officers are rather simple. The regional office of ACAS is sent a copy of the complaint filed with a tribunal, and the conciliation officer then attempts to conciliate. Note that this involvement is *not* arbitration; the objective is to secure a settlement freely entered into and acceptable to both sides. The case workload which this device of individual conciliation has brought to ACAS has been very substantial indeed, as the figures in Tables XII and XIV demonstrate. There can be fluctuations from year to year, particularly as legislation, for example about conditions of eligibility, is amended, and new legislation is introduced. But there is no doubt that, in this new area of individual conciliation, a new and large field of business for this third party function has taken root in Britain.

MEDIATION

In some countries, and for instance in the ILO Guide already mentioned, conciliation and mediation have been regarded as synonymous. This has never been the case in Britain, in the sense that official conciliation services have always been offered on the clear understanding that *the function of conciliation is to assist, but not to lead*. In recent years, particularly since the establishment of ACAS, we can discern a willingness to tread gingerly into this new realm of mediation. When ACAS was established in 1974 as an independent agency, the Service was asked to provide for conciliation and mediation. Section 2 of the Employment Protection Act 1975 did not explicitly mention mediation, but it is covered by the reference to assistance being offered by way of conciliation "or by other means".

Definition
In its first report ACAS set out its response to this new charge. "Disputes sometimes arise where mediation appears to provide the most appropriate method of reaching a settlement." It then added its own definition of the concept. "Mediation is carried out by an independent person who makes recommendations as to a possible solution leaving the parties to negotiate a settlement."[3]

TABLE XIV. INDIVIDUAL CONCILIATION CASES RECEIVED AND DEALT WITH BY ACAS

	Unfair dismissal[1]		Transfer of Undertakings Regs.		Equal Pay Act		Sex Discrimination Act		Employment Protection (Consolidation) Act[2]		Race Relations Act		Totals	
	1982	1983	1982	1983	1982	1983	1982	1983	1982	1983	1982	1983	1982	1983
Cases received for conciliation[3]	41,391	37,123	275	551	862	1,310	533	390	3,397	3,056	538	513	49,996	42,943
Settled by ACAS	16,119	15,591	56	116	21	18	69	91	886	728	60	73	17,211	16,617
Settled privately	1,312	1,241	4	29	3	6	11	6	143	126	3	24	1,477	1,432
Withdrawn	10,640	9,171	31	133	20	26	133	94	1,231	1,034	198	130	12,253	10,588
To tribunal	13,410	12,575	25	197	50	26	122	171	1,034	1,114	271	240	14,911	14,323
Total dealt with by ACAS[4]	41,481	38,578	116	475	95	76	335	362	3,293	3,002	532	467	45,852	42,960

[1] Employment Protection (Consolidation) Act 1978 as amended by the Employment Acts 1980 and 1982.
[2] Including the Employment Act 1980 (other than unfair dismissal) and the redundancy provisions of the Employment Protection Act 1975.
[3] The number of cases received excludes those which were on hand at the beginning of the year.
[4] ACAS was continuing action on 13,496 cases on 31 December 1983.

Source: ACAS Annual Report, 1983

Scale
The figures for the use of mediation in Table XII show that it is still of modest proportions. The number of individual mediation cases has built up slowly, to about 20 a year; mediation boards, which are suited to complex problems on which "wingmen" may be able to offer expert perspectives, are very infrequent.

Mediation in practice
While mediation still assumes that problems will be resolved by the parties voluntarily agreeing, it is a stronger form of third party intervention than conciliation. The mediator "makes recommendations as to a possible solution". A mediator might be lucky enough to "get away" with exercising the function of a conciliator. Judging, however, by the types of case through which mediation is establishing itself in Britain, the function is being applied to complex cases in which an outside lead in the form of recommended solutions is helpful. Typical cases concern matters on which the parties have not clarified the issues, and may be unwilling therefore to go on to arbitration, but are willing to have a neutral chairman helping to hammer out a negotiated agreement; and major matters of substance on which a good deal of in-depth work may be needed, such as a proposed job regrading initiative. The parties may be too bogged down to take the wider view. Mediation is most emphatically *not* arbitration without the power to make an award. It is still for the parties "to negotiate a settlement".

Mediation in other countries
So far mediation has not proceeded, or progressed, in Britain to a prominent involvement in major pay negotiations. We find yet another example of the different ways in which different national industrial relations systems devise their own tools when we turn to the very explicit use of mediation for that purpose in Sweden. The very heavily centralised bargaining in that country has forced the parties to look to possible forms of third party intervention which can facilitate the conclusion of new framework agreements, and mediation has been much used to that end. Mediation facilities are a long established part of the third-party arrangements in Sweden, so that central bargaining has meant an extension of a known technique rather than an innovation. In that setting, mediation commissions can produce very comprehensive and complex recommendations for a central pay and conditions package, and it is not unknown for a party to reject a first mediation proposal. Mediators

do not of course put forward any recommendations whatsoever, without careful testing of the ground as to the likely acceptability of recommendations. Therein lies the art, of producing acceptable recommendations. Yet in complex situations more than one round of recommendations may be needed before the parties agree that there is sufficient common ground for them to be able to negotiate a settlement on that foundation.

Related third party functions

Committees of investigation

Mediation, with the power to make recommendations, has strong affinity with the other third-party resources, committees of investigation or inquiry. Indeed, these latter arrangements have been utilised very infrequently in recent years in Britain, partly because mediation can serve the purpose and also because the advisory activities of ACAS can discharge the function, particularly where more long-term problems, such as adjustment to technological change, are the core issues.

Courts of inquiry

Courts of inquiry are altogether a more dramatic and public matter. Since 1919 it has been possible for the Secretary of State for Employment to appoint an *ad hoc* court to investigate a serious dispute. A court of inquiry is a last resort, coming at the end of the line, for instance after all procedures and conciliation have failed to solve a dispute. Even then the public interest has to be at stake, and for that reason Courts do not require the voluntary assent of the parties before they are launched. Equally, their main purpose is to inform the public and Parliament through their reports, and also to bring pressure to bear on the parties by way of recommendations. Courts depend for their success on being utilised very sparingly, and there have been few courts of inquiry in Britain in recent years. Some have been landmarks, such as the Wilberforce Inquiry into miners' pay in 1972, and the 1955 inquiry into railwaymen's pay which produced the memorable dictum that "*Having willed the end, the Nation must will the means.*" As the figures in Table XII bring out, the sparing use of courts of inquiry may be the "public interest" pressure that is best suited to the British way of resolving "emergency disputes". Work involving mediation and other similar investigations is not undertaken by officials of the official agency, ACAS, but by "independent persons". This applies with equal force to the other third-party function, arbitration.

ARBITRATION

None of the forms of third-party intervention analysed so far involves the *imposition* of a settlement on the parties. Conciliation and mediation depend for their progress on the voluntary involvement of the parties. Even courts of inquiry, which normally do produce recommendations, do not bind the parties, although the very object of the Inquiry may be to put the parties under severe (moral) pressure. Arbitration is different. As our definition brought out, arbitration involves a third party in making a decision, determing a solution, terminating a controversy.

Voluntary arbitration

In fact, the term "imposition of a settlement" is misleading when we consider voluntary arbitration. Where arbitration has been resorted to voluntarily, the parties have, in reality, agreed to surrender their right of self-determination. They have jointly invited an outsider to tell them what is to be done, while specifying very explicitly the terms of reference by which they have handed over to a third party, the arbitrator, their own power to decide. Arbitration is not an open-ended abandonment of self-government in industrial relations. In certain situations it helps the parties to get round an awkward corner. It may help them to save face, even if the arbitrator is left with egg on his; an arbitrator is only as good as his last award.

There is accordingly little point in debating whether arbitration is part of "voluntarism", or its very negation. Some staunch opponents of arbitration regard it as an abandonment of self-government. If the parties can see the device of arbitration to hand they may, it is argued, too readily give up the grind of face-to-face negotiation. Pressure bargaining may often be the best procedure for reaching agreement. We refer later to the particular problem of arbitrating interest disputes.

In practice, and in a pragmatic way, rushing off to arbitration has not been a prominent feature of the British scene. There are several reasons for this, and some of the main ones are as follows:

(*a*) We have already noted that *unilateral arbitration*, by which one side can take the other to arbitration without its consent, is rarely used in Britain.

(*b*) Second, the parties to arbitration do specify terms of reference which prevent an arbitrator from rampaging over too wide an area.

(*c*) Thirdly, arbitration in Britain is a very modest flower, despite the mystique that surrounds it. Even the 1919 industrial court was not in the mainstream of dispute resolution, despite its aspirations to develop principles of industrial jurisprudence.

(*d*) More recently, arbitration, like conciliation, was under something of a cloud in Britain in the early 1970s. The trade unions, in particular, were incensed at the way in which they thought arbitrators seemed at risk of being "nobbled" through the regulatory requirements of prevailing incomes policies. This was one of the main reasons for the establishment in 1974 of ACAS as an independent agency. Its impact was quickly in evidence. Between 1973 and 1975 there was a five-fold increase in the number of arbitrations arranged via ACAS (and the number of arbitrators "on the panel" rose in the same period from 35 to 120). Previously, about 50 arbitrations a year had been organised through official arbitration machinery.

Role of ACAS

Under section 3 of the Employment Protection Act, ACAS may, at the request of one or more parties to the dispute *and* with the consent of all parties, refer the matters at issue to settlement through arbitration. As with conciliation, procedures for negotiation are expected to have been fully utilised, and conciliation has usually been attempted before a dispute filters through to arbitration. Parties may build arbitration in to their procedural agreements as the port of final call. Equally, the conciliation stage may be crucial in distilling the essence of a problem and hammering out the terms of reference which are to form the remit of the arbitrator.

Scale of business

In 1983, 151 arbitrations involving a single arbitrator, and 25 involving a Board of arbitration, were mounted through the facilities of ACAS. This takes no account of arbitration which may be organised privately, or of arrangements which ACAS may service through its good offices. Nevertheless, arbitration is not a major industry. Most of the cases referred to arbitration involve pay cases, the majority of them subsidiary pay issues, such as grading, bonus payments and holiday pay. Few general or national pay claims find their way to arbitration. Arbitration appears to be acceptable for fairly modest pay and pay-related differences. It has less to offer in disputes concerning the problems of principle, such as union recognition or redundancy, where the matters in dispute are much more of an all-or-nothing, right-or-wrong, win-or-lose kind. As one scholar has suggested, there is an "economic calculus" at work in the attitude which parties adopt to their problem-solving arrangements.[4]

Arbitration boards

Boards of arbitration tend to be preferred to single arbitrators for disputes that may have national significance. A board consists of an independent chairman plus two side members, one with a union and one with a management background. The side members are not intended to be the friendly counsel for the relevant side, but to bring to bear in an impartial and objective way an industrial relations expertise which may help the Board. In order to ensure a decision, it is the usual practice for the chairman to have the power of an umpire to determine the issue if the side members, the wingmen, cannot agree a unanimous decision. As we have noted, individual or single arbitrations are much more numerous than boards, in part because they tend to operate more speedily but also because most disputes referred to arbitration do not require the weight of a heavy battery of expertise.

Arbitration procedures

Procedures at arbitration in Britain are explicit, but informal. Terms of reference set the scene. There is a problem or problems to be solved and, in conciliation or in other ways, the parties identify the remit to be given to the arbitrator. This is crucial, both to the standing of arbitration in the light of the voluntary renunciation by the parties of their self-determination for the issue in dispute and for the scope which the arbitrator has to determine an award. He is not free to range; he is asked to resolve a problem. We shall notice subsequently that he has to view the problem and its resolution in the context of the industrial relations realities.

Hearings

Parties to arbitration are asked to prepare, submit and exchange written submissions in advance of the hearing. These, plus the hearing itself, at which all the parties are represented, help to refine and clarify the issues for the arbitrator. Hearings themselves are usually conducted in private, with due regard to basic rules of examination and cross-examination, but without legal trappings based on rules of evidence. The arbitrator may find it useful to visit the "scene of the crime". The award is prepared and submitted by the arbitrator, usually a few days after the hearing, so that he has had time to reflect on the written and verbal submissions before determining his award. Although arbitration awards are not legally binding, they are invariably accepted. After all, voluntary arbitration means that the parties have agreed to let this outsider, the arbitrator, determine the matter which is the subject of his terms of reference.

Continuity of relationship

Arbitration is not about divorce. Rather it is the opposite; the parties have to live together afterwards. This is reflected in the proposition that the arbitrator has to have an eye for the continuity of the employment relationship between the sides. Roy Wilson, a distinguished chairman of the industrial court, argued that industrial relations arbitrators: *"are intended to have, and to bring to the performance of their task, an experience of the facts of industrial life extending far beyond the facts of any particular case."*[5] What can this mean, other than that the arbitrator takes a broad view, but with a keen eye on his terms of reference?

Arbitrators

This leads to general points about the standing and general credibility of arbitration, and arbitrators. First, consider the question: What sort of people make the best arbitrators? Sir Roy Wilson answered: *"the most important of all the qualities necessary for the good arbitrator is the personal capacity to inspire in the parties who come before him full confidence that he will hear and decide the reference with understanding and care and complete impartiality."*[6]

Terms of reference set context

The arbitrator's award has to draw its essence from the context into which the parties place him through the terms of reference and the arguments they put to him. The arbitrator:

> . . . should stick closely to his terms of reference; that is, the arbitrator must answer the question posed and not some other question which he thinks the parties ought to have asked. In coming to arbitration both sides have undertaken to accept the award whatever it turns out to be. They have come on a voluntary basis, on precise terms of reference, and have given no undertaking to accept an award on some other issue which they did not ask to be decided.[7]

Arguments considered

Nevertheless, arbitrators have to think of the industrial relations context. C. W. Guillebaud, in discussing the role of the arbitrator, suggested that he had to take the three elements of equity, economic considerations, and expediency into account in pondering an award. This is somewhat oversimplified. What the arbitrator has to balance is all the elements in the arguments put to him. It all depends on the circumstances of the case. Arbitrators are frequently said to take refuge in "splitting the difference". This is a meaningless statement unless the context of a particular dispute is known. In pay disputes, an arbitrator may have to weigh pros and cons, make trade-offs; but certain arbitration problems require a "Yes" or "No"—this is particularly true of disputes about grading and, where they are still referred to arbitration, disciplinary and dismissal cases, and in demarcation disputes—who does what?

Reasoned awards?
Another way to exemplify the arbitrator's dilemma is through drawing attention to the familiar chestnut—should arbitrators give reasons for their awards? The practice in Britain is not to do so. But this debate has a history. The first president of the Industrial Court, Lord Amulree, did seek to develop a body of industrial relations jurisprudence, particularly on wage principles. He did not succeed. The reasons usually adduced for not giving reasons are that, first, each case is unique, a one-off situation, and, second, case law could breed rigidity and the peril of the precedent. Experience of arbitration in the USA suggests that these fears are overdrawn. Donovan favoured the giving of reasons, but its arguments were so entwined in the environment of incomes policy that it is difficult to assess them fairly. It was evidently haunted by the thought that one would never be able to tell whether arbitrators were paying attention to incomes policy instructions, unless they were forced to give reasons for their awards!

Arbitrators and incomes policies
As we have noticed, the intrusion of incomes policy strictures into conciliation and arbitration did much to undermine their integrity in the early 1970s. ACAS has solved this dilemma very neatly by recommending arbitrators to include in their awards, where appropriate, a statement to the effect that they were not empowered to give an authoritative ruling as to whether an award conformed with pay policy, and that if parties had any doubts about that aspect they should seek the advice of the appropriate authorities.[8]

The Central Arbitration Committee (formerly the Industrial Court) is inclined to favour giving reasons for awards. "Only if reasons are given can a consistent pattern be seen to emerge from the various decisions in the same or related areas. Reasons enable other disputes to be voluntarily settled or parties to disputes which are submitted to prepare their cases more effectively."[9]

When all is said and done, arbitrators in general exercise their judgment about giving reasons, depending on the nature of a case and its complexity.

Arbitration of rights and interest disputes
So far, the analysis of arbitration has been conducted without references to the distinction between "rights" and "interest" disputes.

(a) *Rights dispute*. Where disputes occur that are clearly about the interpretation of an agreement (a "rights" dispute), it is evidently easier to state reasons for an award which draw on the *content* of the agreement and the *intent* of the parties in concluding it.

(b) *Interest disputes*. In interest disputes, by contrast, reaching agreement is the issue in dispute.

Interest dispute arbitration
The point can be put more broadly, however. Just because interest disputes, concerned with new contract issues and argument about what an agreement is to contain, are rooted in the power bases of the respective parties, it is in some countries considered highly inappropriate that interest disputes should be considered at all suitable for arbitration. This is broadly the position in North America and Sweden. On what principles can an arbitration body determine the correct rate of pay for a coming contract period, the critics ask? In Britain, we are not plagued by this fundamental question, since we do not draw the distinction between rights and interest disputes in the first instance. Nonetheless, the fact that arbitration is so little used for major pay disputes suggests that, implicitly and perhaps intuitively, the parties to industrial relations in Britain sense that certain types of disputes, possibly minor (rights?) issues, lend themselves better to arbitration than others.

Arbitration of rights disputes
One can possibly discern a movement, though not yet a trend, towards the greater use of arbitration in Britain on what are, broadly, rights disputes. The Industrial Relations Code of Practice considered that arbitration was particularly suitable for settling disputes of right, and that its wider use for that purpose was desirable. The code on disciplinary practice and procedures (para. 17) also regards arbitration sometimes as an appropriate means of resolving *disciplinary* issues, and possibly as the final stage of procedure. One little known private initiative which has operated satisfactorily is the arbitration agreement in the shipbuilding and

ship-repairing industry for "quickie" arbitration of *demarcation disputes* (an issue on which, as we saw, it is not easy for an arbitrator to "split the difference").

Donovan was very positive towards the use of rights arbitration, once agreements were in a more explicit form. Obviously, the more parties are able to agree on procedures covering particular topics, such as specified types of grievance, disciplinary cases, and demarcation issues, the more they can proceed gradually in that direction, without waiting until such time as their agreements, comprehensively, become suitable for the arbitrator's art.

Private rights arbitration in the USA
There is no doubt that American experience demonstrates the capacity for an industrial relations system to devise a sophisticated private arbitration scheme for resolving interpretation or rights disputes. Private, voluntary arbitration developed substantially in the course of the Second World War, and expanded afterwards on the initiative of the collective bargaining parties. Although the Labor Management Relations Act (Taft-Hartley) of 1947 made collective agreements legally enforceable in the courts it also declared (section 203 (d)) that: "Final adjustment by a method agreed upon by the parties is hereby declared to be the desirable method for settlement of grievance disputes arising over the application or interpretation of an existing collective bargaining agreement."

This declaration confirmed the practice that was gathering momentum, and arbitration has come to feature in well over 90 per cent of collective agreements as the final step in grievance procedures. The operation of this system, a mixture of legally enforceable agreements and private arbitration, has provided a useful corrective to those who equate labour law with the intervention of the courts and the interpretation of legal documents, in this case collective agreements, with legalism. True, strikes still occur during the term of agreements, though they account for only about 10 per cent of the days lost through coercive action. The system relies heavily on individual arbitrators, and a large industry has grown up to service the parties through private arbitration. Overall, this USA experience has demonstrated that industrial arbitration can be low-key and responsive. The ILO has published a guide to grievance arbitration.[10]

In Britain, many of the topics of *individual* grievances are now the subject of employment protection legislation, and this will be taken up in the next chapter. The gap which may primarily exist in dispute resolution in Britain is in the settlement, through peaceful procedures such as arbitration, of group or *collective* grievances which are concerned with rights, and obligations, arising out of terms and conditions or explicit agreements.

CENTRAL ARBITRATION COMMITTEE

Remit

In addition to the *ad hoc* voluntary arrangements in Britain, it is important to remember that the Central Arbitration Committee (discussed in Chapter Three) is the successor to the industrial court set up in 1919, as a standing body available as a voluntary arbitration agency. That function has not featured prominently in the work of the CAC in recent years. Only ten cases were put to it in 1983 under this main and traditional jurisdiction. By contrast, the CAC has acquired or inherited a number of arbitral or near-arbitral functions under various Acts. It used to oversee the fair wages resolution scene, and has a role in the arrangements for disclosure of information for collective bargaining purposes, in equal pay, and in some specific arbitration procedures, e.g., those under the Civil Aviation Act. These statutory functions are vulnerable to changes in governments' legislative philosophies and programmes; in the course of 1980 the CAC lost one of its major sources of business, the referral to it of matters concerning the extension of terms and conditions of employment (the so-called Schedule 11 remit), and one minor though sensitive activity in connection with trade union recognition claims. In 1983 the Fair Wages Resolution was abolished.

Ambitions

Indeed, the CAC is now in search of a new role, preferably by reviving its original role as a standing body available for voluntary arbitration. In its 1979 annual report it hung out its sign:

> The value of arbitration in the process of dispute resolution is acknowledged but not utilized to the extent that would be expected in a modern industrial society. The various modes of arbitration are not fully understood, for example the problem solving approach applied both by the CAC and arbitrators in general which removes many of the risks inherent in the reference of a major issue to arbitration. Further, it permits an extension of the arbitral process by giving opportunity for the parties to present their cases for assessment prior to further negotiation or for the parties to benefit by awards which exploit both sides of the effort-reward bargain. Arbitration has rather more to offer than just an award which bisects claim and offer.
>
> The role of arbitration is not as established as in some other countries. Support for the constitutional approach to the resolution of disputes has declined as less emphasis has been placed upon procedures. This decline

can, in part, be reversed by the establishment of one organization as the focal point for all industrial arbitration. This national arbitration service, together with the conciliation services of ACAS, would serve as the basis of the machinery which the Government makes available to parties to resolve the issues between them without recourse to costly and damaging action.[11]

The message was substantially repeated in its report for 1983.

OTHER ASPECTS OF ARBITRATION

Wages Councils

Certain other points about arbitration in Britain are worth making, not only for the sake of completeness, but because they show the subtlety of third party range of functions at work. Two in particular deserve some thought. First, the independent members of wages councils can come close to wearing all the hats—conciliation, mediation, and arbitration—at different stages of the proceedings of wages councils. Their role is a mixed one—to help the side members to agree, while bearing in mind the remit to set minimum terms of remuneration, and, if necessary, to ensure that a decision is arrived at by voting with one side or the other at the end of negotiations. In some instances the independent members can act as mediators, for example if a particular council decides to take an in-depth look at job-and-pay gradings and requires guidance from the independents.

Co-operative movement

A second example of a mixed remit is the National Conciliation Board of the Co-operative movement. It operates with an independent chairman, and the objective is to arrive at a unanimous, or majority (on both sides), resolution of a case. This agreement then conclusively settles the matter and is binding on the parties to the reference. The chairman may exercise what is in essence a mediatory role, for he is entitled, at his discretion, to offer suggestions or advice. However, he has no vote when the Board is seeking to arrive at an agreement, unanimously or by a majority on each side. What happens if the Board cannot agree? The procedure then explicitly envisages that the independent chairman can arbitrate the difference before the Board, but only after the parties to the difference have been asked whether they agree to this course, and have replied in the affirmative. Such an arrangement, of conciliation—arbitration, has its own particular flavour. In endeavouring to chair the Board to an agreed settlement the chairman has to use the arts of the conciliator already mentioned. It may not be in the interests of an agreed settlement for the chairman to put questions and raise issues which from the beginning he might have wished to pose, wearing an arbitrator's hat. Yet he must all the time keep at the back of his head the possibility that his role may change from that of neutral chairman to arbitrator, at the conclusion of negotiations.

INNOVATION IN THIRD-PARTY FUNCTIONS

Innovation in third-party functions has been approached very cautiously in Britain. This no doubt makes sense, given the sensitivity of industrial disputes. Experimentation has to be handled sensitively. The USA has been the most fertile laboratory for new techniques and for fervent discussion among academics. The following examples illustrate the kinds of "creativity" under discussion in recent years in the USA.

American experience

Boulwarism
After the Second World War, a General Electric Company executive, Mr. Boulware, introduced a collective bargaining strategy which operated with a novel approach, that the management's first offer is also its last. This was intended to indicate an open-dealing stance, for which the management also worked hard by communicating its position directly to its employees. This appeared to be the very negation of collective bargaining, and in fact the courts ultimately ruled that it did constitute bad-faith bargaining. At least it did signify an attempt to avoid the shadow-boxing which collective bargaining sometimes produces.

"Med-arb" (mediation-arbitration)
Here the third-party functions are explicitly recognised to be available as a package, and in sequence, and the neutral third party progresses (moves) from one role to another, as his function in any one becomes exhausted. This method has occasionally been used in Britain.

Advisory arbitration
This issued substantially in public sector rights disputes in the USA. The term is potentially misleading, but indicates an inquiry plus recommendations, which the parties do not have to accept, in contrast to an arbitration award.

Instant (24-hour) arbitration
This has been used effectively in e.g. in the steel industry for a carefully defined range of issues in certain types of rights disputes.

Final-offer-selection
The arbitrator is asked to select as his award the final offer of one side. In principle, this forces parties to negotiate in earnest before they place themselves in a final-offer stance. It is in their interest not to be a substantial distance from the final-offer position of the other side, in case the arbitrator selects that as being the "final offer". Since many arbitration problems concern "packages", and trade-offs may be appropriate on certain matters, final-offer-selection can put the arbitrator in too rigid a position when he selects between the final offers. The term "pendulum arbitration" is sometimes used to describe this arrangement. The arbitrator has to swing to one side or the other. Alternatively, it is referred to as flip-flop arbitration. Heads you win, tails you lose?

Bargaining with a no-stoppage commitment
This is tantamount to compulsory arbitration, for some third-party intervention may be required if the parties cannot reach a voluntary agreement. They then bind themselves to a peaceful outcome, via the third party.

While some of the above initiatives may savour of "gimmicks", they do make the point that third-party functions are flexible, and that they can be used in an inventive way. They can be defended on the ground that any peaceful solution is to be preferred to a stoppage. However, it is important not to push that argument too far. As we saw, there is stout opposition in some countries to any use of arbitration to resolve new contract or interest disputes. One crucial reason for this is that resort to arbitration in such matters removes from the parties the fundamental responsibility for resolving their own differences, and living with the consequences. Built-in arbitration may short-circuit serious negotiation. Put another way, and on a more practical level, the established practice of compulsory arbitration in Australia has not led to the demise of the industrial stoppage, and many students of the Australian scene consider that it has stifled innovation and creativity in their system of industrial relations. The cautious approach to the use of arbitration in Britain suggests there is a healthy awareness that arbitration brings costs as well as benefits.

CONCLUSION

Our analysis of third-party functions, with particular reference to Britain, has shown that, both historically and in the contemporary scene, a wide variety of outside services is available to assist the parties to industrial relations disputes to arrive at agreement. The main unresolved question for the future is whether the British system is likely to move towards dispute-settlement arrangements which use the distinction between rights and interest disputes as the basis for their make-up. The words "conciliation" and "arbitration" convey an enormous potential for supporting an industrial relations system, as this chapter has sought to demonstrate.

SELF-ASSESSMENT QUESTIONS

1. Explain what you understand by voluntary arbitration. How does this differ from compulsory arbitration?

2. Account for the growth of conciliation in Britain in recent years.

3. In what circumstances would you expect an arbitrator to list reasons for the award he has made?

4. Can you suggest new forms of third party involvement to assist the parties of interest to arrive at peaceful solutions of industrial relations differences?

ASSIGNMENT

You are invited to settle a dispute concerning the grading and pay of outside broadcast cameramen employed by a commercial television company. Draft a recommendation that takes into account the various options for restoring the dispute such as conciliation, mediation and arbitration.

REFERENCES

1. International Labour Office, *Conciliation in Industrial Disputes*, Geneva 1973, esp. ch. 9.

2. ACAS *First Annual Report* 1975, p. 8, para. 3.3.

3. *Op. cit.*, p. 17, para. 4.13.

4. For an explanation of "economic calculus", see L. C. Hunter, "Economic issues in conciliation and arbitration", *British Journal of Industrial Relations*, XV, 1977, pp. 226–45.

5. Royal Commission on Trade Unions and Employers' Associations, *Minutes of Evidence 45*, 26th July 1966 (Witness Sir Roy Wilson, Q.C., President of the Industrial Court), p. 1936, para. 9.

6. *Ibid.*, p. 1943, para. 29.

7. John Lockyer, *Industrial Arbitration in Great Britain*, IPM, 1979, p. 81.

8. ACAS *First Annual Report* 1975, pp. 15–16.

9. Central Arbitration Committee (CAC), *Annual Report* 1977, p. 21, para. 4.9.

10. International Labour Office, *Grievance Arbitration*, 1977.

11. Central Arbitration Committee, *Annual Report* 1979, p. 25, paras. 4.13 and 4.14, and *Annual Report* 1983, p. 19.

CHAPTER NINE

The Individual Employee

```
CHAPTER OBJECTIVES

After studying this chapter you should be able to:
* grasp the importance of the individual's contract of
  employment as his main support in understanding
  his terms and conditions;
* understand the importance of settled procedures for
  dealing with disciplinary matters, complaints and
  grievances;
* appreciate how matters such as redundancy and
  dismissal are regulated;
* study the intermingling of legislation and
  negotiations in developing industrial relations
  policies to protect the employee.
```

"We'll make him an offer he can't refuse."
Mario Puzo, The Godfather

THE INDIVIDUAL IN THE COMMUNITY OF WORK

Much of the focus in industrial relations is on institutions and groups. On the side of employees, this concentration on organisation is understandable, since the great mission of trade unions in history has been to support the individual worker and act on his behalf. Trade unions are also, and have to be, alive to the need to keep in touch with the membership. There is none the less a danger that we may forget about the worker as a person; we process him, collectivise him, and make him part of procedures. He may become a means, rather than the person whose interests unions and others are seeking to serve. There is, in addition, the dilemma posed by Commons's definition of a trade union and its role, which we examined in Chapter Five. He argued that the union is a "fulfilling" agency for the individual employee; social cohesion and group solidarity becoming liberating influences for the individual in the world of work. Obviously, this type of approach puts an enormous responsibility on trade unions when they are engaged on the many tasks associated with trying to serve their members.

When the theme of protection of the individual employee was introduced in Chapter Three, we observed that the Factory Acts in particular provided some basic protection in the course of the nineteenth century. Concern for the environment at work has much more sophisticated manifestations nowadays. Legislation on health and safety at work and the activities of agencies such as the Health and Safety Executive ensure vigilance regarding health hazards and safety standards. But the canvas is much broader than that. A great deal of social science research has been devoted to the study of individual and social problems of the workplace, from "psychological motivation" to "group alienation". One of the classic studies of psychology in industry demonstrated the effect of employee attitudes on production in the Hawthorne Works of the Western Electric Company in Chicago.[1] A great deal of practical effort is also devoted nowadays to making work less boring and, if possible, more attractive to those engaged upon it. The activities of the British Work Research Unit are typical of a broad international concern for job-design and the quality of working life. There is a whole onslaught of activity, ranging from techniques of organisational development to work and job redesign and restructuring.

None of these adjustments happens by magic, and they raise problems, cause strains and stresses, for employers, unions and employees. Yet one thing is clear. The individual employee is now seen as having a legitimate involvement and interest in the design of his or her job and the conditions surrounding it.

In the next chapter we shall look explicitly at the ways in which arrangements for joint consultation, co-determination, employee involvement and "participation" seek to take account of the vital interests of the individual at work. In this chapter we emphasise a different approach, namely the rights and obligations which the employee acquires in employment, particularly those which are arrived at through negotiation and by way of legislative enactment. These tend to involve the institutions of trade unions, shop stewards, and management representatives. One of the many paradoxes of British industrial relations is that the main thrust of these rights and obligations and their interpretation derives from a sustained programme of legislative enactment which began to gather momentum from the passage of the Contracts of Employment Act in 1963.

Before we identify the main strands in this package, let us mark out the framework of the industrial relations structure into which the individual has to fit at his or her place of work, whether it is a factory, an office, or a site.

SETTING OF THE WORKPLACE

Management dimensions

On the management side, there are certain obvious elements in such a framework.

An organisational structure

Management has to order its affairs somehow, through functional and departmental arrangements; clearly, one activity or function which has to be organised is the personnel management, the industrial relations, function. Frequently there are problems in relating this function to the line management structure. We noticed in Chapter Four that both the professional expertise and the status of industrial relations personnel within management are increasing. One of the reasons for this is that public policy has pressed programmes of standards and performance on the work situation. From the time of his first interview for a job, to his finally leaving employment, the individual employee is likely to have frequent contact with "Personnel".

A policy of communications

Management has to organise contact with the work force, both directly, e.g., through notice boards, house journals, an internal broadcasting system, and also via meetings with the representatives of the workers, union officials and shop stewards. Under the Code of Practice concerning the disclosure of information, management has an *explicit obligation* to provide certain types of information to trade unions for the purpose of collective bargaining.

Management structure and the shop floor

In particular, a supervisory function has to be provided. The "first line" supervisor is the key link in this chain. The Industrial Relations Code of Practice emphasises that the supervisor is in a key position to influence industrial relations. Management should accordingly ensure that he is properly selected and trained, has charge of a work group of a size that he can supervise effectively, is fully briefed in advance about management's policies as they affect his work group, and is an effective link in the exchange of information and views between management and members of his work group.

Trade union arrangements

Explicit arrangements with representatives of the recognised trade unions, and with shop stewards, are necessary wherever unions are recognised.

Union side

This leads over to the trade union side of the "interface" at the workplace. Here too there are obvious components.

An organisational structure

The union presence has to be clearly identified. The Code of Practice (para. 99) puts it as follows:

> Employees need representatives to put forward their collective views to management and to safeguard their interests in consultation and negotiation. It is also an advantage for management to deal with representatives who can speak for their fellow employees. This function is widely carried out by employees who are accredited as union representatives to act on behalf of union members in the establishment where they themselves are employed [usually termed shop stewards].

The principle of a link, a contact person, a representative to be the spokesman for employees is not in doubt, particularly in larger establishments, where the organisational structure has to be more formal. Functions which require to be serviced include trade union matters, from recruitment to the collection of dues, and industrial relations activities. These latter relate to negotiation, consultation, and handling grievances and appeals of the members. Practice in providing this link does, however, vary a great deal, certainly in Britain.

The shop floor representation function is not always clearly specified in union rule books, which may well confine their provisions about the role of shop stewards to "dues collecting" activity. This is the first cause for concern, and possible bewilderment, when the individual worker looks for a channel of communication. The Donovan Commission was very troubled by the problem, and many of its recommendations for putting the representational functions of stewards on to a more systematic footing found an echo in the Industrial Relations Code of Practice (section 102). It declared that, where there were stewards, the unions should provide for their election, or appointment, define their powers and duties within the union, and also the manner in which they could be removed from office.

Multi-union situations, typical of the British trade union movement, pose other difficulties. In situations where a number of unions may have representation in a plant, none may be adequately represented under the provisions of its rules, and there may be no

explicit and systematic arrangements between unions for steward-
ing. Hence unofficial inter-union shop steward committees, which
may be extremely powerful in the workplace. The TUC is aware of
the problem. "Some unofficial action may arise because of faulty
communication within the union, and unions need to periodically
review their internal machinery."[2] The individual union member
may be puzzled by this; the employee who is not a member of a
union may be even more discomfited.

The right to organise
We have seen in earlier chapters that resistance to union organisation on the part of employers is now exceptional, and that the trade
unions were eventually placed in a very special legal position in
1906. Yet there is no formal declaration in British law of the positive
right to organise; it tends to be taken for granted, until it is challenged. The right *not* to organise is covered in principle by section 4
of the Employment Act 1980, dealing with exclusion from membership of a trade union, and by the let-out "conscience clause" in
section 7, dealing with the union membership (closed shop) agreement. The individualist may seek to contract out of the union
membership agreement—and these are fairly widespread in
Britain, as we noticed in Chapter Five—which the union has
negotiated with an employer.

In less tightly unionised situations trade unions are none the less
likely to enjoy facilities to organise, though the individual will not
then be under the same pressure to become a union member as
would occur, by definition, where a union membership agreement
was in force. Employers may, of course, encourage their employees
to join a union. In that event, the contract of employment of the
individual worker may include a statement along the following
lines:

> Your employer supports the system of collective bargaining in every way
> and believes in the principle of solving industrial relations problems by
> discussion and agreement. For practical purposes, this can only be con-
> ducted by representatives of the employers and of the employees. If
> collective bargaining of this kind is to continue and improve for the
> benefit of both, it is essential that the organisations of the employees
> should be fully representative. You have the right to join a trade union
> and to take part in its activities, and you are encouraged to do so.

Agreed joint arrangements
Management and unions obviously have to agree jointly about
arrangements in a workplace where unions are recognised, in order
to handle the industrial relations matters involved. The number of

stewards, and the facilities which they and other union representatives are to enjoy have to be determined. The Code of Practice
(No. 3) on *Time off for Trade Union Duties and Activities* provides
guidance on these matters. The management also has to work with
safety representatives appointed under Safety Regulations.

Effect on the individual

In principle, then, the individual employee becomes part of an
institutionalised structure. He interacts with the representatives of
management and uses the services to which his union membership
entitles him. The agreements and the procedures between the
various parties, which we studied in Chapters Six and Seven, provide the framework of the substantive and procedural setting in
which he works. As we noted, this environment can be tightly
structured, with standard terms and conditions; on the other hand
there may be scope for the informal system, to use Donovan's term,
for "the work group" to perform. Custom and practice and plant-
based incentive systems may allow a lot of elbow-room, for instance
by way of payment-by-results and wage drift in various forms.

It is quite crucial to recognise that the individual does work in an
organised and group environment, usually regulated by collective
provisions. Whether he is a union member or not, the individual
worker gains the benefits that flow from these arrangements. As we
look in the remainder of this chapter at the main "employment
protection" arrangements which the law has designed to govern the
individual's standing on specified matters, we must never forget
that the collective negotiations and settlement of terms which apply
to the individual employee are still of central significance. To put
the point another way, the role of the trade unions has not been
displaced by employment protection legislation aimed at helping
the individual. Much of the effective use of legislation in fact works
through the unions. Moreover, certain parts of employment protection legislation explicitly protect the rights of trade unions and their
officers and members to go about their union business, including
time off for union business. It would be an odd world if the Employment Protection Act 1975, which the British trade unions did much
to design and promote, as part of their social contract with the then
Labour Government, were to displace the role of unions. In looking
at the range of individual rights and obligations we have therefore
to keep very explicitly in mind that the collective and individual
agreements have to be complementary. We see this very clearly if
we turn to the most central of individual rights, the contract of
employment.

THE CONTRACT OF EMPLOYMENT

Legal setting

Until the first Contracts of Employment Act was passed in 1963 there was no separate contractual law governing the individual's position *vis-à-vis* his employer. Both he and the employer could have recourse to the civil courts concerning their contract, and the individual's terms and conditions could be linked explicitly to a non-legal collective agreement. In certain instances an employee might be issued with a staff handbook setting out his conditions of service, and in the Civil Service, for example, ESTACODE (the Establishment Code) provided, and still does, a very explicit set of rules and regulations governing all aspects of the terms and conditions of the employee. The fact that an Act was passed in 1963 does indicate, however, that not all employees worked in such an explicit state of knowledge about their employment status.

The 1963 Act has been amended on occasion, and its main current provisions are as follows. They are contained in The Employment Protection (Consolidation) Act 1978 which, as its title suggests, brings together a number of the separate pieces of legislation whose features we shall be exploring.

When a contract exists

A contract of employment is in being as soon as an employee demonstrates acceptance of the employer's offer by commencing work, and both parties are bound by the terms offered and agreed. This may be verbal. Under the Act, however, the employer must within 13 weeks give the employee a written statement about the main terms of employment.

Main terms

The statement has to give the names of the employer and employee; the date when the employment began; and say whether any employment with a previous employer counts as part of the employee's continuous period of employment and, if so, the date on which the period of continuous employment began. The statement then has to give the following particulars of the terms of employment as at a date, which must be specified, not more than a week before the statement is given to the employee:

(*a*) the scale or rate of remuneration, or the method of calculating remuneration (including, for example, any terms on piece-rates, or overtime pay);

(b) the intervals at which remuneration is paid, that is whether weekly or monthly or some other period;

(c) any terms and conditions relating to hours of work (including normal working hours);

(d) any terms and conditions relating to:

(i) entitlement to holidays, including public holidays, and holiday pay (sufficient to enable the employee's entitlement, including any entitlement to accrued holiday pay on the termination of employment, to be precisely calculated);

(ii) incapacity for work due to sickness or injury, including any provisions for sick pay; and

(iii) pensions and pension schemes (except when employees are covered by special statutory pensions schemes and their employers are already obliged by those statutes to provide pensions or information about them);

(e) the length of notice of termination which the employee is obliged to give and entitled to receive, or if the contract is for a fixed term, the date when the contract expires;

(f) the title of the job which the employee is employed to do.[3]

The statement must also include a note which specifies any disciplinary rules that apply to the employee, or refers to a document, to which the employee has reasonable access, specifying the rules. It must also state to whom and in what way an employee can apply if he is (a) dissatisfied with any disciplinary decision; and (b) wishes to seek redress of any grievance concerning his employment, and explain what steps follow from an application, or refer to an accessible document which does.

Employers must also provide their employees with itemised pay statements, showing gross pay, take home pay, fixed and variable deductions, and an explanation of these.

Relationship with collective agreements

For all or any of the particulars or information covered by the written statement about the main terms of employment and appeals and grievance arrangements, employees may be referred to documents, such as collective agreements, to which they have reasonable access. These have to be kept up to date. A relevant clause in a contract of employment might then state that the individual's terms and conditions of employment are covered by existing collective agreements negotiated with and agreed with a certain union, recognised by the employer for collective bargaining purposes. This reinforces the point already made about the interlocking of collective agreements and individual contracts.

Obviously, the intention of these provisions is to ensure that each side is clear what their employment relationship principally involves, by way of rights and obligations. For many individuals that may be the end of the matter as far as active use of the information is concerned. However, the whole point of the contract is to establish a base of rights and obligations, should either side find that it wishes to challenge the contract, amend it, or bring it to an end.

INDIVIDUAL RIGHTS IN EMPLOYMENT

Let us now turn to some of the themes concerning the rights and duties of the individual in employment, which enable us to consolidate our grasp of this important matter. We have already mentioned that there is a great deal of legislation covering the broad area of employee protection. For example, most employees are now entitled in Britain to the following rights in their employment:

(a) guaranteed pay;
(b) remuneration on medical suspension;
(c) maternity pay and reinstatement;
(d) time off to look for work or to arrange for training;
(e) notice of termination or dismissal;
(f) a written statement of the reasons for dismissal;
(g) redundancy payment;
(h) not to be unfairly dismissed; and
(i) compensation if unfairly dismissed.

It is not possible in brief compass to examine all these aspects in detail, or in a way which provides adequate information about the law. Our concern is to grasp the main industrial relations sweep of the protection which the individual enjoys in the contemporary employment scene, in a country such as Britain. We have seen that the individual's contract must draw his or her attention to the disciplinary rules and grievance machinery that apply to his situation. We shall first look at these, and then consider some of the aspects of particular rights which have just been mentioned, such as the right not to be unfairly dismissed.

Industrial discipline and procedures
Employers are required to give their employees written information about the disciplinary arrangements and procedures that operate in the workplace. It is obvious that rules of conduct are required in any organisation carrying on work. The employer wishes to have orderly arrangements which promote efficiency. Sometimes, disciplinary rules are then regarded as being of particular concern to

management. Yet employees also have a vital interest in the subject; they wish to be treated fairly, and not arbitrarily, when they undertake work in an employer's premises, and to be protected also against any discrimination by the employer as between groups of workers, or arbitrary action on the part of one employee against other workers.

Disciplinary rules are first and foremost a *positive* element in industrial relations, setting standards of conduct which are reasonable, which are known, and which are certain. It is preferable for the standards and the procedures governing their application to be set by agreement, even if the initiative in ensuring that there is a set of standards and procedures typically rests with management. The Code of Practice on *Disciplinary Practice and Procedures in Employment*, already quoted, puts the position well in para. 5:

Formulating policy
Management is responsible for maintaining discipline within the organisation and for ensuring that there are adequate disciplinary rules and procedures. The initiative for establishing these will normally lie with management. However, if they are to be fully effective the rules and procedures need to be accepted as reasonable both by those who are to be covered by them and by those who operate them. Management should therefore aim to secure the involvement of employees and all levels of management when formulating new or revising existing rules and procedures. In the light of particular circumstances in different companies and industries trade union officials may or may not wish to participate in the formulation of the rules but they should participate fully with management in agreeing the procedural arrangements which will apply to their members and in seeing that these arrangements are used consistently and fairly.

A positive feature
Although adequate disciplinary codes are best viewed as a positive feature of good industrial relations, it is nevertheless only realistic to recognise that disciplinary rules tend to be noticed only when they are infringed. The adequacy of the rules is usually only tested in action; sometimes they become fully known only when action under a disciplinary code is controversial, leading perhaps to dismissal which is then challenged as having been unfair.

Content
Disciplinary rules should be expressed clearly in respect of their content and the procedures under them, and employees should be made aware of them. The legislation requires this, and the Code provides a useful summary, in para. 10.

Disciplinary procedures should:
(a) Be in writing.
(b) Specify to whom they apply.
(c) Provide for matters to be dealt with quickly.
(d) Indicate the disciplinary actions which may be taken.
(e) Specify the levels of management which have the authority to take the various forms of disciplinary action, ensuring that immediate superiors do not formally have the power to dismiss without reference to senior management.
(f) Provide for individuals to be informed of the complaints against them and to be given an opportunity to state their case before decisions are reached.
(g) Give individuals the right to be accompanied by a trade union representative or by a fellow employee of their choice.
(h) Ensure that, except for gross misconduct, no employees are dismissed for a first breach of discipline.
(i) Ensure that disciplinary action is not taken until the case has been carefully investigated.
(j) Ensure that individuals are given an explanation for any penalty imposed.
(k) Provide a right of appeal and specify the procedure to be followed.

Categories of offences
Disciplinary procedures frequently distinguish categories of offences. For instance, "gross misconduct" may cover such offences as stealing, falsification, fighting, smoking in prohibited areas, intoxication, and refusal to comply with legitimate instructions. Such misdemeanours may involve immediate suspension, subsequent enquiry, and summary dismissal from employment if the offence is found proven. There may be other categories of offence—"serious misconduct" could embrace poor performance, abnormal wastage of materials, poor time-keeping, unnecessarily noisy behaviour, loitering in toilets. The provisions governing the handling of such offences may "escalate" from oral warnings to formal written warnings, culminating, if the offence is repeated, in dismissal.

Practical considerations
Experience suggests the following main points about reasonable and effective disciplinary rules and procedures.

(a) The penalties for categories of offences must be known and explicit.
(b) Nevertheless, each instance which calls the disciplinary rules into operation usually has its own distinctive features. Each case is unique.

(*c*) This means that the rules have to be applied with judgment and discretion. In addition, the employment record of the individual concerned has to be taken into account in assessing the gravity of an offence.

(*d*) It is highly desirable that trade union representatives should take part in procedures.

(*e*) The application of disciplinary procedures *to* trade union representatives must studiously avoid any hint of victimisation. The Code of Practice advises (para. 14 (*b*)) that disciplinary action against a trade union official can lead to a serious dispute if it is seen as an attack on the functions of the union. Although normal disciplinary standards should apply to their conduct as employees, no disciplinary action beyond an oral warning should be taken in respect of a trade union representative until the circumstances of the case have been discussed with a senior trade union representative or full-time official.

(*f*) Criminal offences outside employment can cause difficulties. Again the Code (para 15. (*c*)) counsels that these should not be treated as automatic reasons for dismissal, regardless of whether the offence has any relevance to the duties of the person in his job. The main criterion should be whether the offence makes the individual unsuitable for his or her own type of work, or unacceptable to other employees. "Employees should not be dismissed solely because a charge against them is pending or because they are absent through having been remanded in custody."

(*g*) The crime sheet should be wiped clean after a specified period of time, accompanied by satisfactory conduct, has passed since an individual, still in employment, committed a disciplinary offence. An "offender" must be encouraged to work his passage back into good standing as an employee.

(*h*) Successive levels of management should be involved in processing serious offences. The other side of this coin is the right to appeal to a higher stage or, to put the point another way, the need for steps to be followed in processing disciplinary offences, particularly through an appellate arrangement. This leads to a brief consideration of grievance machinery.

Grievance procedures

Grievances may arise over a much broader field than matters relating to disciplinary rules. As we have seen, discipline has its focus in standards of conduct and sanctions for their abuse. An individual employee or a group may, however, file a genuine complaint or grievance about a pay problem, a matter of job grading, or allocation of work which is quite a different kind of industrial relations matter from a disciplinary one. The employee may be perfectly entitled to take the initiative in seeking a change or redress.

We have already referred to grievance procedures in Chapter Six, and in particular in Chapter Seven we discussed procedures, noting how in Britain these are capable of dealing with, or processing, both disputes about interest and about rights. On the whole, grievances tend to lie closer to rights disputes than to differences of interest, since grievances frequently concern the interpretation or application of an agreement or a custom and practice which is already operating. We saw also in that chapter that individual grievances may contain the seeds of a dispute involving others. To that extent disputes and grievance arrangements, with their various procedural steps or stages, should be in harmony.

Link with disciplinary procedures
Concerning appeals about disciplinary matters, the relevant Code of Practice (paras. 16 and 17) states that grievance procedures are sometimes used for dealing with disciplinary appeals, though it is normally more appropriate to keep the two procedures separate. Disciplinary issues are in general best dealt with internally, and usually require speedy determination. However, the external stages of a grievance procedure may be appropriate for handling appeals against disciplinary action where the matter has not been resolved within the organisation, or where it has become a collective issue between management and a union. It also suggests that independent arbitration may sometimes be an appropriate means of resolving disciplinary issues, by agreement between the parties concerned.

It is for the parties of interest in industrial relations to design the arrangements which they find suit their needs. What is important is that disciplinary, grievance and appeals processes should be explicit and known to everyone who may be affected by them. In addition, however, we have to recognise that, whatever parties may agree as private procedures between them, matters of discipline can involve *statutory* rights. Such rights do, however, have to be invoked, by a party making a complaint. This usually leads to the involvement of ACAS, which seeks to conciliate—individual conciliation. If this fails, an industrial tribunal will consider the complaint. The origin and nature of these tribunals were outlined in Chapter Three.

CERTAIN IMPORTANT INDIVIDUAL RIGHTS

We now turn to examine some of the particular rights which employment protection legislation provides for the individual employee. This will enable us to see the way in which the law and industrial relations practices are interwoven, and the role of unions and public bodies such as industrial tribunals in operating the protective measures. We take up in turn:

(*a*) the period of notice;
(*b*) maternity rights;
(*c*) redundancy; and
(*d*) unfair dismissal.

Period of notice

One of the most obvious rights and obligations arising out of the individual's employment relationship is that he or she should receive, and also give, adequate notice of termination of the contract. The Contracts of Employment Act, as amended, has provided certain ground rules:

(*a*) after being employed for four weeks, an employee is entitled to a minimum period of notice of one week;
(*b*) length of service entitles the employee to longer periods of notice—at least two weeks for two years' service or more, and one additional week for each further year, up to a maximum of twelve weeks for twelve years' service or more;
(*c*) entitlement to pay during the period of notice.

An employee who has been employed for four weeks is also required to give his employer a minimum of one week's notice. This is not affected by length of service.

Statute sets minima

These statutory minima may be improved upon by agreement. There are numerous qualifications to this general set of rules, to take account of particular types of employment and contract. Nor does the Act prevent the employer or the employee from waiving their right, or from accepting pay in lieu of notice. In certain circumstances, the contract may also be terminated without notice if the conduct of the other side justifies it.

These arrangements are intended to remove from the employment relationship the arbitrariness and inconvenience which could occur if employment could be terminated at the whim of either side. As between employer and employee, the balance of equity favours the worker, in that he or she is bound by less rigorous requirements regarding the length of the period of notice than the employer.

Maternity rights

One of the major shifts towards greater equity in industrial relations in Britain in recent years has concerned the equal treatment of women in the labour market. The Equal Pay Act 1970 is an obvious vehicle for that purpose. As part of a widening of employment protection measures, there are now in addition explicit rights pertaining to maternity. These provide four rights for an employee who is expecting a baby:

(*a*) paid time off for ante-natal care;
(*b*) the right to protection against dismissal on account of her pregnancy;
(*c*) the right to return to work with her employer after absence on account of pregnancy; and
(*d*) the right to maternity pay.

Ground rules

Provided she has been in the employment for a year (the same minimum period of eligibility as that provided for the general rules governing unfair dismissal) a pregnant employee can complain of unfair dismissal if she is dismissed because she is pregnant or for a reason connected with her pregnancy. If her condition makes it impossible for her to do her job adequately, she has to be offered a suitable alternative job if one is available. She is also entitled to time off with pay for attendance at an ante-natal clinic.

After her confinement, the employee has the right to return to her job within a period of twenty-nine weeks. However, she must satisfy certain procedures for this entitlement to be watertight. First, she must have been employed for two years, and have remained at her job until at least the eleventh week before the baby was due, and must have told her employer in writing, at least three weeks before she began her absence, of the circumstances and of her intention to return to work afterwards.

After seven weeks have passed following her confinement, the employer is entitled to ask her in writing to give him written confirmation, within two weeks, of her intention to return. One obvious reason for such a requirement is that the employer may have had to make alternative temporary arrangements, as indeed the law allows, for a replacement. The employee must also give at least three weeks' written notice of the date when she plans to resume work.

Maternity pay is payable for a period of six weeks by the employer (who can reclaim from the special Maternity Pay Fund) to an expectant employee who has been in his employment for two years.

Assessment

These complicated arrangements are subject to the general rule of what is "reasonably practicable" in the circumstances. Some of the obvious problems that can arise, and which may lead to cases before industrial tribunals, concern the following problems. Pregnancy protects against dismissal: but supposing a pregnant employee is off work frequently due to sickness, and this is not necessarily attributable to the condition of pregnancy? What happens if at the time of her pregnancy or on her return an alternative job offered to her is not "suitable"? The arrangements for temporary replacements may also have to be very explicit, if problems are to be avoided on the prospective return of the mother. Some 180 cases arising under the maternity provisions reached ACAS in 1983, but as a consequence of conciliation, private settlement, or withdrawal of the case, fewer than one-third went on to be considered by industrial tribunals. Despite the complexities of the provisions, the protection provided for the condition of pregnancy is a significant addition to arrangements for the equitable treatment of female employees who become pregnant.

Redundancy

Since 1965, there has been a national scheme in Britain which provided rules, procedures and financial compensation where employment is terminated on account of redundancy. Generally, this is a situation in which an employer's need for employees to do certain work has ceased or diminished or is expected to do so. More precisely, redundancy can arise when the employer has ceased or intends to cease to carry on the business for which the employee was employed, or in the place so employed; or where there is or is expected to be a reduction in the requirements of the business for employees to carry out work of a particular kind, or in a particular place. An employee being declared redundant, "surplus to requirements", is naturally entitled to receive due notice of termination in accordance with his contract. Redundancy raises certain additional points, however.

Redundancy causes dislocation to the individual affected by it, and financial provision is made to ease the adjustment; it poses adjustment problems for labour markets, and for trade union members. The redundancy scheme therefore seeks to provide a practical and sensible set of arrangements for reducing the harsh impact of workers being told that their jobs are about to disappear.

Procedures

An employer is required to consult appropriate recognised trade unions when he proposes to make even one employee redundant. This is intended to give the unions an opportunity to discuss the situation and see whether the numbers affected can be reduced or the effects of redundancy mitigated. While the general rule is that the employer is required to consult at the earliest opportunity, *consultation must begin at least 30 days before the expected redundancy where 10 to 99 employees are involved, and at least 90 days in advance if 100 or more employees are involved in an establishment.* The union is entitled to reasonably full information about the proposals. Provision is made for exceptions where it is not "reasonably practicable" for an employer to meet these requirements; but an employer's good faith can be tested before a tribunal if the union thinks that an employer has not done everything possible to consult as required.

An employer is also required to notify the Secretary of State for Employment if he plans to make 10 or more employees redundant at an establishment within a specified period, and to give the same notice as that to which unions are entitled. This is intended to enable the Employment Service to assist with advisory, placing and training services. These obligations on an employer apply even in situations where the persons to be made redundant are volunteers.

An employee given notice of dismissal because of redundancy is entitled to reasonable time off, with pay, to look for a job or to arrange training. Again, this is intended to smooth the adjustment into new employment. Financial compensation arrangements provide another cushion to ease the adjustment process.

The original Redundancy Payments Act 1965 introduced the principle that an employer should pay a lump sum by way of compensation—a redundancy payment—provided the employee has at least two years' reckonable service. The payment is calculated by reference to age, length of service (with a maximum of 20 years), and weekly pay (the maximum figure is reviewed from time to time). The scale of entitlement weights compensation in favour of workers over 40, but the maximum scale of entitlement is 30 weeks multiplied by the weekly maximum rate of £140 (in 1983). The employer has to show in writing to the employee how the redundancy payment has been calculated. Redundancy pay may also be claimed in certain circumstances for layoffs and short-time working. The redundancy scheme is financed by allocations from social security payments, from which an employer can claim a rebate of a proportion (presently 41 per cent) of the payment he has made.

Some key issues

Redundancy case law is now fairly settled, and about 300 cases reached ACAS in 1983. There are a number of classic problems which have arisen over the years in applying the redundancy provisions:

(*a*) What is meant by "the place where" the employee was employed?

(*b*) How is "work of a particular kind" to be interpreted?

(*c*) When is the dismissal wholly or mainly because of redundancy?

(*d*) How is a case to be assessed where dismissal may allegedly be for other reasons, such as inefficiency, unsuitability, or ill-health?

(*e*) Has the employee been unfairly selected for redundancy?

Disputes can find their way, via ACAS, to industrial tribunals, where the onus is on the employer.

Industrial relations aspects

It is open to employers to operate more advantageous voluntary schemes for redundancy than that set out in law, and it is quite common for unions to negotiate more favourable terms for redundancy "handshakes". Schemes then become analogous to the severance pay arrangements, negotiated through collective bargaining, which are so common in the USA. The statutory scheme in Britain does, however, provide a floor, and it does seek to ensure that employers do not act arbitrarily. The provisions for involving unions and the public employment service are aimed at facilitating the transition from a job that is disappearing, into new employment. They show the industrial relations machinery at work, both collectively through the involvement of unions, and individually, in giving the employee some protection. In the period 1977–1982, 2.7 million people received statutory redundancy pay, an average of 452,000 a year. The recession in the early 1980s brought an increase in advance notice of redundancy and, in 1982, in the number of confirmed redundancies and redundancy payments. Despite the legislation, redundancy still features as an important cause of stoppages. In 1982, 8 per cent of stoppages and 16 per cent of days lost related to redundancy questions; in 1981 the figures were respectively 11 per cent and 15 per cent. There is a clear need therefore for the kind of protective legislation we have discussed above.[4]

Unfair dismissal

Provided an employee asks for it, verbally or in writing, he is now entitled to receive from his employer, in writing, a statement of the reasons for his dismissal from employment. This entitlement is clearly crucial in general terms. It increases the certainty on the part of the employee as to the causes of termination of his employment, which could be helpful to him in his subsequent search for a new job. It puts the onus firmly on employers to ensure that their industrial relations managers are able to set out clearly what factors weighed in dismissing an employee. Above all, however, the entitlement to a written statement of the reasons for dismissal enables an employee to determine whether he wishes to take advantage of the statutory provisions which give him the right not to be unfairly dismissed.

Towards a legal code

Donovan wanted to see satisfactory voluntary procedures governing dismissals developed and extended; and a majority of the Commission went further and recommended early legislation to establish statutory machinery to safeguard employees against unfair dismissal. The White Paper, *In Place of Strife*, declared in favour of statutory machinery. The Industrial Relations Act 1971, Sections 22 to 31, responded by providing a statutory scheme. Even when that Act was repealed in 1974, its partial replacement, the Trade Union and Labour Relations Act 1974, re-enacted the essentials of the 1971 scheme. That was quite a compliment.

Amid all the controversy in recent years about the nature of industrial relations law in Britain, there has then been a remarkable consensus about this one enormously important protection for the individual employee, against arbitrary dismissal from his employment. While the precise design of the provisions governing unfair dismissal has been modified from time to time, the key provisions have remained substantially unaltered.

Fundamental concept

The basic concept is that every employee with at least a year's service (the qualifying norm has varied over the years from six months to two years) has the right not to be unfairly dismissed by his employer. The onus is on the employer, *if challenged*, to establish that the dismissal was fair. He then has to demonstrate what the reason, or principal reason, was for the dismissal, and that it was for one or more of the following reasons:

(*a*) the capability or qualifications of the employee for performing work of the kind which the employer engaged him to do;

(b) the employee's conduct;
(c) redundancy;
(d) some other substantial reason which justified the dismissal of an employee holding that position.

The employer may have to satisfy an industrial tribunal that in the circumstances, including the size and administrative resources of his undertaking, he acted reasonably. The tribunal assesses reasonableness or unreasonableness with regard to the above circumstances and also "in accordance with equity and the substantial merits of the case". Since 1980, employees in firms with 20 or fewer employees only become eligible for this protection after two years, instead of the normal one.

Three types of remedy

What sanctions may be deployed against an employer if a dismissal is found to have been unfair? What are the remedies? The arrangements distinguish three:

(a) reinstatement;
(b) re-engagement; and
(c) compensation.

In considering the remedies of reinstatement and re-engagement, the tribunal will explain to the employee what it can do, and ask the employee whether he wishes it to issue an order. The tribunal will also have the discretion to consider whether it does wish to order reinstatement, in the light of three criteria—the wishes of the employee, the practicability of reinstatement, and the justice of the reinstatement, this depending on the extent to which the employee caused or contributed in part to the dismissal. If reinstatement is decided against, the less rigorous alternative of re-engagement is then assessed on the same criteria. Reinstatement means that the employee is to be treated by the employer "in all respects" as if he had not been dismissed. Re-engagement means the employee is taken back and placed in comparable or other suitable employment, but not necessarily with the same terms and conditions. If neither of these two alternatives is appropriate (and in practice re-engagement and reinstatement are not common) the tribunal makes an award of compensation for unfair dismissal. One part, the basic award, is related to age, pay, and length of service (by analogy with redundancy pay), subject to reduction if the employee has unreasonably refused to go back, or on account of the employee's conduct before the dismissal.

A second part, the compensatory award, takes account of the

amount which the tribunal considers just and equitable in all the circumstances, having regard to the loss which the complainant has sustained. Again, the extent to which the complainant caused or contributed to the dismissal can be taken into account. A maximum sum (£7,500 in 1983), reviewable from time to time, is prescribed. The compensatory award takes account of five different categories:

(a) immediate loss of wages;
(b) the manner of dismissal;
(c) future loss of wages;
(d) loss of protection in respect of unfair dismissal or dismissal by reason of redundancy; and
(e) loss of pension rights.

The Employment Appeal Tribunal has ruled (*Tidman* v. *Aveling Marshall Ltd.*, Industrial Cases Reports 1977, p. 507) that an industrial tribunal must itself raise these five categories of compensatory award in making its assessment.

As we have already noticed, particular circumstances, such as pregnancy, are also covered by these procedures, and trade union membership or activities on behalf of a trade union are protected against dismissal. It is also open to parties to seek to handle matters associated with discipline and dismissal through negotiations and via their own voluntary procedures. But the statutory protection does set a safety net which an employee can use.

Significance of cases
Unfair dismissal cases give rise to about 90 per cent of the individual conciliation business before tribunals. Over the years the tribunals have had to contend with a vast array of unfair dismissal and related business. In 1982, for instance, they dealt with 11,500 claims concerning unfair dismissal. About 30 per cent of claims succeeded. Both figures are typical for recent years. Many of the leading cases see the light of day through tribunal decisions being appealed against on points of law to the Employment Appeals Tribunal. We outlined in Chapter Three the activities of the tribunals and the Employment Appeal Tribunal (*see* below). Some interesting cases have been settled concerning the interpretation of capability, the procedures followed by the employer in the count-down to dismissal, and the very difficult terrain covered by the concept of "constructive dismissal". This relates to situations in which an employee may resign where the employer's conduct shows an intention not to be bound by the contract of employment. The employee can then seek to prove that he was, in essence, unfairly dismissed because of the way the employer behaved. The code on

disciplinary practice and procedures is relevant, as a basis of good industrial relations practice, to the interpretation which tribunals may place on the grounds for such matters as dismissal and the way in which they were handled.

Industrial tribunals

As outlined in Chapter Three, industrial tribunals originated at the time of the Industrial Training Act 1964, and they have sub-sequently acquired numerous additional functions relating to aspects of employment protection legislation and its application. Tribunals sit in different parts of the country. Each has a legally qualified chairman and two lay members with knowledge or ex-perience of industry or commerce. Tribunals operate within a statu-tory scheme. But they are intended, as their composition indicates, to take account of industrial relations realities. This is obviously necessary in interpreting such concepts as "fair and reasonable", and in assessing the industrial relations aspect of remedies such as reinstatement.

It is the intention that this machinery should provide a readily accessible, speedy, inexpensive and realistic industrial relations approach to the equity of individual employee protection. Employers and employees may also put their own cases to a tribunal, or be represented legally, or by union officials. A framework of formality is of course necessary, and this is provided through the regulations as to the procedures of tribunals on such matters as evidence, and the award of costs.[5]

Employment Appeal Tribunal

The Employment Appeal Tribunal (EAT), consisting of a legal chairman and two other members drawn from a panel of names submitted by the CBI and the TUC, acts as a watchdog over tribunals, in the sense that appeals on points of law concerning tribunal decisions are channelled to the EAT, and not to the ordin-ary courts of law. Its origins were outlined on p. 54.

CONCLUSION

It has only been possible in this chapter to select some of the important themes which are germane to the rights and duties of the individual employee and the world of work. Nor is the discussion of statutory provisions governing such subjects as redundancy and unfair dismissal intended to provide more than an outline of the principles and procedures. It is certainly not to be regarded as an adequate alternative to the various legal commentaries and guides on the statutes and their application.[6]

Key industrial relations points

Our concern is with the industrial relations dimensions. In that setting, certain points stand out.

(a) Firstly, there has been a major social change in the acceptance of what is a reasonable balance of equity ("fairness") between the rights of the employer and the worker. The balance has swung in the direction of greater regard for the interests of the employee while he or she is in employment and also when the employment, for whatever reason, comes to an end. Workers are now recognised to have "property rights" in their jobs. This interest in job control and job regulation is, however, a good deal wider than the internal management of trade unions which we discussed in Chapter Five with reference to the objectives of trade unions. The various statutes concerning employer protection go far beyond the defence of particular jobs; in many respects they are intended to ensure equity as change to new jobs in the world of work occurs. The question of whether a *"balance of equity"* has been achieved is necessarily subjective, and there is no reason to assume that the precise "mix" of arrangements achieved in Britain is permanent or sacrosanct. There have been significant changes in that balance, and also adjustments at the margin, in the past decade. We must expect the theme of equity in individual employment rights to continue to attract interest.

(b) Secondly, the arrangements for *promoting equity* involve various parties of interest, in addition to the individual employee. We have noticed in particular that the trade unions are explicitly and rightly involved in protecting the interests of their members. Equally, the arrangements seek to strike a balance between statutory minima and adequate elbow-room for unions and employers to make alternative voluntary arrangements through collective bargaining. However, it would be true to say that employee protection legislation has in fact substantially added to the workload of union officers and officials, and has called in addition for them to develop new types of expertise.

(c) Thirdly, employment protection emphasises, rightly, the need for procedures, and much of this chapter therefore has been taken up with that theme and its various expressions over the range of matters on which the employee needs protection.

(d) Fourthly, the various surveys of workplace industrial relations to which we have referred already throughout this book bring out clearly that in the 1970s there *was* a growth in formal arrangements covering procedures of various kinds. Law and codes of practice were clearly very influential in this process, which has done much to enhance the standing of the individual employee "at the coal face".

That is not the whole story, however. There are other and mainly more positive features concerning the individual in employment; these relate to job satisfaction and involvement in the affairs of the workplace. How are the energies, expertise and interest of the workforce to be harnessed as a creative resource in industrial relations? That is the theme we will now examine in the next chapter.

SELF-ASSESSMENT QUESTIONS

1. Explain the main features of an individual's contract of employment under British arrangements.

2. How far do you agree with the suggestion that disciplinary rules provide a positive feature of a company's industrial relations policy?

3. Check your grasp of the industrial relations ramifications of a redundancy situation. Can you suggest improvements in the British arrangements?

4. Distinguish the legal and the industrial relations aspects of unfair dismissal. Are the current remedies for unfair dismissal in Britain satisfactory from an industrial relations standpoint?

ASSIGNMENT

You have just been appointed personnel officer of a small company which wishes to dismiss an employee who has been guilty of persistent bad time-keeping. Advise your employer of the formal procedures he should go through to ensure that the employee cannot claim unfair dismissal. (Consult the Department of Employment leaflets referred to in this Chapter under References.)

REFERENCES

1. F. J. Roethlisberger and W. J. Dickson, *Management and the Worker*, Harvard, 1939.

2. *TUC Guides*, 1979, p. 4.

3. Department of Employment, Employment Protection leaflet 1, *Written Statement of Main Terms and Conditions of Employment*, 1978, p. 5.

4. See Statistics of redundancies and recent trends, in *Employment Gazette*, Volume 91, 1983, no. 3, pp. 245–56.

5. *See* Linda Dickens, "Unfair Dismissal Applications and the Industrial Tribunal System", *Employment Gazette*, March 1979, pp. 233–5.

6. The Department of Employment has a series of leaflets on the theme of employment protection which set out the main features of the statutory schemes and procedures. There are in addition various commentaries, published by the Institute of Personnel Management and by individual authors too numerous to list here.

CHAPTER TEN

Democracy in Industry

CHAPTER OBJECTIVES

After studying this chapter you should be able to:
* tell the differences between collective bargaining and joint consultation;
* describe alternative routes to employee involvement;
* explain the difficulties associated with participation in decision-making;
* understand the need for adequate information if participation is to flourish.

"The rank is but the guinea stamp;
The man's the gowd for a' that."

Robert Burns

HISTORICAL BACKGROUND

In previous chapters we have touched upon the theme of industrial democracy. The definition of industrial relations in Chapter One which concentrated our attention on "social relations in production" hints at the theme. At the conclusion of Chapter Three it was suggested that demands for greater democracy and power-sharing in industry were opening up a new vista for public policy-making in industrial relations. In Chapter Four we pointed out that pressure for greater participation by employees in decision-making in their workplaces was a new and pressing challenge for management. In discussing procedures in Chapter Seven we also noticed that joint consultative procedures could be regarded as a component of a more positive outlook on problem-solving in industrial relations. Now we turn to the theme in its own right.

There is undoubtedly an aura of nostalgia about the term "industrial democracy". It has meant many things to many men. Chartism, Christian Socialism, Utopian Socialism, Fabianism, Guild Socialism, Workers' Control, Nationalisation, Workers' Co-operatives, all have in their various ways been seeking to make industry (in the widest sense) more democratic. The issues of power and influence in employment have produced specific schemes, ranging from Whitleyism, through joint consultation to co-partnership, profit-sharing, job enrichment, work restructuring, and employee directorships.

Trade unions as an instrument of industrial democracy

Trade unionism itself can be viewed as one sustained surge of pressure aimed at making the running of industry less autocratic and more democratic. Indeed, the idea that employees should be able to play a more active part in the running of the enterprises in which they work seems a rather sensible one in its own right. People are not passive. The EEC speaks about "the democratic imperative", of people becoming, and wanting to become, more actively and positively involved in the businesses that employ them.[1]

The point can of course be put another way. As the processes of production and decision-making have become more complex, so people in employment have increasingly found themselves distanced from the overall purpose and products that flow from their labours. Specialisation of function has meant a narrowing of perspective. Industrial democracy seeks to change this, to humanise the process.

Defining industrial democracy

The EEC defines the theme as "the various ways in which employed persons influence the decisions of the enterprises for which they work".[2] The 1978 British White Paper, *Industrial Democracy*, defined it as "the means by which employees at every level may have a real share in the decisions within their company or firm, and therefore a share in the responsibility for making it a success. The objective is positive partnership between management and workers, rather than defensive co-existence."[3]

These are narrower definitions than some. They concentrate on the *enterprise*, whether it is in manufacturing industry or any other sector of economic activity. A wider perspective could cover the whole process of employee involvement in national economic and industrial affairs. One recent study paints on a broad canvas of that kind.[4] That is not our purpose in this chapter. Equally, the above definitions of industrial democracy imply no dramatic change in ownership and control; and certainly do not suggest anything about a major movement, based on class, towards an employee-dominated society. This low-key view of what is meant by employee participation or industrial democracy has tended to dominate the discussion in Britain, and we shall analyse the theme from the centre of this mainstream of pragmatic interest. The Donovan

Commission provides a useful vantage point from which to look back and forward.

The Donovan perspective
The Commission itself, apparently almost as an afterthought, or as a belated gesture to some of the testimony it had received, devoted its last chapter, nearly four pages of its report, to the subject. In its evidence, the TUC had stated that "It is generally true to say that no great emphasis is being placed at the present time on the need for more firms to embark on joint consultation as generally conceived and practised."[5]

The Commission argued that its proposals for the reform of collective bargaining, on the basis of comprehensive agreements at factory and company level, would do more than any other change to allow workers and their representatives to exercise a positive influence in the running of the undertakings in which they worked. It acknowledged that workers' participation in management was important, but considered it subsidiary to the reform of collective bargaining. A majority of the Commission could not support a TUC proposal for worker directors.

The term "joint consultation" was the one most frequently used to denote industrial democracy from the time Joint Production Committees were set up in the First World War, through the Whitley Reports to the committees set up in the Second World War to promote co-operation in production in support of the war effort. In addition to the Joint Industrial Councils for collective bargaining, which we discussed in Chapter Six, the Whitley Committee proposed the appointment of Works Committees representing management and workers in individual establishments. Such committees were seen as having primarily a consultative role; they were not to meddle in the industry-wide collective negotiations which Whitley was inclined to confirm as the pattern in Britain.

Consultation and bargaining
The distinction between collective bargaining on the one hand and joint consultation on the other was being clearly signalled in this approach. It has never disappeared from the centre of the stage. Even when, in pursuit of some of these ideas of industrial democracy, the British Labour Government nationalised various key industries after 1945, the nationalisation statutes distinguished the two. All the authorities which were set up were given the statutory obligation to have consultative machinery. The relevant Act usually dealt with this by specifying industrial relations functions under two separate sub-sections, one dealing with the familiar negotiations

about "terms and conditions", the other with joint consultation. The railways were the exception, though even there the machineries of negotiation and consultation were kept apart by having separate agendas and separate meetings.

Section 46 of the Coal Industry Nationalisation Act 1946 was typical in its identification of what the substance of joint consultation was. It covered questions of safety, health or welfare, the organisation and conduct of the operations, and other matters of mutual interest. Training and productivity featured in other remits.

As we have noticed, Donovan did not in any way seek to shift the centre of gravity of the British industrial relations model by promoting joint consultation. Rather the reverse. It saw collective bargaining as the prime avenue for advancing democracy in industry and participation on the part of the employees. This is a perfectly respectable position. In the USA, for example, the received doctrine is that collective bargaining *is* industrial democracy in action; the notion of some kind of additional consultative machinery or forum, or some kind of separate agenda for business which is handled via a different route from the collective bargaining way, is not regarded with enthusiasm. On this approach, the way to promote employee involvement is by advancing, widening and deepening the scope and content of collective bargaining. This tends to happen anyway, because of the sheer dynamic nature of employer–employee relations in changing economic, social and political environments.

Forward from Donovan

Yet if we move forward from the Donovan vantage point, it is clear, in Britain and elsewhere, that many practitioners in industrial relations and numerous theorists have not been content with the Donovan approach. They have felt the need of something in addition to collective bargaining. What that "something" is has proved rather elusive, as this chapter will bring out. There is, then, ample evidence to suggest that collective bargaining does not in itself exhaust the content or the aspirations associated with employee involvement.

In the early 1970s the TUC in Britain and, for example, the Confederation of Swedish Trade Unions, began to push for much more explicit arrangements for new types of involvement and machinery, from worker directors to new principles governing management prerogatives. Part of the Social Contract which the British Labour Government made in 1974 with the TUC covered the promotion of industrial democracy. To that end the Government in 1975 appointed the Committee of Inquiry on Industrial Democracy which produced the Bullock Report in 1977.[6] This investigation "stirred the pot", and stimulated a whole range of alternative proposals, ranging from the "top down" solution, based on worker directors, to the "bottoms up" stance, adopted by the CBI, favouring a more gradualist approach to this phenomenon of employee participation. We refer to these strands in more detail below.

KEY THEMES IN THE INDUSTRIAL DEMOCRACY DISCUSSION

There are certain key themes in the subject of democracy in industry, and we proceed now to consider them in the following order.

(*a*) The relationship between collective bargaining and participation.

(*b*) Decision-making.

(*c*) The provision of information.

(*d*) Forms of employee participation.

(*e*) Constituency arrangements for employee involvement.

Collective bargaining and participation

We have already suggested that the expansion of collective bargaining is frequently regarded as the most appropriate route along which to advance employee participation. Collective bargaining can certainly penetrate into areas which were previously the preserve of management decision-making. This has been happening in Britain, for example in some of the areas of employee protection discussed in the last chapter, in joint involvement in such matters as job grading and evaluation, in disputes procedures which may erode the management right to take decisions about allocation of work, and in employee participation in the management of company pension funds. It has happened on an even more extensive scale in recent years in other countries, not least in Sweden. The USA has traditionally allowed collective bargaining to carry the main weight of advancing employment security and protection measures which are frequently the subject of legislation in Europe. Collective bargaining can be, and is, inventive.

Adversary aspects

There is no doubt, however, that collective bargaining does involve the possibility of the entrenchment of differing points of view. Expanding the scope of collective bargaining may well increase the number of matters on which the parties may confront one another, and have to invoke disputes procedures, outside third party assistance, such as arbitration, or the use of coercive sanctions. It is at this point that one of the key differences between bargaining and participation surfaces. The whole ethos of the theme of industrial democracy is that of a more positive and co-operative attitude to the interaction between employers and employees, managers and managed. That is not to say that employee involvement is to be viewed as a bed of roses; but it is identified with positive involvement, not the potential adversary role crucial to a bargaining stance.

Union involvement

In addition, as we already know, the existence of collective bargaining machinery presupposes the acceptance and recognition of negotiating agents, such as trade unions. This in itself implies something about the representativeness of trade unions: yet the pressure for and against union membership agreements (the closed shop) brings out vividly the point that unions may "own" the machinery of collective bargaining and yet not be regarded as fully representative of all employees. One of the key issues in the employee involvement debate, to which we return later, has been the basis of representation of employee interests. Should the unions own this? Countries, and sectors within countries, differ in the degree of unionisation, and in the strength of trade unionism at the grass roots level. This obviously influences the type of representational arrangements which are feasible. It poses a problem in drawing the line between collective bargaining on the one hand and employee participation on the other. There is a grey area.

One can put the point another way. Nothing can be more damaging to industrial relations in a unionised setting than any attempt, open or concealed, to use "joint consultation" as a vehicle for by-passing or weakening trade unions.

Selective involvement in decision-making

Unions on the whole have been willing to extend the frontiers of bargaining, while stopping short of "fundamental managerial decisions". Major matters such as investment decisions, plant location, takeovers and mergers, product mix, and closures are usually regarded as management functions. A union will push and prod in areas concerned with manpower planning, recruitment, utilisation and deployment, as well as the traditional areas of pay and other terms and conditions which work through in particular to the pay packet. Yet it will not wish to penetrate, or be sucked into, management decision-making which compromises its position as the traditional "opposition" to management.

A trade union will be reluctant to allow itself to become an explicit party to investment decisions which lead to job losses, if its members are then able to accuse it of having failed to defend their interests. The union will insist on being consulted, having the right to be informed, but resist accepting joint responsibility for a decision which can put it in a situation of "conflict of interest". For its part, management may welcome the additional infusion of employee expertise which participation may bring: but it, too, will wish to draw the line somewhere between consultation and co-determination. This leads to the next and main theme, decision-making.

Decision-making

Traditionally, industrial decision-making and management prerogatives have been viewed as the industrial equivalent of political sovereignty. Management has the right to manage, to allocate the work. This is not a particularly helpful stance in clarifying the problems and investigating the grey area between consultation and collective bargaining. One fairly pragmatic view of employee participation is that employee involvement can extend gradually to joint decision-making, co-determination, in matters about which employees have accumulated experience and which directly affect their immediate interests. This can embrace the work process and manpower matters, ranging from the planning of manpower to the physical and social environment at the workplace. Even these matters can involve aspects of cost and efficiency, and differences of view, which may pose conflict rather than co-operative approaches. This difficulty in identifying concrete types of problem for co-decision-making encourages many people to argue for a gradualist approach, broadening down "from precedent to precedent".

Shaping decisions and making decisions

Underlying this is the distinction between *shaping* decisions and *making* decisions. The process of "working towards", or distilling, a decision can stop short of responsibility for the decision which is eventually taken, and implemented, by the management. Many of the participants in the debate about democracy in industry attach prime importance to involving employees at an early, and certainly an earlier, stage in shaping a decision, before plans and programmes have begun to crystallise. This has the great merit of generating confidence at the grass roots. However, it also argues against pushing the participative process to the point at which there is co-responsibility and co-accountability with management for the decision which is taken and put into effect. On this view, involvement and participation *precede* but do not pre-empt the actual decision-making. The management still makes the final decision, and is responsible for executing it. In the final analysis the decision and its implementation are management tasks.

Improved quality of decisions

To sceptics who say that this is mere window-dressing, one can answer that this process does enable employees to put points, while management has to listen, evaluate, and discuss jointly with employees and their representatives. There has been involvement on the part of the employees: but they have not "moved over" to the role of manager with its associated responsibilities. Obviously, however, if participation is to be meaningful it should be the case that the decisions then arrived at are, in some senses, superior to, and of better quality than, those that would have been reached without this kind of involvement. This is frequently very difficult to establish. If participation is to mean anything, the decisions must in some sense reflect the consultative process. This is not the same as saying that management has to become a rubber stamp: but there is a clear onus on management to explain why a decision it takes may not be in line with the shape into which discussions with employees were moulding the likely decision. Another difficulty in this process of working towards decisions is that, on occasions, management decisions have to be made quickly. That poses risks, in that it may appear to stampede a consultative process.

Networks for decision-shaping

Decision-making is clearly complex, involving many variables and impulses from both outside and inside a firm. There are also numerous layers and strata within an organisation in the build-up of decision-making, from shop floor, through supervisory strata, to senior management. Decision-shaping does not occur only at board level. Channels of communication do not run in one direction alone, from the top down, in collecting the information on which decisions are to be based. Decision-making has therefore to be *informed*, and the process of assembling information can range throughout an organisation and a host of networks, depending on the complexity and ramifications of the problem, all helping to mould or shape the decision.

An organic view

Thus participation precedes decisions, and the execution of these decisions by the hierarchies of management. The approach can usefully be labelled an organic one. Let participation grow and develop in well-cultivated industrial soil, gradually and carefully. How far it eventually penetrates into co-determination on some of the difficult substantive matters of management, such as investment and financial planning, will be determined by the success at each stage. Gradualism of this kind may not, however, go as far or as fast as advocates of employee participation wish to see, particularly when they ask how progress is to be guaranteed in the face of a hostile management. How can pressure, a momentum, be maintained for closer involvement? Models of participation which involve the board-room representation of employees may provide the answer, and this is discussed below.

The provision of information

A diet of information fed by management to its employees is clearly essential if employees are to be able to become involved in any meaningful way in shaping decisions. Control over information is frequently a vital component of the power which an individual or group enjoys within an organisation. Middle management, supervisors, and shop stewards may acquire and exercise power through the control which they have over the selective filtering of information down and up a company's system of communication. In recent years there has been strong pressure in Britain on companies to provide information to their negotiating counterparts in the unions about the standing of the company. The Industrial Relations Act 1971, section 2, provided that the proposed code of industrial relations practice, to which we have already made several references, should meet the need, by providing practical guidance with respect to disclosure of information by employers.

Statutory basis
Sections 17 and 18 of the Employment Protection Act 1975 placed on ACAS a duty to provide a code of practical guidance about the disclosure of information by employers to trade unions for the purpose of collective bargaining. A code was produced in 1977 and it expanded on the general provisions on the subject set out in the industrial relations Code of Practice, first issued in 1972. The arrangement provides for sanctions against an employer in the Central Arbitration Committee if he does not provide "relevant information". There has been little recourse to the CAC under these provisions. Few cases are referred, and most are withdrawn. The CAC has a statutory obligation to explore whether the matter can be resolved via conciliation. This is done by means of an informal hearing attended by an ACAS conciliator. A large proportion of the cases are then passed to ACAS to promote a settlement.

What kinds of information?
The scope of information which is provided for bargaining purposes can clearly be sensitive. The code gives examples of information on pay and benefits, conditions of service, manpower, performance and financial matters as relevant to collective bargaining. Although this is subject to the constraint of confidentiality, and possible injury to the undertaking through disclosure, the intent is clear. Employers are expected to be as open and helpful as possible in meeting union requests for information; unions are asked to identify their requests for information with precision. Obviously, if collective bargaining cannot be conducted realistically without information, how can the more positive activity of participation thrive if it has no adequate diet of comprehensive information?

Two key problems
Everyone recognises the validity of the question. Information has to pass. Where difficulties arise, just as they do in information for negotiating purposes, is with regard to two matters. There is, first, the problem of commercial confidence. Companies can shelter behind this: progressive companies do not. The second problem concerns the capacity to comprehend information. The more the range of information widens out beyond topics with which employees can be expected to be familiar, such as terms and conditions, and aspects of their immediate jobs, the more the need to invest in training about information and its comprehension is accentuated.

Information about performance, and concerning financial matters in particular, is often specialised and complicated. The trend towards the preparation of Employee Reports in addition to the conventional annual reports and accounts of companies is a straw in the wind in this regard. A very explicit effort is needed to "get across" fundamentals about the make-up of production and sales, income and its allocation. It goes without saying that the capacity to comprehend information is pertinent at all levels of an organisation, not just on the shop floor. How many directors understand the finer nuances of balance sheets?

Forms of employee participation
Involvement in their places of employment can take a wide variety of forms for the employees—from membership of a canteen committee to participation in an *ad hoc* meeting on a particular problem; from regular committee meetings dealing with health and

safety to working parties on job evaluation. Briefing meetings, and attendance at regular assemblies at which management reports the state of business, are other forms of involvement. The most formal and powerful of the structures that have been proposed for involvement is, however, that of employee representation on boards of directors.

Employee directors as proposed by Bullock

Participation at board level can be seen as the keystone of the building. The Bullock Committee was not asked to consider whether there should be employee representation on boards of directors, but how best to bring such representation about. Its model was not a mandatory one; it proposed that legislation should be enacted which made it possible for employee representatives to be appointed to boards of parent companies and subsidiaries which employed more than 2,000 persons. Its proposal did not go so far as the 50-50 parity of membership of boards as between shareholder and employee representatives which the TUC had envisaged. Nor did it adopt the two-tier board structure which is the pattern in the German co-determination model. The Bullock majority opted for a unitary or single board solution, and proposed a "$2x + y$" formula for the composition of the board.

Shareholders and unions would each select x members of a board, and together the $2x$ members would then co-opt a third group of directors, y. Y would always be an odd number, and not less than 3. Y would also be less than one-third of the total membership. Thus a board could never have fewer than 11 members, its size varying above that figure with the size of the labour force. The x employee-directors of the board would have to be employees of the firm, and they would almost certainly be trade unionists. The y group could be drawn from people with particular expertise outside the firm, including trade union officials. In principle, all directors would have the same legal duties and responsibilities. Boards would determine their own rules with regard to the much debated matter of confidentiality of board information, and they would also decide whether the chairman should have a casting vote.

The model did not require such restructured company boards to be established. Employees would have to ask for it, through unions. The proposal envisaged that the initiative in "triggering" a new-style board would rest with a union, or unions, in a company which covered at least 20 per cent of all the employees. If a union did take the initiative there would then be a ballot of *all* employees to test their opinion about the principle of employee board representation. Provided at least one-third voted in favour, the arrangement could then be set in motion for reconstituting the board in accordance with the $2x + y$ formula.

The union base

From that point on, however, the Bullock proposal in effect built on trade unionism. The proposal envisaged that the recognised trade unions would elect trade union members as their board representatives. To deal with the typical British problem of multi-unionism, it proposed that a joint representation committee covering all the unions that were recognised would be set up. This committee could, if it wished, determine that the appropriate method of selecting the employee-directors would be through a ballot of all employees, and not just union members. Bullock also proposed that a new national agency, an Industrial Democracy Commission, would be set up, to give advice, provide conciliation and if necessary resolve controversial issues. A comprehensive training programme would be mounted out of public funds.

Descent from Bullock

The Bullock scheme is the strongest and most explicit general board room model of employee participation which has been proposed in Britain. Yet the proposal never commanded sufficient support for it to be used as a basis for a legal enactment. Employers insisted that the correct approach was to build upwards, gradually, and not to put the keystone on the building of participation before walls had been put in place. The then Labour Government produced an altogether weaker document in the Industrial Democracy White Paper, published in 1978. It admitted that there was no consensus about the principle whether employees should be given statutory right to representation at board level. At the time of Bullock, not all trade unionists had been persuaded that it made sense to add to the existing channels of collective bargaining. For its part, the CBI was willing to see a legal obligation placed on larger companies to negotiate participation agreements with their employees, with an arrangement for imposing an agreement through arbitration if no agreement could be reached voluntarily, within a specified period of time. That position was subsequently modified in favour of a low-key voluntary process of extending participation.[7]

Providing information about involvement

This voluntary approach can be given a nudge to "deliver", and the 1982 Employment Act, section 1, did precisely that. Companies with more than 250 employees are now required to include in their annual report to shareholders a statement describing what they have done to introduce, develop and maintain employee involvement arrangements. The CBI responded by publishing in 1983 *Reporting Employee Involvement*, which offered employers practical guidance in fulfilling this obligation. It also published in 1983 a report on *British Employee Involvement Today*, which brought together information about a range of practices on employee involvement.

Unitary or two-tier boards?
Four points are important in considering the forms of employee involvement. First, the single-tier board versus the two-tier company board has proved a controversial issue. Bullock opted for retaining the traditional unitary board. Much Continental experience, of which the German is the best known, does, however, work with a two-tier board system. The top tier, the supervisory or policy board, does have employee representation, and its function is to oversee the running of the company, but not become involved in it. With the exception of the coal and steel industries, in which parity co-determination does exist, the recently revised German law on co-determination still gives the chairman, who is chosen by the shareholders, the casting vote in cases of deadlock in the supervisory board. The second, lower, tier is the management board, concerned with the day-to-day running of the business. It is composed of executives, and there is no employee representation on that board. The authors of the British White Paper already cited were evidently persuaded that there was merit in the two-tier board. It does appear to resolve the problem which we discussed earlier, that of employees and their representatives having a say, but without becoming involved in executive decision-making and its implementation.

The outcome with regard to the structure of company boards in Britain may eventually be resolved by pressure from the EEC. The 1975 EEC document considered that the dual structure for company management was the most appropriate; but it accepted the need for a transitional period of undefined length, during which other forms of representative institutions within companies might develop. Nevertheless, government, unions and employers in Britain are united in their vehement opposition to any imposition of legally based models. They prefer the voluntary approach, nudged on by legal requirements to provide information, and by the changes contained in the Companies Act 1980. This also brought the concept of employee participation into the open, by prescribing that directors are to have regard to the interests of employees as well as shareholders in performing their functions on behalf of a company.

No strong case has been put forward in Britain for extending the experiments with worker directors which have been conducted in the steel industry and the Post Office. The latter, which is the more recent, operated a board structure which used the Bullock formula of $2x + y$, and gave full corporate responsibility to all 19 board directors. The experiment at national board level was discontinued in 1980, after a two year experimental period. There is a general reluctance in Britain to regard the experience of nationalised industries, and experiments in them, as helpful for the learning process concerning industrial democracy in private industry. The circumstances of monopoly nationalised industries, with a high public accountability profile, are not regarded as typical.

Structures below board level
The second main point about forms for employee involvement concerns the sub-board structures that may provide the detailed framework for facilitating involvement. Is there any obvious blueprint? We have noticed already that *joint consultative committees* have had a long and varied history as an institution running alongside, but not supplementing, collective bargaining. There is nothing in principle to prevent a tiered structure of consultative committees from being set up alongside the existing line management and negotiating structures. The important *caveat* is that the structures must not compete or overlap. If that is achieved, there could be merit in using two systems, negotiating and consultative, as complementary. Matters could be initiated in consultative processes which were "too hot to handle" as bargaining matters at an early stage. As progress was made certain matters could move from the consultative to the negotiating channel.

Dangers in informality
Unless some kind of formal structure, however flexible, is erected for the conduct of employee involvement, there is a distinct danger of progress in participation becoming desultory and lacking in any form. This is the third point. If people are left "to do their own thing" in participation, the arrangements may be too loose; it could simply mean a lack of direction. It is precisely because of that kind of fear that Bullock and others have argued that board representation is the key that unlocks the door to participation in depth, throughout an organisation.

The CBI has tried to meet this difficulty associated with a flexible approach by suggesting that guidelines for employee involvement should cover the following six major factors in management's action:

(*a*) defining the objectives of involvement;
(*b*) reviewing existing practices to identify employee involvement needs;
(*c*) identifying the key elements of involvement;
(*d*) assessing training needs;
(*e*) establishing arrangements for involving employees; and
(*f*) checking for results.[8]

That does at least provide an agenda. Whether it produces a sufficiently positive response to the "democratic imperative" remains to be seen, at any rate in Britain.

Importance of industrial relations environment
A fourth point has already been touched upon, but it is worth developing a little. It concerns the national industrial relations environment within which participative arrangements are being designed. We have noticed the German solution at the "high level" of board participation. Within the infrastructure of German enterprises, this high level involvement runs alongside a weak trade union presence and the dominance of the Works Council representing all employees. Traditionally, unions have been weak within the plant in Germany; Perlman noted many years ago how they neglected workshop rules, by contrast to British and American unions.

One recent study of British versus German management suggests that the German Works Council has greater potential for consultation than union representation via shop stewards.[9] Such generalisations can be dangerous. Yet this one does raise an important question for the British context about the 'ownership" of industrial democracy. Is it to serve the interests of the unions and their members, or those of all the employees in an organisation?

Constituency arrangements

Single channel?
There is general agreement in discussion about industrial democracy that consultation should not seek to displace established collective bargaining arrangements. We have already noticed the point that consultation may, however, involve wider interests than those covered by trade unions. The EEC document stressed that employee participation was meant to cover involvement by all employees, not only members of trade unions. Without seeking to

bypass established union channels, it then becomes essential to ensure that ways are found of harnessing the involvement of every employee in industrial democracy. Established trade unions prefer the "single channel" of communication via the unions for both bargaining and consultation. It is understandable that they insist that workers' representation must be fully based on trade union structures, so that representatives can report back "through properly accredited channels". Survey evidence suggests that in Britain the joint consultative arrangements *are* most commonly linked to trade union representation.

Middle management matters

One group in particular, middle management, has always been a sensitive one in the continuing discussion about industrial demo-cracy. In organisations, most people are both managers and man-aged, since there is a vertical hierarchy of decision-making. Yet middle managers and supervisors have particular interests at stake. They can be by-passed both by a scheme of board representation, unless they are given constituency and electoral rights, and by any scheme of participation which is simply a dialogue between the shop floor and top management. The more formal the participative structures, the more necessary it may be to provide particular "constituencies" for various groups within an organisation. Ironi-cally, however, that in itself may build a new set of formal arrange-ments which clog the process of participation in any meaningful sense.

Alternative forms of employee involvement

Before we sum up the content of this chapter, we must pause, however briefly, to salute two distinctive forms of employee in-volvement which have had chequered careers. There is, first, a respectable if modest range of experience with *worker co-operatives*, and *labour co-partnership* arrangements; these involve a restrained expression of the old radical idea of "workers' control". With the exception of some distinguished runners, such as the John Lewis Partnership, such schemes have never entered the main-stream of employee participation in Britain. Nor has a second form of involvement, that based on financial inducement, through *profit-sharing and incentive schemes for the purchase of shares by employees*. In Britain, recent tax incentives have given them a boost. Again, however, the various forms of employee profit-sharing and shareholding have not quite caught fire as yet.

One very radical trade union scheme, which combines elements of workers' control and a financial pay-off—to the unions though not to the individual members—was launched for discussion in Sweden some years ago.[10] While this drew a great deal of its intellectual parentage from Germany and Denmark, it proposed a scheme under which collectively-owned investment funds, receiving annual allocations out of company profits, could eventually acquire majority ownership stakes in Swedish companies. Critics have attacked the scheme, and variations upon it, on the ground that it is not about employee involvement but union takeover. It continued to be controversial after a modified scheme was introduced in 1984.

CONCLUSION

We can now pull together the threads of the participation theme in the following summary points.

(*a*) The *democratic imperative*, based on an urge for greater social, political, and economic involvement is now working through to a continuing demand for more employee involvement in the affairs of the organisation for which they work. The EEC is likely to sustain this momentum in Europe.

(*b*) Employee involvement, *industrial democracy*, claims to fill a gap which is not covered at plant level by collective bargaining, and to do so through a more positive involvement than that represented by the traditional "adversary" posture of collective bargaining.

(*c*) How is this to be achieved? Various alternatives have been suggested, from "bottoms-up" gradualism to bold, director, "top-down", schemes. Britain has backed away from the Bullock boardroom model.

(*d*) In Britain, any forms of participation have to mesh with the machinery of collective bargaining, and complement the existing work and ambitions of trade unions. It would be foolish to endeavour to by-pass trade unions.

(*e*) As between countries, the strength and structure of unionism at the plant level will affect the shape of in-plant representation arrangements for employee involvement.

(*f*) What is the role for government in promoting participation? Can it best proceed via amending company law, by encouraging codes of practice, or by producing model structures for adoption by publicly-owned and private industry? Is it sufficient for it simply to make encouraging noises?

(*g*) Tests of success for employee participation are elusive. Management may see success as greater efficiency, speedier decision-making, improved communication. For employees, concerned with job satisfaction and a sense of well-being and security, the pay-off may be more subjective, finding expression in a gradual *process* of increased immersion in the affairs of the company. For the public, the gain may lie in the knowledge that the human resource is being encouraged to participate constructively, rather than defensively, in economic activity. That too is a legitimate objective for industrial relations.

(*h*) Finally, what part, we may ask, can employee participation play in the much-debated and publicised *era of technological change* into which the microchip is allegedly leading, or plunging us? Taking up this last point, the TUC has recognised the need for technological progress and for a constructive response.[11] It sees collective bargaining, involving the whole workforce through established procedures, as providing the most effective and suitable vehicle for the union response to technological change. Nevertheless, it thinks that the unions can also bring the discussion of new technology into the area of industrial democracy. If trade unions had rights to be represented on company policy boards, and some statutory basis for being fully involved in drawing up company strategic plans, the TUC considers that there would be significant gains in the acceptable introduction of new technique and equipment. But it is also aware of the wider theme, that full involvement means participation at all levels of corporate decision-making, and therefore facilities for the development of the kinds of in-depth involvement which we have discussed in this chapter.

In fact, technological change is simply a very vivid, modern and popular example of our wider theme. If we return to our low-key definitions of industrial democracy at the beginning of the chapter, we can see that the agenda for involvement set out there is perfectly capable of coping with the microchip as one agent of change in industrial relations. Industrial democracy in its various forms is seeking to ensure that employees have an opportunity to take part in, and be consulted about, the changes in their situation at work, however these are brought about and whatever they contain. Any particular form of change can then be brought into the participative dialogue; the more dramatic and far-reaching the change, the greater the need for earlier and more constructive anticipation of the adjustments that will be needed. In principle, however, there is no difference between the "chip" and other innovations.

As this chapter has brought out, the theme of democracy in industry has been "in the air" since the early 1970s, and the various codes and legal requirements to provide information and report have promoted involvement at the workplace. The recent survey evidence produces the encouraging conclusion that most employees now have access to both trade union and consultative facilities. The latter deals with work practices, health and safety, and related matters. The contrast between the workplace in Britain as a *union* base and the Continental workplace as an *employee* centre of representation is being eroded.

SELF-ASSESSMENT QUESTIONS

1. In what areas of management do you consider it is appropriate for trade unions to become involved?

2. Assess the problems associated with the provision of company information for purposes of bargaining and for consultation.

3. What are the pros and cons of unitary as against two-tier boards of directors of companies?

4. Can participative arrangements hope to cope with rapid technological change and, if so, in what ways?

5. Suggest ways in which a government could promote employee involvement, and how you would bring this about.

ASSIGNMENT

Using the CBI Guidelines set out on p. 204, construct a document which could act as a participative agreement between a company and its employees.

REFERENCES

1. *Employee Participation and Company Structure in the European Community* (Green Paper), COM (75) 570, Commission of the European Communities, November 1975, p. 5.

2. *Op. cit.*, p. 5.

3. *Industrial Democracy*, Cmnd. 7231, London 1978.

4. John Elliott, *Conflict or Co-operation? The Growth of Industrial Democracy*, 1978.

5. *Trade Unionism*, TUC 1966, p. 100.

6. *Report of the Committee of Inquiry on Industrial Democracy*, (chairman: Lord Bullock), *Cmnd. 6706*, London, HMSO, January 1977.

7. *Guidelines for Action on Employee Involvement*, CBI 1979.

8. *Op. cit.*

9. Jean Miller, *British Management versus German Management*, Teakfield Ltd., 1979.

10. Rudolf Meidner, *Employee Investment Funds. An Approach to Collective Capital Formation*, Allen & Unwin, 1978.

11. *Employment and Technology*, TUC, 1979.

CHAPTER ELEVEN

Incomes Policies

CHAPTER OBJECTIVES

After studying this chapter you should be able to:
* understand the importance of relative pay as a pressure on pay determination;
* recognise the complexities of adopting a single pay norm or standard in a modern economy;
* see the difficulties in developing a continuing policy for guiding the growth of incomes;
* understand the industrial relations implications of interventions in "free" collective bargaining.

"He who pays the piper calls the tune."

INTRODUCTION

What do we mean by incomes policy? We can bracket the target for this chapter by defining incomes policy as *a concerted policy for making decisions about the level and structure of pay and other incomes for a whole national economy, in the light of its overall economic situation.* This concerted policy need not be the creature of the national government. We discuss that later. On a historical view of incomes policy as one important element in industrial relations, the scope of the policy was originally conceived as being limited to wage incomes: gradually it has come to include other forms of factor incomes, such as profits. Sometimes it goes beyond that, to embrace price policies as well, and also to try to sweep into its net some treatment of capital. The introduction of a capital gains tax in Britain in 1965 was part of a deal with the unions.

GENESIS OF INCOMES POLICY

Beveridge and full employment

In Chapter Two it was suggested that an early and clear landmark for the post-Second World War industrial relations scene was Beveridge's policy study about full employment in a free society. Beveridge argued, it will be recalled, that countries could reasonably aspire to full employment policies after the war. The analysis of total or macro economics deriving from John Maynard Keynes was confidently thought to offer countries a useful box of tools. They could pursue policies which would ensure that total or aggregate demand, total spending, in an economy was kept at a level high enough to employ its resources to the full. In particular, the labour force would be fully employed, in the sense that about 97 per cent could expect at any time to be in jobs. Monetary and fiscal policies would be fine-tuned to ensure that the flow of spending met this happy condition. Hence full employment policies, which enjoyed a vogue for a whole generation after 1945.

Beveridge was aware, however, that full employment held out the prospect of a bargaining bonanza for trade unions. After all, if governments, through full employment policies, keep the manpower of a country fully employed, they are in effect guaranteeing that the demand for labour will be kept high. This is a highly favourable wicket on which a trade union can go to bat. By the same token, employers may not find it too painful to concede pay claims in that kind of climate; the policy which is providing a flush of jobs is at the same time making it easy to sell their products. So their resistance is low.

Beveridge did, however, place a particular responsibility on the unions in his analysis and policy recommendations. He suggested that the TUC should seek to bring about a unified wage policy. Reason, rooted in a strong reliance on arbitration, should be the basis of wage determination, rather than the give and take and muscle of free bargaining. All this is history: but it is not in the least dated. As this chapter will bring out, we continue the search for solutions to control the rate of growth of incomes in our societies, ensure responsible union behaviour, and discover criteria to guide pay fixing.

Post-war experience
In the post-war years it soon became evident that full employment economies were having difficulty in reconciling their full employment goal (say 97 per cent employment, or 3 per cent unemployment) with two other objectives: stable prices, and free collective bargaining. *The Economist* newspaper wrote of the "uneasy triangle" which these three variables made up. Subsequently, the triangle became enlarged into grander geometry, when additional policy objectives were added, such as satisfactory economic growth, and balance of payments equilibrium. Economists had a field day wrestling with the irreconcilable. Nevertheless, it is important to remember that for many years after the war, countries such as Britain maintained remarkably full employment, and indeed

over-achieved very markedly in relation to Beveridge's 3 per cent norm for unemployment. Until 1967 the average annual level of unemployment was hardly ever above 2 per cent, and frequently nearer 1 per cent. In the 1970s it has only rarely been below 3 per cent, and tended strongly upwards after 1974. With the benefit of hindsight, pay increases until the late 1960s were also low, compared to their tempo since. Table XV gives the main statistics on pay, prices and unemployment since 1966, incomes policies were launched in earnest in 1982.

TABLE XV. PAY, PRICES AND UNEMPLOYMENT 1966–83

Year	Average annual increase in manual hourly earnings%	Annual increases in retail prices%	Average annual unemployment%
1966	6.2	3.9	1.6
1967	5.3	2.5	2.5
1968	7.2	4.7	2.5
1969	8.0	5.4	2.5
1970	15.3	6.4	2.6
1971	12.9	9.4	3.4
1972	15.0	7.1	3.8
1973	14.1	9.2	2.7
1974	21.4	16.1	2.6
1975	26.8	24.4	4.1
1976	11.4	16.5	5.7
1977	8.3	15.9	6.2
1978	14.6	8.3	6.1
1979	16.6	13.4	5.8
1980	17.8	17.9	6.8
1981	13.3	11.8	10.5
1982	11.2	8.6	12.2
1983	9.0	4.6	13.0

Sources: British Labour Statistics Historical Abstract 1886–1968, HMSO 1971; British Labour Statistics Yearbook 1975, HMSO 1977; Department of Employment Gazette; ILO Yearbook of Labour Statistics.

One apparent discovery in the 1950s was the so-called Phillips curve, which established the proposition that there was an inverse relationship between the level of unemployment and the rate of increase in wages. This was simply another way of stating the problem that Beveridge had identified. Tight labour markets (low unemployment) facilitate pay increases.

Incomes policy not required

Despite the emphasis which Beveridge had placed on reason and on responsible trade union behaviour, main stream economics did not for many years concede the case for trying to get a grip on incomes through some kind of concerted policy. It was argued that appropriate monetary and fiscal policies in themselves would suffice. Provided they were correctly aligned to bringing demand into balance with the economy's potential supply at "full employment", all would be well. The demand-pull, cost-push debate was usually resolved in favour of the demand school. Unions could not push pay increases through, it was thought, unless demand was kept sufficiently buoyant to finance them. As is often the case in economics, one side was stressed, the other neglected. Yet it was always clear to industrial relations practitioners that demand was sometimes adjusted to accommodate the pressure coming from unions. This was true not least in the public sector, in which pay increases were sometimes conceded in response to union pressure. If this necessitated more government borrowing (an increase in what is now called, more delicately, the "public sector borrowing requirement"), and a growth in public debt, which therefore had consequences for the supply of money in the economy, so be it. Demand ruled.

Incomes policy becomes respectable

A landmark in bringing incomes policy into the legitimate fold of economic policy was the report published in 1961 by what is now the Organisation for Economic Co-operation and Development or OECD (at that time the Organisation for European Economic Co-operation), entitled *The Problem of Rising Prices*. Produced by an internationally reputable group of economists, this report argued that *both* excess demand (demand pull) *and* excessive negotiated wage increases (wage or cost push) were of predominant importance in explaining the rise in prices in major economies in the period they studied, from 1953 to 1960. Countries such as the USA, Britain, the Netherlands, and Denmark, Norway and Sweden were "convicted" of the charge that excessive wage increases constituted both an important *and* independent inflationary force.

Since that time it has been legitimate to include incomes policy as an appropriate part of a nation's overall economic and social strategy. The question with which this chapter is concerned is, accordingly, the industrial relations aspects of incomes policies; we take for granted that incomes policies can help. As we shall discern, it is not easy to devise and operate a concerted policy of the kind envisaged in our introductory definition; but for our purposes the search for such a policy is a relevant task. And it has profound industrial relations connotations. Indeed, on no other subject in industrial relations has so much debate raged, so much ink been spilled and so many hairs split in academic debate since the war. Beveridge was right: there *is* a problem.

An international search

Britain has experienced a continuous search for an appropriate incomes policy since 1961; there were sporadic incursions into the arena prior to that year. Table XVI on pp. 232–3 sets out a summary chronology and chronicle of the saga.[1] Britain has not been alone. Either occasionally, or on a continuing basis, other countries have sought to develop mechanisms for ensuring that pay and other incomes grew in an orderly fashion in relation to the national economic situation. We refer briefly to experience in two other countries, Australia and Sweden. Their approaches and mechanisms have distinctive and interesting features. There is, however, plenty of grist to the mill in British experience, and the interplay between industrial relations and incomes policy is a vivid example of the inter-disciplinary interests that are involved. There are strong political and social, legal and historical, as well as economic phenomena in the mix. We look first at some of the main problems with which incomes policies have sought to come to grips, and then consider alternative policy arrangements that have been tried or proposed.

PROBLEMS

Incomes policy problems include the following:

- (*a*) wage structures and pay relativities;
- (*b*) pay rounds;
- (*c*) wage drift;
- (*d*) anomalies;
- (*e*) comparability;
- (*f*) low pay; and
- (*g*) expectations.

Wage structures and pay relativities

We begin deliberately with the problem of "differentials", in order to avoid the trap of thinking in too simple and aggregative terms about wages. As we shall see, many incomes policies suggest a single norm—such as 3 per cent—as a target for annual pay increases. It is important to grasp that such a norm is made up of

changes in the myriad of pay structures, wage and salary rates
determined throughout the whole range of labour markets by the
parties of interest.

Why do wages differ?

Even if pay were to be set in a world without employers' associations and trade unions, there would be a variety of rates of pay,
in different industries and occupations, in different parts of the
country and, frequently, as between men and women. Adam Smith
set out an analysis of why wages differed in different employments.
He drew attention to factors such as:

(a) the agreeableness or otherwise of the jobs;
(b) the ease and cheapness, or difficulty and expense, of learning
them;
(c) the constancy or instability of employment;
(d) the integrity or trust required; and
(e) the risk factor associated with the probability of success in the
occupation.

His analysis has been developed and refined, but it still provides a
useful list of factors that explain differentials in pay. To put the
point another way, we would expect the information about the
occupational mix which was set out in Table IV in Chapter Two to
throw up a similar variety of information about relative pay for the
occupations.

The modern world of industrial relations is not, however, one in
which this host of wage rates is set by individual employers bargaining with individual workers. We have seen the driving force behind
trade unionism which presses for "the going rate", and "the rate for
the job". Employers, too, wish to hold this line, at least in principle.
Under collective bargaining the setting of pay often becomes indeterminate, in the sense that no one knows what the correct price is,
but a wage is arrived at through the give and take of pay negotiations.

We have then in a modern labour market a complex structure of
pay, and many differentials emerge in occupational, industrial,
geographical and other forms. Even between firms in the same
industry in the same local labour market there may be subtle and
significant differences regarding their pay structures.[2]

Relativities and leap-frogging

It is a well-known feature of pay determination that groups of
workers are interested in relative pay—differentials—as well as in
the pay levels they obtain. They wish:

(*a*) to maintain differentials which they have established; and

(*b*) to close differentials *vis-à-vis* groups whom they think are unjustifiably paid more than them.

These understandable group interests can lead to the well-known phenomenon of *leap-frogging*, by which a group may seek to overtake another. It can also lead to efforts to *whipsaw* employers, a tactic which consists of picking off one employer, preferably a profitable one, and then using the pay increases extracted from him to put pressure on other employers in the same locality, occupation, or industry, to match the increase obtained.

Dynamics of pay structures

This type of pressure, "coercive comparisons", to maintain or restore differentials, has long been in evidence. Much scholarly work on wage structures discusses these problems of "wage dynamics". For purposes of incomes policy ambitions, the additional point which has been infused into the brew has concerned the wage-wage spiral at the time of tight (full employment) labour markets. Additionally, chronic inflation has tended to make people even more conscious of the need to keep up or, preferably, get ahead. Much discussion and debate about incomes policy focuses on this force of pay relativities. Can wage-wage spirals be broken by co-ordinating bargaining? Would a national job evaluation scheme help to produce the "correct" structure of wages for the economy? What is crucial is to grasp the point that the wage adjustment processes between and within sectors of the economy are a key part of the problem of incomes policy. And these processes are the meat of industrial relations.

Pay rounds

Fixed-term agreements

In a country such as the United States, with a tradition of fixed-term pay agreements, it is possible to predict when agreements are due for re-opening, i.e., re-negotiation. Since not all the major contracts are re-negotiated in any one year, the process of collective bargaining tends to be spread over time. There are, nevertheless, key bargains or contract negotiations, e.g., within the steel industry and in the automobile industry. The terms settled in negotiations for (say) General Motors will affect not only the other car manufacturers, but can have an influence over a period of years on settlements in other industries. This is true not only of the size of pay increases, but also of innovations in the non-wage provisions of agreements, covering such matters as pensions, sickness pay, protection against increases in the cost of living, and severance pay.

British pay round

We saw in Chapter Six that British agreements are typically open-ended, re-negotiable whenever the parties decide to review the terms. In recent years, however, as a consequence of inflation and various successive attempts to run an incomes policy, a "pay round" has tended to develop, in the sense that at intervals of twelve months there is a review of terms and conditions throughout the economy, agreement by agreement, sector by sector. *Within* each twelve month period, however, there has as yet been no systematic attempt to synchronise bargaining, through concentrating major negotiations into a particular season of the year. This has been proposed from time to time. Within the twelve-month period, there is none the less some kind of ordering of a queue, a sequence, wage leadership. This is not predictable in any precise way, but sectors such as engineering, including the motor car industry, coal mining and other energy industries, tend to take the lead in the autumn, to be followed throughout the winter by the public sector, including local authority negotiations. Occasionally, the sequence may be distorted by a particular stoppage, or by some settlement suggested by a court of inquiry, or a public body. This rough-and-ready sequence lends some order to pay rounds in Britain, but it is not an order which has been arrived at by a consensus, based on a national economic strategy. Much of it reflects tradition, the seasonal demand for the product of the sector, and a canny assessment of bargaining strength. We consider later the case for a more synchronised approach.

Wage drift

In Chapter Six we noticed that wage drift is an important component of wage dynamics. It manifests itself readily in sectors with minimum pay agreements, since the underlying assumption of such agreements is that they set a floor, on which the parties will erect a superstructure at company, plant and shop level. We noticed that some elements of wage supplementation are strongly rooted in enhanced productivity and incentive schemes. We noted also, however, that wage drift causes two serious tensions in pay determination:

(a) between those workers in a sector who do and do not obtain supplementation; and
(b) between sectors.

In many white-collar forms of employment, particularly in the public sector, wage systems are tight, and any erosion of pay differentials which follows from wage drift elsewhere will encourage demands for compensation. The arguments are not all one way, however. In many white collar jobs there is opportunity for annual pay increments for employees on a pay scale, and the phenomenon of "incremental drift" has thus been identified as an inequity between blue- and white-collar workers. Secondly, it is sometimes possible for workers on fixed pay schemes to be upgraded, hence the term "grade escalation" or "grade creep".

Wage or salary drift is best regarded as one component of the pay relativities problem discussed above. Its control has proved ticklish, not least in models and experiences of incomes policies in other countries, such as Sweden.

Anomalies

Though there is strong historical evidence that inter-occupational pay may change only slowly, there are sufficient instances of "anomalies" to make the point that occupational and industrial pay relativities may sometimes get "out of line", and require some kind of restoration to a previous position in the league table, on grounds of equity, and possibly even supply and demand. Experience in Britain since the war has been strewn with *ad hoc* situations in which anomalies have been recognised or forced to public attention, and resolved by *ad hoc* fire-fighting through courts of inquiry (e.g. the railwaymen, in 1955, the local authority workers, in 1970, and the miners in 1971–2), and specialist inquiries (into teachers' pay, e.g., in 1974–5). Some of the specialist institutions set up from time to time have also had to handle hot potatoes which raised questions of anomalies. The Pay Board (1972–4) produced specific reports on anomalies and relativities. Experience suggests, then, that on occasion some *ad hoc* or standing machinery may be required to deal with particular problems of this nature.

Comparability

Civil service origins
Adjustments of wage structures, anomalies, and compensation for wage drift are all manifestations of some kind of view of equity in pay fixing. However, an explicit principle, *comparability*, was inserted into British pay determination in 1955, and has been snowballing through the argumentation about pay increases ever since. The concept was introduced by a Royal Commission on the Civil Service, 1953–5.[3] It sought to grapple with the problem of how civil

servants should be remunerated, particularly when the output they produced was difficult to measure, and government has to try to observe economy in public spending. There had been previous enquiries, and various pay policy arrangements. The 1955 Commission proposed what it thought was an equitable principle; "the primary principle of civil service pay is fair comparison with the current remuneration of outside staffs employed on broadly comparable work, taking account of differences in other conditions of service."[4] This primary principle should be supplemented by considerations of internal relativities (*differentials*).

Fact-finding machinery for establishing the outside situation was set up in the form of a Pay Research Unit. This formed the input to the second stage, negotiation. Beyond that lay the possibility of arbitration through the Civil Service Arbitration Tribunal. In 1981 the government repudiated this arrangement.

A new approach had therefore to be worked out, and a committee (the Megaw Committee) made proposals for a new system, based on wholly independent pay data collection followed by "informed collective bargaining". There was to be no arbitration device in the event of failure to agree, nor any ban on the right of civil servants to strike. The arrangement proposed was an open-ended one. Meantime, the discipline of "cash limits" is meant to provide a proxy in the public service for "ability to pay".[5]

Four important aspects
Four aspects of comparability are important for the wider vista of incomes policies which concerns us here.

(*a*) First, comparability can be, and has been, widened out beyond the technical comparisons of like-with-like to embrace a far wider notion of equity.

(*b*) Secondly, parts of the public sector not originally covered by the fair comparison concept, and in particular the nationalised industries, have regarded the concept as applicable to them as well. Since they are not always governed in their behaviour by commercial considerations, implementation of fair comparison in nationalised industries often works back to government borrowing, to meet the deficits they incur through financing pay increases.

(*c*) Third, comparability, as a device for catching up as well as for keeping up, has tended to facilitate the transmission of pay increases, however initiated, throughout the pay system.

(*d*) A fourth consideration is that any productivity-based policy for pay makes heavy weather in the public sector, since many forms of public service activity are labour-intensive, difficult to measure, and have a history of low productivity gains.

Low pay

Wages Councils have, by definition, been preoccupied with low pay sectors and with setting pay floors. Insofar as they raise pay floors, however, they may also raise the structure of the pay building which is erected upon them. The same point applies to the use made of the device of extending terms and conditions. This was permissible in Britain under the 1959 Act on Terms and Conditions of Employment, and the subsequent arrangement under Schedule 11 of the 1975 Employment Act, now repealed, for extending terms and conditions in areas where pay is "comparatively" low. This could cover both absolutely and relatively low pay. Low pay was also discussed in Chapters Three and Six.

Expectations

In the early post-war discussions of pay under full employment, the Phillips relationship suggested that wages would rise more rapidly as unemployment fell, and conversely. In the early 1960s, the relationship was seen as a very useful policy aid for fine-tuning pay policy norms. As the tempo of inflation increased in the 1970s, however, it appeared that this relationship, even in a weak form, was no longer applicable. Indeed, at one stage pay appeared to be rising faster as the level of unemployment increased. In part, at least, this reflected the phenomenon of inflationary expectations at work. As pay negotiators anticipated and expected that inflation would speed up, their pay demands increased accordingly. This had two policy implications, the recognition that any incomes policy would also have to take account of price movements quite explicitly and, secondly, that inflationary expectations had to be broken somehow, through gradual de-escalation, through pay freezes, or by some appropriate mixture of carrot and stick.

One characteristic that dominates this review of the mechanics and methods of pay development is the *transmission mechanism* for passing pay increases, however initiated, through the national economy's pay structures. Wage increases have tended to be generalised. Incomes policy has therefore concentrated on techniques which:

(*a*) set low general norms, in the hope that these will apply throughout the system; and/or

(*b*) institute machinery which sets criteria to govern exceptions.

It is hoped thereby to insulate them from the "generalising effect" by ensuring that special cases really are regarded as exceptions.

INCOMES POLICY APPROACHES IN BRITAIN

A variety of approaches

A whole host of variations on the theme of incomes policies has been played in Britain. Table XVI provides an overview. More explicitly, the following main strands can be drawn out of the practical experience.

Explicit norms

Explicit national pay norms, or guiding lights, have on occasion been set. During the period 1965 to 1970, when the National Board for Prices and Incomes held sway, a serious effort was made to establish a credible core for the growth of incomes by reference to the overall average growth in real output in the economy. The range of 3 to $3\frac{1}{2}$ per cent was used as a benchmark, though circumstances changed so rapidly that frequently a nil norm or a freeze intruded, before and after as well as during that period. (In the USA a guidepost of 3.2 per cent, reckoned to be the historical long-term growth rate of productivity for the whole economy, was proclaimed as the datum for a voluntary policy of non-inflationary wage and price behaviour, between 1962 and 1966.)

In Britain, it never proved possible to keep the 3 per cent light burning brightly for any extended period. Table XVI shows the fluctuations in the criteria used from time to time. As inflation gathered momentum in the 1970s, a norm of 3 per cent based on the real underlying performance of the economy proved absurdly low in relation to the rate of price increases, and unrealistically high in respect of the poor real growth of the economy.

A persistent snag about any single norm was that the norm tended to become the minimum, rather than the average, to be used as a starting-point rather than an average for the outcome. For that reason, controversy persists as to the wisdom of enunciating a single norm as a guide. A single norm masks the myriad of pay mentioned earlier.

Exceptions to a norm

Exceptions to pay norms have been recognised from time to time, for a variety of reasons which are explicit or implicit in the debate on pay at particular times. In 1975–6, efforts were made to assist low-paid workers by enforcing a flat, across-the-board increase of six pounds per week. On occasion, the public sector has been used, as in the pay pause of 1961–2, to initiate a reduced tempo of pay settlements. Some of the barrage of incomes policy White Papers has grasped the nettle of exceptions by specifying a list of criteria

TABLE XVI. BRITISH VARIATIONS ON AN INCOMES POLICY THEME

Year	Government	Policy model	Comment
1947	Lab.	White Paper on personal incomes, costs and prices	Intended to persuade: economic crisis
1948	Lab.	Wage freeze	For one year
1950s	Cons.	Various courts of inquiry, e.g., engineering and shipbuilding, 1954, 1957, railways, 1955	Raised need for incomes policy
1956	Cons.	White Paper (Cmd. 9725), economic implications of full employment	Nation must will the means
1957–61	Cons.	Council on prices, productivity and incomes	To educate and influence TUC unhappy
Summer 1961			
1962–4	Cons. Cons.	Pay pause in public sector White Paper: incomes policy, the next step National Incomes Commission established	Start of education campaign Guiding light (2–2½%) 1963 (3–3½%) productivity basis To review claims, offer advice
1964 (Dec)	Lab.	Joint Statement of Intent on Productivity, Prices and Incomes National Board for Prices and Incomes established	Set scene for tripartite consensus
1965			Norm of 3–3½% TUC voluntary early warning system
1966 (July) 1967 (first half) 1967 (July)	Lab.	Prices and incomes standstill Period of severe restraint Nil norm, plus productivity and low pay criteria	During period 1965–70 Prices and Incomes Board produced

Date	Party	Policy	Notes
1968 (Apr.)—		Ceiling of 3½% on wage and dividend increases	
1969 (March)—		Exceptions for productivity and low pay	
1969–70 (March)			numerous case studies on pay and prices
1970–2	Cons.	No official policy	Prices and Incomes Board abolished
		1971 effort at n −1 policy for public sector	
1972 (Nov)—1973 (April)	Cons.	Wage and price freeze (stage one)	Statutory
1973 (April)—Nov	Cons.	(Stage 2) −£1. + 4% per week: ceiling of £250 per annum	Pay Board and Price Commission set up
1973 (Nov)—	Cons.	(Stage 3) −£2.25 per week, or 7%, maximum of £350 per annum	Ended by General Election Feb., 1974
1974 (Feb)—	Lab.	Social contract—free-for-all, despite restraint policy with TUC	Pay Board abolished
1975 (Jul)—1976		White Paper, attack on inflation Flat increase of £6 per week	Voluntary, but possible sanctions on prices and contracts
1976 (Jul)—1977		5% limit, in range £2.50 – £4. per week	Self-financing productivity schemes allowed
1977 (Jul)—1978		10% guidelines	
1978 (Jul)—		Proposed 5% norm, rejected by unions	
1979 (March)		Standing Commission on Pay Comparability	For public sector problems
1979 (May)—present (1984)	Cons.	Market to determine pay	Comparability frowned upon; cash limits used for public services, based on notional 3% norm for pay increases. No formal incomes policy

which would justify some departure from the norm. From the start of its mission, the Prices and Incomes Board was instructed to think of exceptional pay increases for the following kinds of circumstances alone—increased productivity as a consequence of improved work practices; the need to redistribute manpower; the low pay, reasonable standard of living, criterion; and situations where pay had fallen out of line with remuneration for similar work. As we noticed in Chapter Six, the productivity criterion subsequently enjoyed a "high noon", both in its own right and as a means for obtaining and giving higher pay increases than the national norm permitted.

Particular exceptions have from time to time been justified by other methods, such as *ad hoc* courts of inquiry, the Pay Board, and the Comparability Commission established in 1978 to handle the accumulation of pay problems in various segments of the public sector. Governments have proved adept at devising such *ad hoc* arrangements for lancing particular nasty boils on the industrial relations body politic.

A variety of sanctions

The sanctions deployed in support of policy have been very varied. Until the early 1960s, the main emphasis was on an educational approach and appeals to the national interest, couched in positive and on occasion sharply critical tones. Sometimes there have been periods of legally enforceable norms, as in 1966/8. Law was kept in the background, to be used as and when required, from 1975 to 1978.

Political opportunism

The acceptability of any kind of institutional machinery for incomes policy, and certainly that espoused by a rival political party, has been used as a political football. On occasion, as with the attempts by the then Conservative Government between 1957 (the Council on Prices, Productivity and Incomes) and 1964 (the National Incomes Commission, 1962–4), the Trades Union Congress has refused to take part. At other times, the unions have eventually felt that a particular policy had exhausted its usefulness and acceptability; the Social Contract died on the vine in 1978/9. For their part, employers have preached responsibility and solidarity, but have found them difficult to practise. This is hardly surprising, in the light of what was said in Chapter Four about the bonds that bind employers together.

Absence of private consensus

Whether because of the political expediency which has pervaded the incomes policy initiatives, the private parties of interest at national level—the CBI and the TUC—have never sought themselves to establish, between them, a "privately owned" incomes policy. While it is possible, as Swedish experience demonstrates, for the national government to be kept at arm's length for long periods, it is certainly exceptional for bipartisan policies to be developed without some explicit tripartite presence of government. One of the problems in Britain is that *either* the unions *or* the employers have been favourably disposed towards the government of the day, rarely both at the same time. Perhaps if the private parties were to establish their own bipartisan framework this would induce some more responsible and stable response by the political parties when in government? This speculation leads to an outline of some of the incomes policy schemes which circulate in Britain.

POSSIBLE APPROACHES

It is a measure of the importance attached to the problems which incomes policy poses that, instead of shying away from a search for solutions, the debate about appropriate arrangements shows no sign of abating. Various recent proposals cover much the same ground, and contain rather similar ingredients.[6] The following summary sketch is typical of recent lines of thinking.

Incomes policy agenda

(*a*) An annual overview of the growth of the national economy and the monetary and fiscal framework is needed. This could flow from a kind of consultative national economic forum involving government, unions, management and the public interest. It would assess the outlook and consider priorities, and also provide information for subsequent dialogue.

(*b*) Such an assessment would help to place expectations in a framework of the resources likely to be at hand. Another aim would be to identify the scale and financing of government's own affairs, and therefore the likely pay profile of the public sector.

(*c*) An indicative norm *might* be set for pay increases. Some see such a single norm as too rigid, and unrealistic for the widely varying needs of labour markets and special situations. Others argue that some kind of benchmark has to be set in order to influence bargaining at the grass roots. Likewise, any machinery for exceptions or anomalies has to have some kind of national datum, if only to see by how much it is making "a special case".

(*d*) The annual bargaining round should be compressed, for example into the period January–March, tying in with the annual government Budget proposals. One advantage seen for this compression, or synchronisation, is that it would make the consequences of particular pay settlements more evident, and would avoid the dribble of leap-frogging pay settlements throughout the year. There seems to be general agreement that the public sector would settle later in the round.

(*e*) Some scope or elbow room for negotiation by sector and by company would be needed. No central guidelines can possibly identify and regulate the detail of pay systems in local labour markets. Put another way, it is essential that some element of bargaining by the "parties of interest" should be retained. In any case they alone know the circumstances of their case. They are accustomed to bargaining.

(*f*) A national body, whether a permanent arbitration device, an anomalies board, or a reincarnated Prices and Incomes Board would be set up, to deal with the problems of anomalies, relativities, and distortion of differentials.

(*g*) More sophisticated versions envisage an explicit link between pay and fiscal policy, in two particular forms. First, the precise progression of the income tax scales is regarded as crucial to negotiations for lower-paid workers, and for incentives for more highly-paid, skilled employees. Second, corrective tax measures could be taken to penalise parties which exceeded the broad consensus for pay movements.

(*h*) A variation proposed by James Meade would retain the system of collective bargaining. Unsettled disputes would not, however, be resolved by coercive action, but by resort to an impartial arbitral body or commission. It would have to award in favour of the final position (offer or claim, i.e., final offer selection) of one of the two sides. In addition, it would be expected to attach great weight in its selection for its award to the criterion of promoting employment. This wage-fixing policy would run alongside monetary and fiscal policies aiming at a steady rate of growth in aggregate money spending in the economy.[7]

(*i*) Most solutions recognise that pay policy also has to have regard to social goals for low-paid groups. Some kind of social equity or fairness is acknowledged to be necessary.

(*j*) Little discussion takes place about the use of a job evaluation scheme for ranking jobs in the national economy, these then being related to some kind of pay line or curve.

In recent years no one concept has matched the boldness of Elliott Jaques's time-span of discretion theory in the 1950s.[8]

(*k*) Trade union schemes insist that no pay policy will work without some scheme to control the retention and distribution of profit. More ambitious schemes envisage, along the lines of the Swedish scheme for employee investment funds, that some element of collective ownership of resources will be needed in order to establish an acceptable consensus. The taxation of property as well as of income then enters the discussion and adds to the complications.

(*l*) Most controversial of all, an *indirect* approach to an incomes policy is suggested by those who start from the balance of industrial relations power as the key. This argument assumes that trade unions have excessive, and monopolistic, bargaining power. This must be reduced, for instance by reducing trade union legal immunities and containing their power to resort to coercive bargaining sanctions. Pushed to its logical conclusion, this approach would redress the balance, and then leave the pay negotiating process to itself.

(*m*) Even if a private concensus on pay and profits were to be negotiated between the CBI and TUC, critics ask whether the two sides could make their members toe an incomes policy line? As we have seen, neither the TUC nor CBI is a strongly centralised body, with constitutional powers that provide an *entrée* to the control of their members in bargaining. Even if they had the control under their rules, it does not follow at all that they could then ensure that any privately agreed national incomes policy was adhered to. The pressure of market forces might defeat the provisions in the rules. This approach does, however, at least raise the question whether we have to assume that a national incomes policy must be inspired, led and enforced, by government.

INCOMES POLICY IN OTHER COUNTRIES

As a final perspective on the dimensions of incomes policy, let us consider briefly the arrangements in two other countries, Australia and Sweden. Both, like Britain, are very open economies, heavily dependent on international trade. Yet there are very vivid differences and contrasts in their approaches.

Australia
Ever since the legislation establishing the Commonwealth Conciliation and Arbitration Court (now Commission) was enacted in 1904, the Australian industrial relations scene has presented an intriguing mixture of compulsion and collective bargaining. The legislation helped to institutionalise trade unions and employers through recognition arrangements, and the Australian trade union movement,

with some 280 unions, covering 2.8 million members, is still fragmented. A stable 55 per cent of the labour force is unionised.

The content of wage polices within the arbitration framework has varied over the years, yet the Commission continues to have a key part to play. For many years, the content of the policy embraced two parts: the idea of a basic *social minimum wage related to need*, which was revised from time to time, latterly annually; and *"margins" for skill, experience and conditions*. One recurring element, understandable in the context of a social minimum, was the explicit use of cost-of-living adjustments. Between 1921 and 1953, for instance, the basic wage was adjusted quarterly by reference to a consumer price index.

In the 1950s this cost-of-living approach was abandoned, and the emphasis on pay settlement shifted to market forces. In 1967 the concept of the basic wage was also abandoned, and the two-part approach to wage-fixing was replaced by a total wage concept. The system in the 1950s and 1960s acquired hybrid features of bargaining and arbitration, with a three-tier structure—industrially negotiated or arbitrated pay increases, plant increases, and "consent awards" by which industrially negotiated increases were confirmed at arbitration. "Over-award" payments became rife.

The consequences of OPEC price increases in 1973 and the subsequent price explosion forced a revision in these Australian rules. A Prices Justification Tribunal was set up in 1973 as a semi-voluntary watchdog, and in 1974 it announced that it would disregard pay increases in excess of those set at arbitration. This shifted the weight of the three-tier system to arbitration. The implementation of equal pay for women also put strains on the system, and in 1975 the Commission reintroduced wage indexation, partly in response to an approach by the Federal Government.

The new strategy had interesting features. Indexing was to take place quarterly (subsequently the interval varied), in the light of movements in the consumer price index. Full compensation was not automatic. Equally, the form of indexing was variable; it could be tapered (plateau indexation) to protect low-paid persons. A general national productivity increase criterion was also included. These criteria were applied in national wage cases examined before the Commission. Other increases could be granted, provided they related to job content (work value), skill, responsibility and community relativities. Claims on these detailed criteria were handled by individual industrial Commissioners.

Historically, the Australian approach used the conciliation and arbitration machinery to set standards, and awards became legally binding minima. This principle has continued. The interesting consequence is that it is customary for unions, employers *and* the Government to appear before the Commission, to plead for a particular course of action. The Commission has also been in the habit of sponsoring regular conferences in relation to the application of the principles for wage fixing.

This 1975 version of Australian incomes policy was terminated by the Commission in 1980, and a search for a new set of criteria initiated. Following a wages pause in the first half of 1983, and the agreement on a kind of Social Contract between the unions and the Labour Party, a new, centralised system of wage determination based on six-monthly indexation was introduced in September 1983.

The system has always been much more than a compulsory arbitration model. It can cover pre-arbitration and post-arbitration negotiations, negotiations instead of arbitration, and the explicit function of conciliation when a "log of claims" is submitted to the Commission. National institutions are not readily transferable; yet the Australian arrangements have some graphic features:

(*a*) the durability of an arbitration agency;

(*b*) flexibility, through reliance on negotiation, conciliation and arbitration at different times;

(*c*) the capacity of the system to deal with a minimum social standard and some element of (but not necessarily complete) indexation;

(*d*) the use of the Commission as a forum in which all the main pressure groups, including the Government, plead their sectional interests.

Sweden

By contrast to Australia, Sweden has a traditional abhorrence of arbitration of "interest disputes". The parties of interest are heavily organised and strongly centralised, largely as a result of their own efforts. Government stood back from this private horse-trading.

After one or two tentative attempts at centrally co-ordinated bargaining, the two main groupings in the private sector of the economy, LO (the Confederation of Trade Unions) and SAF (the Swedish Employers' Confederation) initiated a sequence of co-ordinated bargaining deals in 1956 which has continued without interruption. Centrally negotiated agreements have been concluded for periods of one to three years, depending on the bargaining and economic climate.

Over the years, agreements have become more complex, to take account of the need to provide for general increases, some scope for supplementary bargaining at industry and plant level, compensation for wage drift, the demands of the trade union movement for egalitarian pay structures based on the notion of "solidarity" and, on occasion, cost-of-living compensation clauses.

Particularly since full collective bargaining rights were conceded for public sector employees, including civil servants, in 1965, the Swedish bargaining system has become more complex. Public activity has accounted for a large and growing share of the economic activity in the country, and public employees have proved adept at putting pressure on to receive compensation, sometimes in advance, for wage drift in the private sector. Controversy has raged about the wage leader question, as between the private and the public sector. In the early 1970s a consensus appeared to be emerging based on the concept that the "competing" or export sector should provide the benchmark for what the economy could afford by way of scope for pay increases. The increase in productivity in this open sector plus changes in world market prices for internationally traded products would set a *corridor* within which bargaining could occur.

This was not intended as a guiding light in any rigid sense, but as a framework, and one that would provide elbow-room for negotiation, with some give and take from one year to another. It certainly did not allow the scope for pay increases to be determined by a governmental agency. In recent years, the government's involvement has however increased, because of the growth in its own activity and in the strength of the public sector unions, and also because fiscal, particularly income tax, policy has proved more and more relevant to efforts to obtain increases in *real* pay.

The "corridor" concept has also lost much of its support since the international economic crisis of 1973. Violent price fluctuations in world markets and variable exchange rates have altered the fundamentals for estimating a corridor with any precision.

Sweden represents a prime example of an industrial relations system which has endeavoured to find a form and a format for incomes policy through a private forum consisting of the main parties of interest. This has provided a continuity to the search for negotiated solutions. The opportunism prevalent in Britain has singularly failed to match this sustained effort.

It is well not to be too laudatory, all the same, about achievement in other countries. In 1984 the Swedes reverted to decentralised bargaining, industry by industry. The government did not like the implications, fearing that a wage explosion might undo the benefits reaped from a large devaluation of the currency in 1982 which had brought a remarkable recovery in Sweden's external balance. The government imposed a price and dividend freeze, and threatened to intervene in the pay process.

CONCLUSION

Efforts to design and operate incomes policies have brought a new dimension into industrial relations since the Second World War, particularly (in Britain) since about 1960. As Table XVI brings out, there has been an onslaught of official policies since 1961. "Free" collective bargaining, whether at national, industry, company, plant, or shop level has repeatedly and persistently been put under pressure to conform to wider national economic, social and political objectives.

The list of specific challenges, advice, guidance and constraint has been formidable.

This has put industrial relations under continuing stress. The discretion and scope for self-determination and self-seeking enjoyed at various strata have been restricted. Tight criteria have made life difficult for local union officers; flat-rate norms or ceilings have irked the more skilled elements in the labour force. Productivity elements have been easy to accommodate in some areas of the labour market, but not in others, in particular the public sector.

The environment for pay negotiations has sometimes been predominantly economic, at other times social, and on occasion downright political in flavour. Some criteria, such as a national average productivity norm, have been economic; some have been social, appealing to solidarity, social equity, fair comparison, or priority for those on low pay; other criteria have been unashamedly political, particularly when a freeze or standstill has been imposed.

Typically, the criteria have come "down the line" from the top, and have been couched in simple or crude general terms. This is understandable. It is a dilemma of incomes policy that policies cannot be expressed in a complex form, with numerous exceptions and riders attached to them. There is a problem of communication; messages have therefore to be crisp.

However, national policies, while setting a framework, have to avoid imposing a straitjacket if they are to be credible "at the coal face", where day-to-day bargaining is carried on. The concept of a wage corridor tries explicitly to allow some scope for bargaining, and kitties or pots reserved for local bargaining echo the point.

While the direction of national policy-making has, inevitably, been from the top down, a great deal of the industrial relations pressure has been generated at and from the grass roots, through efforts to maintain and restore differentials. It has been increasingly recognised that a firm's "internal labour market" is to some extent a small world on its own, insulated in part from the outside, external, labour market. Any persistent attempt to run an official policy has had to invent casual or standing machinery to deal with anomalies, exceptions to the rule.

The private sector/public sector comparability issue poses sensitive problems, especially for the trade unions in public employment. A productivity bargaining criterion tends to accentuate this stress, since so many public sector services are labour-intensive, and it is not easy to achieve rapid increases in productivity, for instance through heavy capital investment.

Incomes policies have also put great strains on the power structures within organisations. Within the trade union movement, the TUC has had to try on occasion, with very limited powers, to keep its member unions in line; within member unions there have been stresses between national and local officers; and the shop floor has sometimes jousted with the forces of union government. Employer organisations have faced a similar dilemma.

Increasingly, the "balance of power" in industrial relations has been scrutinised, in order to test whether it holds the key to resolving the problem of non-inflationary pay determination. If unions were made less powerful, and were stripped of some of their power to coerce, would that dampen cost-push out of existence? The union monopoly bogy keeps recurring.

Particular models of incomes policies have had a brief life span in Britain. New variations on second-hand models have had to be improvised. The late George Woodcock, a distinguished former General Secretary of the TUC, once remarked that the search for an acceptable incomes policy would of necessity involve many "shoddy, shabby compromises". So far he has not been proved wrong.

SELF-ASSESSMENT QUESTIONS

1. Examine the importance of pay comparisons in devising an appropriate incomes policy. How would you define "fair comparison"?

2. How would you handle the problem of allowing exceptions to an incomes policy which had set an average productivity norm of 3 per cent for the whole economy?

3. Assuming that synchronisation of negotiations on pay would assist in solving the problem of excessive growth in money incomes, indicate the ways in which you would bring about the synchronisation of pay bargaining in Britain.

4. What lessons, if any, can Britain learn about incomes policy both from her own recent experience and that of other countries?

ASSIGNMENT

You are a civil servant and your Minister wants to argue the case for an incomes policy which sets a single norm for pay increases of five pounds per week for everyone in employment and which allows exceptions only for demonstrable anomalies and labour shortages. Prepare a brief for him which sets out the arguments for *and* against such a scheme.

REFERENCES

1. The *Industrial Relations Handbook*, ACAS, 1980, pp. 35–8, gives a brief summary of post-war efforts.
2. Derek Robinson (ed.), *Local Labour Markets and Wage Structures*, 1970.
3. Royal Commission on the Civil Service (chairman Sir R. Priestley), 1953–5, *Report, Cmd. 9613*, 1955.
4. *Op. cit.*, p. 25.
5. Inquiry into Civil Service Pay, *Report, Cmnd. 8590*, 1982.
6. *See*, e.g., *National Institute Economic Review*, No. 85, 1978; *Pay: the Choice Ahead* (CBI proposals for reforming pay determination), CBI, 1979; *A Better Way* (proposals by a group of British trade union leaders), 1979.
7. J. E. Meade, *Stagflation, Vol. I. Wage-fixing*, London 1982.
8. Elliott Jaques, *Measurement of Responsibility*, 1956.

CHAPTER TWELVE

Facing the Future

The Prussian army lost the battle of Jena to Napoleon in 1806 not because it was no longer the army of Frederick the Great, *but because it still was*.
Quoted by Kahn-Freund

At the conclusion of this journey through the terrain of industrial relations it is appropriate to take stock. We do this not by rehashing the content of the various chapters, but rather by seeking to discern what path industrial relations is likely to follow in the future. Can we see some obvious pointers? And, if so, how can the system adjust or, more accurately, be made to change? It is to the future that our informed studies beckon us, not the past.

Change and adaptability

The first point to take up is the need for an industrial relations system to be *adaptable in the face of change*. Chapter Two concluded with an observation about the need for an adaptable labour force, in the light of changing industrial and occupational manpower needs. Does the industrial relations system facilitate this? We noticed in Chapter Ten that the theme of technological change is relevant not only to industrial and occupational adjustment but to the employee participation discussion. People wish to be consulted, to advise and consent, about change.

In addition, people are still concerned to improve their living standards, to shift the balance of advantage gradually in the direction of more leisure and less work, and less demanding work at that. In other words, they want an improvement in the quality of work, as well as in the overall style of life they enjoy. Despite some prophets of doom and gloom—and they had their forerunners during the first Industrial Revolution—there is little to suggest that the work ethic has been eroded, that people are desperate to reach and settle in the Land of the Lotus Eaters. They are worried more about job opportunities, and about the availability of education and training to prepare them for these. It is *fitness for work* that is the real issue, not the spurious notion of preparation for a workless society. To put the point another way, people are more willing to share jobs and undertake part-time work. They have not abandoned the idea of work.

The industrial relations system cannot be expected to carry the entire burden of adjustment. Change in society involves sensitive adaptability on the part of all kinds of policies and institutions, ranging from education to religious institutions, from National Health Service to civilised social welfare, and accompanying political and legal frameworks which facilitate the workings of a society. But an industrial relations system clearly has a part to play in helping to ease the movement of the economy and the society. After all, people spend a quarter of their adult lives in the world of work, immersed in the arrangements for governing the "social relations at production" which we have been exploring in this study.

Disquieting British performance

How does the British system match up? There are no absolute criteria for judging this. Yet several indicators have been disquieting. We saw how Donovan fretted about the gap between the formal and informal systems of industrial relations, and it and others have shown deep concern about the problems of shop floor industrial relations and their meshing with the activities of national unions and the overall institutions, such as the TUC. Equally, we noticed how ambivalent employers' organisations are about leading from the front, or simply forming groupings according to the issue of the day.

Collective bargaining has shown remarkable durability in the face of attack from both legislative and incomes policy quarters. We have seen that collective agreements in Britain are still a hotch potch. Donovan and others have searched for a solution which would modernise collective agreements. The problem has been diagnosed: but the tempo of change is sluggish.

Paradoxically, Britain has not been indifferent to the problems. The onslaught of legislation which has sought to get a grip on the balance of power in industrial relations, the feverish experimentations with incomes policies, the search for a way forward towards more positive employee participation, all have involved an enormous input of energy, ideas and, understandably, controversy. Yet the balance of power remains unstable, the search for an incomes policy makes little ground, and participation percolates imperceptibly through.

Promising features

There are some credits on the balance sheet, all the same. In the broad area of industrial relations law, we have seen that *employee protection* has made remarkable strides, and there is a well-developed set of programmes and procedures for handling a broad sweep of employee security matters. Some critics say that the pendulum has swung too far in the direction of security, and that reasonable flexibility and mobility of labour are being hampered. On balance, protective measures such as redundancy compensation cushioned the effects of the severe recession in the early 1980s.

The presence of ACAS has brought a revival of interest in the scope and potential of the third-party function for assisting industrial relations. This can be relevant not only in fire-fighting, but in the much less dramatic and patient efforts at improving peaceable procedures for industrial relations. Britain does not demonstrate the buccaneering willingness to innovate that we noticed in the USA; yet innovation *is* occurring. However, it needs to be publicised more.

Who generates new initiatives?

The reader will have noticed that the initiative for change in British industrial relations has tended to come from governments. As we have noted, the emerging shift to company bargaining in the 1970s was brought about mainly through the climate created by government—via law, Codes of Practice, and a general pressure to formalise work relationships. True, the "parties of interest" in the labour market have quite unashamedly used governments to obtain the legislation they favoured. Many of the third-party interventions have originated with the "parties". Yet one of the most obvious routes to advance a system of adaptable industrial relations tends to be neglected. The TUC runs to government; the CBI does the same. While talking of voluntarism, they are in fact pleading for government intervention. They are adept at putting items on the agenda of government. Yet they seldom run to each other. What is the prospect for a TUC-CBI concordat?

A TUC-CBI compact?

In what proved to be the last of his many incisive contributions to illuminating British industrial relations, Sir Otto Kahn-Freund asked, more in hope than expectation, whether the TUC and CBI might become collective bargaining partners.[1] He envisaged two things. First, on wages, a *general pattern* for negotiations could be set nationally, as in Sweden and other countries. We saw some of the dimensions of this in Chapter Eleven. Some kind of centrally agreed framework would facilitate synchronisation, a new "rites of spring". It would at least expose leap-frogging. It could also force out into the open the meaning of solidarity. This national pattern or wages framework can be regarded as the substantive part of Kahn-Freund's proposal.

Secondly, however, he asked whether the central organisations might not enter into central, basic, agreements on conditions other than wages. He pointed to the Scandinavian countries, and, to a certain extent, the Belgian, French and Italian experience. Matters covered by such an agreement could include negotiating procedures, rules regarding coercive action, such as picketing, arrangements for handling national emergency disputes, notice arrangements, works councils, and protection of various kinds, such as that against unfair dismissal. As we have seen, some of this is already governed in Britain by legislation.

Kahn-Freund suggested that if this kind of development is to come

it can only come through a change of voluntary bargaining methods, a change of *mores*, in a sense, and this, as we all know, is infinitely harder to achieve than a change in the law. In a sense it would be a transformation of the present political negotiations between Government, TUC, and CBI into something more regular and more regulated.[2]

No doubt the TUC and CBI would retort that they do not have the power over their members to conclude such agreements. Or they could say that they can only proceed as far and as fast as the membership allows. This is the convoy principle—the speed of the slowest ship determines the speed of the convoy. Equally, they could argue that they do not *seek* to have concentrations of power at the centre. Here, however, there is a wider public policy interest which is frequently overlooked. The public has some right to expect that such central and respected bodies do exercise leadership, and do put pressure on their membership. If, for instance, the TUC were to have a very explicit plan of organisation, its inter-union disputes settlement arrangements, which we saw to be low-key and "one-off" in their approach, would have a positive framework within which to operate. There is a legitimate public interest in such matters. The same applies to the elimination of multi-unionism. Donovan put the responsibility for change on management. In doing so, it failed to distinguish between responsibility and the source of new initiatives. It is reasonable to expect management to lead and propose changes; but that does not excuse trade unions from making constructive proposals. Responsibility rests on everyone, not just one of the parties of interest.

Custom and practice are often paramount in the industrial relations process in Britain. By definition, custom and practice are retrospective, backward-looking, in their thinking and workings. If custom and practice are to be dragged into the present, and prepared for the future, the need for a consensus between the top dogs, the TUC and CBI, is all the more pressing.

The typical British way to reach such an accord is by a case-by-case approach. Yet a step-by-step approach may be quite the wrong one, to take Kahn-Freund's point. A comprehensive basic agreement, ranging over the whole strategy of an industrial relations framework, rather than the tactics of any particular issue, may be the kind of bold initiative which the British system of industrial relations needs.

The European dimension

If the pressure for change cannot be mounted from within, what is the prospect for change being introduced from the outside? In principle, an integrating market ought to mean greater opportunity for the movement of persons between national labour markets. This leads to the European Economic Community theme. In the first chapter we drew attention to the classification of the industrial relations systems in the member countries of the EEC which Jack Peel recently analysed. There is enough variety there for us not, at first sight, to see any clear thread. Peel does, however, offer a thought-provoking list of key Continental practices which in his judgment could transform the industrial scene in Britain:

> higher productivity, legally-binding agreements, better fringe benefits, works councils, industrial unionism, good-conduct bonuses, worker participation, concerted action programmes, better trade union education facilities, no closed shops, national minimum wages, and no strike clauses in public service agreements.[3]

Britain is unlikely to take these suggestions on board as a simple shopping list or agenda. Industrial relations innovation, if it is needed in quite the sweeping way Peel suggests, happens in subtle ways. Yet pressures from the Community are at work. Although much of its energy and effort is consumed on the problems of the Common Agricultural Policy, integration is happening, as intended, in other parts of the social and economic fabric. Harmonisation of certain tax matters, elimination of barriers to trade, and freedom of movement of labour are nibbling away at the insularism even of Britain and France. It may be too grand to label this convergence; yet some drawing together should occur in an integrating economic community.

Three particular EEC pressures can bear on British industrial relations. First, legislation on company law, which will eventually see the light of day, has already provided an *entrée* to the worker participation theme. We saw in Chapter Ten that the controversial topic of company board structure is part of this agenda. If solutions to that impose requirements about board representation and about supporting structures of works councils, the pressure on British industrial relations could be substantial. Interestingly, the British government, unions and employers are agreed in their opposition to a statutory approach to this. They see no value in directives which conflict with well-established differences between countries in policies and practices.

Secondly, particular parts of our industrial relations machinery may be sensitive to change as a consequence of the sheer movement of goods and people within the Community, and the growth of trade and commerce. It is not too far-fetched to envisage that other Community countries doing business with Britain may eventually be a source of new ideas on collective agreements, not least on the sensitive topic of their legal enforceability. Can Britain in the long run remain an international exception to the pervading rule that collective agreements are contracts? Similar harmonisation may occur in other areas of employee protection, such as the rules governing unfair dismissal. The British Equal Pay Act 1970 had to be amended to conform with Article 119 of the Treaty of Rome. This need not be a one way street. We have had substantial experience in the past decade of programmes aimed at employee protection. Others can learn from us.

The third pressure is a much more general one. From having been one of the rich uncles of the Community, Britain has declined to the status of a poor relation. That in itself gives sufficient cause to suggest that we now need to think more explicitly about the European dimension. This is true of our social and economic affairs in general; it is surely also relevant to the ways in which we organise our social relations in production. And that is the very essence of industrial relations.

REFERENCES

1. Otto Kahn-Freund, *Labour Relations. Heritage and Adjustment*, 1979, esp. p. 85 *et seq*.

2. *Op. cit*. p. 87.

3. Jack Peel, *The Real Power Game. A Guide to European Industrial Relations*, 1979, p. 174.

Appendix

FURTHER READING

> In addition to the references given at the end of each chapter, the reader will find the following works help to consolidate the subject matter of industrial relations.

Books

G. S. Bain (ed.), *Industrial Relations in Britain*, 1983.

H. A. Clegg, *The Changing System of Industrial Relations in Great Britain*, 1979.

John Elliott, *Conflict or Co-operation?*, 1978.

Alastair Evans, *What Next at Work?*, 1979.

Kevin Hawkins, *A Handbook of Industrial Relations Practice*, 1979.

Michael P. Jackson, *Industrial Relations*, 1977.

Otto Kahn-Freund, *Labour Relations. Heritage and Adjustment*, 1979.

Jack Peel, *The Real Power Game. A Guide to European Industrial Relations*, 1979.

Henry Pelling, *A History of British Trade Unionism*, 3rd ed., 1976.

E. H. Phelps Brown, *The Growth of British Industrial Relations*, 1959, and *The Origins of Trade Union Power*, 1983.

E. Owen Smith (ed.), *Trade Unions in the Developed Economies*, 1981.

Official publications

Advisory, Conciliation and Arbitration Service (ACAS), *Industrial Relations Handbook*, 1980.

Royal Commission on Trade Unions and Employers' Associations 1965–1968, chairman Lord Donovan, *Cmnd. 3623*.

International Labour Office, *Collective Bargaining in Industrialised Market Economies*, 1973.

The Department of Employment Gazette (monthly), has regular feature articles on developments in industrial relations.

Journals

The British Journal of Industrial Relations, published three times a year, carries research and review articles.

Index

For a full list of titles and prices write for the
complimentary Macdonald & Evans Business Studies/
Legal Studies catalogue and/or complete M&E Handbook
list, available from Department BP1,
Macdonald & Evans Ltd., Estover Road,
Plymouth PL6 7PZ

Basic Law:
An Introduction for Students
L.B. CURZON

This M&E HANDBOOK is intended for students, especially at "O" and "A" Level, who wish to understand the fundamental principles and procedures of English law. The author has also taken into account the needs of other readers, both in the UK and abroad, who require an overview of our legal system, its purposes and structure. For this edition the content has been brought up to date, recent developments have been noted, and the number of case references has been increased. It is hoped that students will use this material as an introduction to the vast store of cases in which so much of English law is recorded. ". . . the author is to be congratulated on the skill with which his material is presented." *Education and Training* L.B. Curzon, a barrister and Vice-President of the Hang Seng School of Commerce in Hong Kong, is an established author in the field of law and economics.

M&E Handbook Series

Business Administration
L. HALL

This HANDBOOK has been specifically written for students preparing for examinations in business management, and in particular those set by the ACA, ICMA, ICSA and certain BTEC higher level courses. It is also recommended reading for the Association of Accounting Technicians Level III examination in Business organisation.

The author gives a detailed analysis of the general principles of management, including the most up-to-date techniques, and the organisation and control of office procedure.

M&E Handbook Series

Business and Financial Management
B.K.R. WATTS

This M&E HANDBOOK is intended primarily for students preparing for the examinations of the Institute of Chartered Accountants, the Association of Certified Accountants and the Institute of Cost and Management Accountants as well as the Diploma in management studies where a knowledge of industrial structure, investment and financial management is required. For this fifth edition several chapters have been rewritten to incorporate recent developments, dealing particularly with the sources of finance for small firms, break-even techniques useful for marketing managers, treatment of tax in published accounts and current cost accounting. ". . . thoroughly recommended." *ALIA Bulletin* ". . . tremendous value for money." *The Accountant* The author is Principal Lecturer in Finance, Faculty of Management, Slough College of Further Education.

Commercial and Industrial Law
ANNE R. RUFF

This M&E HANDBOOK provides a comprehensive and succinct outline of the relevant features of business law. As such it will prove invaluable to students whose examination syllabuses require a detailed knowledge of this wide ranging area of law, particularly those set by the Institute of Legal Executives, the Institute of Chartered Secretaries and Administrators and the Institute of Cost and Management Accountants. It will also be useful as a basic introduction to relevant areas of law for personnel officers, office and factory administrators and owners of small businesses. For this latest edition the text has been thoroughly revised and brought up to date in the light of changes in legislation since the previous edition. ". . . thoroughly recommended." *Legal Executive* ". . . clear and succinct style." *The Accountant* The author is a Lecturer in Law at Middlesex Polytechnic.

M&E Handbook Series

Human Resources Management
H.T. GRAHAM

This M&E HANDBOOK covers a subject which appears under a variety of titles in a growing number of professional and technical courses. It provides a framework for the combination of elements of industrial psychology and sociology, personnel management, training and industrial relations which make up this wide-ranging area of study and will be suitable for students taking BTEC National and Higher Diplomas and Certificates and those taking professional examinations such as those of the Institute of Chartered Secretaries and Administrators, the Institute of Administrative Management and the Institute of Personnel Management. For this new edition the text has been thoroughly revised and updated. Recommended by the Institute of Administrative Management, the Institute of Bankers, the Institute of Commercial Management and the Institute of Management Services. The author is Principal Lecturer in Personnel Management at the Faculty of Business and Social Studies, Croydon College.

M&E Handbook Series

Labour Law
M. WRIGHT & C.J. CARR

This M&E HANDBOOK is intended for all those preparing for examinations in labour law or industrial law, whether at college, polytechnic, university or professional level. The text also provides a concise statement of the main rules relating to employment and industrial relations which will also be of value to the general reader. For this new edition the book has been thoroughly revised to take account of recent legislation such as the Employment Act 1982 and the Trade Union Act 1984. Michael Wright is Assistant Principal at Napier College of Commerce and Technology in Edinburgh. Christopher Carr is Principal Lecturer in Law at Lancashire Polytechnic.

M&E Handbook Series

Economics: A Student's Guide
JOHN BEARDSHAW

This major new work is designed to meet the needs of students of economics who require a wide and rigorous presentation of the subject. Presupposing no knowledge of the subject, the book has been carefully designed through its graduated approach so that it will be suitable for "A" level, BTEC National and Higher level examinations, professional examinations, and for first year degree students. While the subject matter of economics remains broadly unchanged, there are periodic shifts in emphasis in its presentation and these trends have to be kept in view in any general treatment for student use. Special attention is drawn to the international aspects of economics with particular reference to Africa and India. The author, who has had long teaching experience, has also acted as a consultant in economic affairs to business concerns, and combines theory and practice to good effect from each of those spheres. An awareness of student requirements in relation to examination syllabuses (which has been the author's first consideration) is linked in his text with a sense of the importance of bringing the student into touch with the realities of the industry, trade and commerce. The treatment covers, among many other topics, mathematical techniques, demography, markets in movement (with an appendix on computer programmes), consumption savings and investment, comprehensive studies of current economic problems, economics and welfare and the economics of underdevelopment. Each chapter ends with questions and problems to help with the development of essay technique and data response. The author is Senior Tutor in Banking Studies and Lecturer in charge of Economics at Southgate Technical College. He is also, with David Palfreman, the author of the successful M&E Business Studies title, *The Organisation in its Environment.*

Industrial Administration and Management
J. BATTY, *assisted by specialist contributors*

This book gives concise coverage of the subject of industrial administration, emphasising the latest ideas such as ergonomics, value analysis, work study, marginal costing, budgetary control, the Seven-Point Plan and job evaluation. Although primarily aimed at students preparing for professional examinations, its practical slant should make the book very useful to working managers. "There is no hesitation in recommending this book to every person engaged in or studying for any branch of management and administration." *Work Study* Recommended by the Institute of Bankers, the Institute of Management Services and the Institute of Marketing.